A BUSH CAPITAL YEAR

A Natural History of the Canberra Region

Ian Fraser and Peter Marsack

CSIRO

PUBLISHING

National Library of Australia Cataloguing-in-Publication entry

Fraser, Ian, 1951–

A bush capital year: a natural history of the Canberra region/by Ian Fraser and Peter Marsack.

9780643101555 (pbk.)
9780643101654 (ePdf)
9780643102248 (ePub)

Natural history – Australian Capital Territory.
Botany – Australian Capital Territory.
Zoology – Australian Capital Territory.

Marsack, Peter.

578.09947

Published by

CSIRO PUBLISHING
36 Gardiner Road, Clayton VIC 3168
Private Bag 10, Clayton South VIC 3169
Australia

Telephone: [+613] 9545 8555
Local call: 1300 788 000 (Australia only)
Fax: +61 3 9662 7555
Email: csiropublishing@csiro.au
Web site: www.publishing.csiro.au

Front cover: White-winged Choughs by Peter Marsack

Back cover: Macleay's Swallowtail by Peter Marsack

Set in 10.5/17 Adobe Goudy and Trajan
Edited by Janet Walker
Cover and text design by James Kelly
Typeset by Desktop Concepts Pty Ltd, Melbourne
Printed by Ingram Lightning Source

CSIRO PUBLISHING publishes and distributes scientific, technical and health science books and journals from Australia to a worldwide audience and conducts these activities autonomously from the research activities of the Commonwealth Scientific and Industrial Research Organisation (CSIRO).

Jan26_RP_ILS

CONTENTS

AUTUMN

Australian Magpie, see page 178

ARTIST'S ACKNOWLEDGEMENTS

For me this project began with my ill-defined interest in painting a wider range of natural history subjects and working more in the field. My special thanks go to Ian Fraser for immediately saying yes when a total stranger approached him to collaborate on a book on the natural history of the ACT, and for showing me around his home range. His wonderful essays gave me more material to illustrate than I could possibly manage. Thanks also to John Manger at CSIRO Publishing, and to Penny Olsen for her continuing support and encouragement to me and to Australian wildlife artists in general. Most of all thanks to my family, Janet Gardner, Kate and Nick – you know how much I owe you.

The artwork for this book was prepared with assistance from an ACT Government Environment Grant. Over the past 15 years many people have helped to put me in touch with the area's natural history, taking me to particular places, showing me the species they were studying, providing advice, reference material or photos and patiently answering my questions. Others have been kind enough to commission work or buy paintings from me and will recognise some of the images used in this book. I hope I've remembered you all. In alphabetical order, my thanks to: Richard Allan, David Andrew, Pat Backwell, Nadina Beck and Mike Double, Simon Bennett, Leo Berzins, Alistair Bestow, Michael Braby, Graeme Chapman, Mark Clayton, Andrew Cockburn, Bill Cooper, Isobel Crawford, Geoffrey Dabb, Fred Ford, Healesville Sancturary, Rob Heinsohn, Tony Howard, Leo Joseph, Julia Landford (and all the members of Wildlife and Botanical Artists ACT), Ashley Leedman, Bob Lewis, Dianne Logg, Sarah Legge, Rob Magrath, Christine and Pamela Marsack, Ian Mason, Jamie Matthew, Anthony Overs, Harvey Perkins, Anne Peters, Gil Pfitzner, Stuart Rae, John Rawsthorne, Perry and Alma de Rebeira, Trevor Richards (Morpeth Gallery), Danny Rogers, Alison Rowell, Dave Rowell, Dick Schodde, Melody Serena and Geoff Williams, David Shorthouse, Denise Sutherland, John Wombey, Naomi Wynd.

Peter Marsack
May 2010

AUTHOR'S ACKNOWLEDGEMENTS

I shall be forever grateful to Peter Marsack for asking me to collaborate with him on this project; I had long admired his work from afar and was delighted to be invited to work with him. It was a book I'd thought about doing for a long time, and it was with the greatest enthusiasm that I joined the project.

In the course of writing and researching the text many people assisted, some unwittingly through their published research, others more directly by generously commenting critically and helpfully when asked. Among these were Ross Bennett (frogs and reptiles); Ted Edwards (moths and butterflies); Mark Lintermans (aquatic animals); Penny Olsen (various birds of prey); Will Osborne (frogs and reptiles); Greg Richards (bats); Dave Rowell (spiders, centipede, peripatus). It should be needless to say that any remaining errors or unknowable speculations are despite their best efforts.

The text was written with assistance from the ACT Government's ACT Environment Grants.

I was delighted when CSIRO Publishing, through John Manger, agreed to publish the results of our labours. We are both most grateful to them.

Most of the plants and animals you will meet in these pages dwell in the superb system of national parks and nature reserves that cover the ACT from the northern to southern borders, and from east to west. Like all of us I am in debt to those who manage them on our behalves.

A long time ago my father, Fred Fraser, set me on this path and I wish he could have seen this book.

But perhaps above all my thanks are due to Lou, through and with whom all things are possible.

Ian Fraser
May 2010

INTRODUCTION

The Australian Capital Territory is a treasure trove for a naturalist, though it is rarely mentioned as a destination for nature-lovers. One measure of this wealth is the number of bird species found here. In excess of 280 species have been recorded in the ACT, compared with some 820 species on the Australian list, which includes rare vagrants to the far north and residents of oceanic islands. That is, some 35% of the bird species ever seen by Europeans anywhere in Australia have been found in an area representing less than 0.03% of the total Australian land mass – and it is an area without a coastline, without rainforest, without deserts.

An important reason for this diversity is in the immediate juxtaposition of three major habitat types, a most unusual situation. In the tiny territory the great western woodland grassy plains bump up against the inland edge of the coastal hinterland mountain forests, while the whole south-eastern Australian Alps system reaches its northern limit in the Brindabella Ranges. Mount Coree, clearly visible from the national capital, is the northernmost peak of the Alps. Each of these habitats has its own rich suite of plants and animals, so a great diversity of life can be found within an hour's drive of Parliament House. That drive can take us through the remnants of ancient Yellow Box-Red Gum woodlands with their associated grasslands, across the Murrumbidgee with its special riverine habitats, up through the dry open flowery forests of the lower ranges, higher into the wet fern gullies and tall eucalypt forests and finally into the Snow Gum woodlands and bogs more than 1200 metres above Canberra.

The relatively high altitude of the region (by Australia's modest standards at least!) and the absence of an ameliorating coastal influence means that it is more markedly seasonal than much of the country, and major annual movements occur among birds in particular, between the plains and the mountains and in many cases to places thousands of kilometres to the north. The high mountains burst into colour and movement when the icy shackles are finally released in late spring. This book seeks to reflect that seasonality.

When the site of the future national capital was determined in 1908 there was no particular need for a territory to go with it, but there was a need for a guaranteed water supply, and this was a major incentive for the declaration, on 1 January 1911, of the Federal Capital Territory. The funny wiggly line that makes up much of the western boundary of the now Australian Capital Territory (the name changed in 1938) is wildly at odds with the sternly inflexible delineations cherished by surveyors. In fact it marks the boundary of the Cotter River catchment – the ridge line of the Brindabellas. The need to protect that catchment was seen as paramount; the 1914 Cotter River Ordinance virtually made it an offence to eat a sandwich in the catchment, and all toilets along the border are carefully located in NSW!

In time, and with vigorous public nudging, notably by the National Parks Association of the ACT, it was recognised that the best way to manage the forested catchment was as nature reserve. The Gudgenby Nature Reserve in the south of the territory was declared by the Commonwealth Government in 1979; in 1984 it was expanded to become the 94 000 hectare Namadgi National Park, which with subsequent additions now covers 106 000 hectares, 46% of the ACT. Today, under self-government, the overall ACT reserve system represents approximately 55% of the territory. Significant among this is Canberra Nature Park, a unique reserve of over 30 separate units, protecting the hill forests of the suburbs, the Jerrabomberra Wetlands, and perhaps most importantly some nationally significant grassland and woodland reserves in the north of the territory. These habitats are to the ACT what the rainforests are to Cairns.

In the mid-1990s it was realised belatedly that the proposed Gungahlin Town Centre was to be located in the middle of some of the most significant remaining lowland native grassland in south-eastern Australia. After some wrangling and increasingly tedious cracks about 'legless lizards, wingless moths and earless dragons', the decision was taken to move the centre to protect the habitat. Many people saw this as a sign that civilisation was still possible.

Indeed, despite some setbacks, notably the degazetting of part of the Black Mountain Nature Reserve in 2003 to build a freeway, the ACT reserve system in 2010 is an excellent one.

This book seeks to help anyone who is interested to discover and celebrate the plants and animals that make the Australian Capital Territory, and indeed Australia, so very special. It introduces many parts of the reserve system, and places outside it, in the hope that more people, Canberrans and visitors, will get to know it better. Every story is set in a real place.

I have made every effort to ensure that the information is both accurate and as up-to-date as possible, but understandings change and in some fields they are changing quickly; it is possible that in some cases we will come to see the lives of the characters somewhat differently.

It is hard for a writer to admit that a picture is worth a thousand words, but Peter Marsack's beautiful paintings most certainly tell their own deep stories. I like to think that together his brush strokes and my words can bring these wonderful fellow inhabitants of our territory to life in the rooms of your mind.

I love this land and its ancient, teeming and subtle life passionately. We are extraordinarily privileged to be living here and now, but with that privilege comes the responsibility of stewardship. Sadly, it is not a responsibility that we have fully shouldered yet. Based on the premise that with better understanding comes greater appreciation and respect, my hope is that this book may, in a very small way, help to increase our sense of stewardship. Not to mention our simple pleasure in this most wonderful world into which we've stumbled.

Ian Fraser
May 2010

Macleay's Swallowtail on Pimelea ligustrina, *see page 14*

SUMMER

SUMMER IS A TIME OF ESTABLISHMENT, OF GROWTH AND MATURING, OF TEACHING AND LEARNING; HOW WELL THOSE LESSONS ARE LEARNT, OF SURVIVAL AND FORAGING AND LIVING WITH ONE'S OWN KIND, WILL DETERMINE WHETHER LIFE OR DEATH IS BROUGHT BY THE DAYS AND YEARS TO COME. IT IS A BUSY TIME AND THE WORK IS HARD.

High in the mountains the flowering is only now reaching a peak, and the meadows and Snow Gum understorey blaze with colour and are alive with insect life; grasshoppers, butterflies, beetles, flies and wasps all emerging, feeding and mating. Bird breeding has started later than on the milder lower slopes, so the high forest and woodlands still ring with their calls. Lizards and frogs have emerged from their winter torpor and are feeding in preparation for their own breeding.

Lower down in the temperate grasslands the flowering comes later than in the adjacent forests, and the northern reserves are blue with Chocolate Lilies and Blue Devils, yellow with Billy Buttons and Rush-lilies. Later in summer a great richness of grass seeds feeds finches and parrots and small mammals.

At these lower levels, most young birds have left the nest and are learning vital life lessons. With each tentative flight they get more confident, land less clumsily, and increase their chances of surviving an attack from above or below. By following their parents they are learning where to find food, how to deal with it if it wriggles or runs, or is just hard or prickly. They learn quickly what the alarm calls mean – those of their own kind and of many other kinds – and what to do when they are heard.

Less obviously, young kangaroos and wallabies, wombats and possums, native rats and antechinuses, are all learning the same general lessons.

One lesson they must all eventually learn is how to respond to the fires which are an integral part of their world and which come with summer lightning storms.

The frogs are less prone to fires, but in a thousand small ponds the race is on for a million tadpoles to grow and develop legs in order to escape before their home dries out and becomes a death cell. Above their oblivious heads dragonflies dart and mate. Over hills and on the ranges butterflies whirl and court and millions of eggs are laid on food plants. In gardens and bushland wasps hunt these caterpillars and spiders to feed their hatching larvae. In turn millions of spiders spin webs every night to hunt the dragonflies, butterflies and wasps. In some summers the air seems to vibrate to an almost painful degree with the roaring song of cicadas which attract flocks of birds, including Little Ravens from the granite peaks, to the feast.

Later in summer some birds which have successfully raised young to independence have now begun again, to try to increase their success still further; every young animal which reaches adulthood is a tangible measure of the success of its parents' gene line. This time, some of those repeat breeders, including Kookaburras, will have the very important advantage of the help of their earlier offspring. In turn those siblings are learning essential lessons in childcare.

In the last hot summer days there is a restlessness in the air, with the days of movement at hand for many animals. And for many smaller animals, these days are the last of their lives.

Sugar Glider, see page 166

DECEMBER

SACRED KINGFISHER (*Todiramphus sanctus*)

LOWER SLOPES OF MOUNT AINSLIE, CANBERRA NATURE PARK. It is a hot still mid-morning. The tangled webs of the colonial Christmas Spiders, small but brilliantly coloured in black, red and yellow with white thorns on their carapace, make walking difficult.

Above them a small brilliantly blue-green bird with buffy breast and heavy black bill is waiting, still as the air. Earlier the forest had resonated with its harsh 'ek-ek-ek', repeated for minutes at a time. Now it is silent, sitting on a low bare branch, focused on the ground below. Almost anything small that moves is grist to the kingfisher's mill, but despite its name, fish rarely feature. Most kingfisher species throughout the world are essentially woodland and forest insect eaters, but some came to specialise in fish, which had hitherto been a minor part of the diet. By chance the sole European member of the family is one of those fish specialists, so 'kingfisher' is applied to the whole group. Our bird is indifferent to any of this, as it is to the fact that we call it 'Sacred' because many Polynesians revered its supposed ability to control the waves. Rather its attention is directed to a large grasshopper on which it pounces, landing briefly alongside it before bearing it back to the branch and battering it savagely into submission. Unhesitatingly it then flies with its catch to a small hollow high in an old Brittle Gum, from within which come the desperate screams of four fat chicks who eat well and often and wish to keep doing so.

Both parents maintain a shuttle of food throughout the day to the chicks for three weeks, increasing the frequency and size of the offerings as the babies grow. Many species of insects, spiders, worms, skinks and even the occasional frog and small bird go down their throats. Unlike most birds the kingfishers are not very subtle about disguising the nest site – the chicks are noisy, it smells very badly and droppings ooze down the trunk. Presumably the highly developed aggression of the parents leads to this complacency. Threatening intruders are met with harshly shrieking dive-bombing furies, which cause most to withdraw rapidly.

The bird's adventures during the seven months it is absent from Canberra are remarkable. Every year it leaves when the chicks are fully independent – usually during March – and follows the coast north, all the way to the very tip of Australia at Cape York. Some of its fellows stop when they get to northern Australia, but many others, including this bird, push on across Torres Strait. Some stop when they reach the shores of New Guinea but again some are driven still further. Our bird continues east and remarkably heads out again across the ocean until it reaches Trobriand Island to the north-east – and it does so every year. Some of its fellows from Western Australia even cross the Timor Sea and keep going to Borneo and Sumatra, a round trip of up to 10 000 kilometres. Youngsters are not apparently guided by the adults; in fact they often precede the adults on these odysseys.

But for now the sole concern is getting food into the nest hollow, which is bad news for unwary skink or grasshopper but good news for Canberra bird-watchers.

SNOW COUNTRY FLOWERS

MOUNT FRANKLIN ROAD, BRINDABELLAS, NAMADGI NATIONAL PARK.
The high mountains are cold, windswept, and snowy for much of the year, not the sort of place we'd choose to search for wildflowers. But, on a glorious early summer day, as we climb steadily through the Snow Gums from Bulls Head at 1200 metres to Mount Ginini some 550 metres higher up, the roadsides are increasingly a cascade of colour. Daisies, tiny or imposingly large, in mauve, white and yellow, both soft herbs and woody shrubs, cluster numerous minuscule flowers on globes or discs for visibility, surrounding themselves with brightly coloured pseudo-petals, or with bright papery bracts to increase their chances of being noticed. Bright glossy yellow native buttercups reflect light like a mirror to attract the attention of passing insects. Banks of mauve and white Eyebrights are busy with butterflies and wasps jostling for position. Meadows of yellow Bulbine Lilies and pink Triggerplants appear, and banks of purple Black-eyed Susans. In the December immediately following the big fires of January 2003, the blackened soil was snowy with an unprecedented display of sprawling Pricky Starworts for tens of kilometres of road. Their job, replenishing the soil seed bank for next time, is now done. Today, from the top of Ginini, the whole side of Mount Gingera across the valley is stained yellow with the myriad small pea flowers of Leafy

Bossiaea. Subtle scents add to the invitation, while orchids mimic native peas or lilies to trick insects into seeking a nectar treat which they won't find.

Those few species – Narrow-leaf and Gorse-leaf Bitter-peas for example – which grow all the way up from Canberra to here are flowering some two months later than they do a kilometre lower. But why the exuberant profligacy of it all?

The reason lies in the same harsh winter conditions that might lead us to doubt the existence of a summer bonanza. In milder climates, such as in coastal heathlands, there is enough warmth to support plant growth and encourage pollinating insects and birds all year round. Different plant species can spread their flowering throughout the year to minimise competition. In the mountains though, there are only about three months when it is warm enough for flowers to develop and then for plant growth to take place, so most flowering is crowded into the early weeks of summer and competition is frenetic.

There is another difference too from flowering at lower altitudes – the predominant colours of the flowers. At lower Australian altitudes birds are important pollinators of flowers and reds and oranges are the colours that they see best (and which insects don't see). Up here though we find only whites and yellows, blues and mauves, the colours in which insects see the world. It seems that there are virtually no bird pollinators among the Snow Gums; perhaps there isn't the surplus solar energy available to produce the quantities of nectar needed to attract birds. One of the very few exceptions is the lovely leathery-leaved Royal Grevillea, whose red spidery flowers attract the uncommon Crescent Honeyeater into the mountains as soon as the snow starts to melt.

So, time to get out of the car and wander along the road to enjoy this brief cornucopia of colour, scent and texture while it lasts.

RED-BELLIED BLACK SNAKE (*Pseudechis porphyriacus*)

LOWER MOLONGLO RIVER CORRIDOR. Among the rocks of the river edge a satin-black flicker brings us up short. Centuries of superstition – plus a few bad experiences – have instilled a near horror of snakes in many of us, but this Red-bellied Black Snake is typical of her species in being apparently utterly oblivious to us. She continues probing in a leisurely fashion into crevices in an eternal search for frogs. She is a heavy-bodied slow-moving snake, but her food-gathering strategy does not require speed or agility. She is adult and a metre long, though her recent mate was twice that length. If she becomes aware of us she will slip away as inconspicuously as possible, swimming strongly if necessary. If we were to be foolish enough to corner her she would respond vigorously, raising the front of her body and even pretending to strike with flattened neck and hissing loudly. It is all bluff though, and she will not bite unless no other options are left. Furthermore, her venom, though quite adequate for frogs, lizards, mice and fish, is not particularly toxic and as a result no adult human is known to have died from a Black Snake bite.

Other snakes hunt ACT river banks too, and both Highland Copperheads and Tiger Snakes have more toxic venom. The Copperhead has a similarly amiable nature, while the Tiger likes to appear ferocious and bluffs accordingly. Both are also loath to actually bite – venom is a valuable commodity and the risk of breaking a tooth on a large animal such as a person is a very serious one indeed. (Stories of Tigers chasing people are based on misinterpretations of the snake's desire to make for safety, and particularly water.) On the dry hills above us Eastern Brown Snakes hunt mice; their venom too is extremely potent, and while not aggressive they are very nervous and highly strung and will lash out dangerously if threatened.

Our gleaming Black Snake, however, continues her hunt, sliding over rocks like water. She does this by looping her body and using the loops to push back against the ground, assisted by muscular pressing onto it by individual scales. Her non-blinking stare, which people can find disturbing, is due to the fact that she doesn't need to blink – a transparent scale covers each eye, protecting it from dust, wind and water. She learns more about the world by tasting it, however, than she does by seeing or hearing it. Her constantly flicking tongue is 'tasting the air', gathering a rich kaleidoscope of chemicals from it and drawing them in to be analysed by a pit, known as Jacobsen's Organ, in the roof of the mouth. Mere humans have nothing like it.

Goannas do have it, as well as the oddly forked tongue, and this is no coincidence. Goannas are more closely related to snakes than they are to other lizards (and in some ways snakes are best thought of as a very specialised group of lizards). Goannas and snakes probably both trace their ancestry back to the long-extinct giant marine legged mososaurs, though there is still debate about whether the ancestral snake lived in water or underground. Either way fossils tell us that very early snakes, over 130 million years ago, still had legs. Venom – simply modified saliva – came much later, as a further aid to a hunting animal without grasping hands or claws. Originally it was probably used to stop prey from struggling just by chewing. The use of grooved back fangs to inject venom into muscle or blood vessels may date from only 15 million years ago and the more efficient front fangs from even more recently.

Just two days ago 'our' snake mated with the big male that patrols this section of the river. After pressing his chin along her body and testing her readiness, they lay quietly joined for over an hour before he slipped away. (Reports of much more dramatic encounters between snakes, with two equally-sized animals wrapped around each other like a plait, actually refer to two rival males testing their strength; the victor gets mating rights in the area, the loser slips away unharmed to try again when he's grown bigger.) Later in summer she will cease feeding and stay near the burrow until she gives birth to 18 young, each about 15 centimetres long. Like most other local snakes – but unlike most snakes elsewhere in the world – baby Black Snakes are born live in a transparent sack from which they must escape before starting life alone.

As we have been musing she has suddenly vanished, in the way that snakes do, but the day feels brighter for her company.

REDEYE CICADA (*Psaltoda moerens*)

URIARRA CROSSING, MURRUMBIDGEE RIVER CORRIDOR. On a River Oak branch a Redeye Cicada is dying. It is mid-morning and it's hard to distinguish between the vibrations caused by the heat pulsing in our ears and the waves of sound that beat against our heads. It is a few years since the Redeyes last emerged en masse, but this is their year again. For days the males have been gathering in the Casuarinas along the river, the newcomers attracted by the hordes already calling. Their intent of course is not to attract each other but the silent females. This is their only chance to pass on their genes to another generation and they have waited years for the opportunity.

The dying cicada is in the beak of a Dusky Woodswallow; he is almost as big as the bird's head and she is battering him on the branch. Her chicks will soon be leaving the nest and she has been regularly harvesting the seemingly endless crop of cicadas to meet their noisy demands. Were he capable of such concepts, the cicada might take comfort in the fact that his task is done; a female is even now carrying his genes in her fertilised eggs. As his unknown mother did a few years ago, this female will slice into the wood of a branch and lay over a hundred eggs in the grooves. As their father did, the nymphs will hatch in early spring and tumble to the ground where they will burrow to a root and settle down for years – for most of their lives in fact – to grow, to feed and to await their brief time in the sun.

Just three weeks ago the now doomed cicada, spurred by triggers understood by neither cicada nor human, emerged as a nymph from the soil and crawled up the trunk of the tree, where he stopped and began to attain adulthood by splitting the skin along his back and pushing out. For days the region was dotted with uncountable cicada nymph shells, on trunks, fence posts and grass stems, not to mention a few shed walls and car tyres. In the 20 minutes his emergence took, many of his fellows were taken by waiting birds, but not him. Still he had to wait, at terrible risk while his wings filled with fluid and hardened, but he was a survivor. Until now.

Australian cicadas, over 200 species of them, are bugs. This is not another word for 'creepy crawly' but is a whole order of insects, the Hemipterans, characterised by a long feeding tube through which they suck up liquids. The cicada's tube sheath extends along the full length of the underside of the body, in both nymph and adult. It contains four hollow needles which pierce the wood and take up sap for nutrient. It is a dilute food and the surplus water, with all the goodies extracted, is sprayed out, pattering around us as 'cicada rain', nearly as pure as cloud rain.

And as soon as he was able, he began to sing, raising his wings clear of his body that nothing might muffle his performance. Much of his body was designed for this, with his abdomen forming a formidable resonating chamber, to amplify the vibrations of a pair of corrugated membranes (timbals) on the sides of his body just in front of the abdomen.

Contracting muscles crackle the membranes in and out like a wobble board – the sound can be painfully loud to human ears. The timbals can operate together or separately; no two cicada species sound the same. The energy required to drive this mighty percussion at up to 100 vibrations a second is considerable, and only the heat of a summer day can sufficiently supplement his internal energy supply.

But now his song is silenced forever. In years to come though, his children will again roar the same pulsing love ballad to fill and define the stillness of a summer morning.

EASTERN WATER DRAGON (*Physignathus lesueurii*)

MOLONGLO GORGE. Wandering down the track along Molonglo Gorge, just above the rocks of the Molonglo River, we are suddenly aware of being watched … Well, everywhere we go that is the case, but there is something compelling about the gaze of the big lizard, with mediaeval crested back and head, green body and orange throat. To add to the impact, he is nearly a metre long. (In eastern Victoria in fact the species is sometimes known as the Gippsland Crocodile.)

Water Dragons are found along the eastern seaboard from Gippsland to Cape York, as well as in New Guinea, but never far from water. Virtually every permanent stream in the ACT has a population. The famous Australian National Botanic Gardens population probably had its origins in water dragons living along the Molonglo before it was flooded to make Lake Burley Griffin in 1964. They would have been pushed back by the rising waters, perhaps making their way up Sullivans Creek and thus across to the Gardens.

A lizard for all situations, the water dragon seems to be equally comfortable on land where it can run very rapidly indeed, including on its hind legs, in water where it swims powerfully and can stay under for up to two hours, and in trees. It will lie out on a branch, from where if disturbed it will drop into the water from heights of six metres or more. In fact we are more likely to hear the splash than see the lizard.

A formidable hunter, it will take insects and crayfish, frogs and tadpoles, ducklings, small mammals and lizards – even baby water dragons – as well as berries and fruits. Consumption of this varied diet is enabled by the typical dragon lizard teeth, permanent triangular cutters along the sides complementing long sharp gripping canine-like fangs at the front; these are regularly replaced. Pick up a dragon, if you must, very cautiously indeed.

Up to 20 soft-shelled eggs are laid in the bank, or in flat soil far enough from water to avoid flooding, buried in a burrow to hatch in two to three months. The youngsters are 15 centimetres long at hatching, and must look after themselves from the start. They shelter in the home burrow, sunning themselves alongside it, at risk from many sources, not least their aunts and uncles.

This lizard is of a lineage as ancient as he looks; 20 million year-old water dragon skeletons from the Riversleigh fossil mines of north-western Queensland are apparently identical to modern ones. In fact the dragons are regarded as the most ancient group of lizards. This assessment is based in part on their unique teeth arrangement; no other lizard has those fang-like front teeth and flattened triangular side cutters. Only the ancient dinosaur-related reptiles, the two Tuataras of New Zealand, have similar teeth. It is believed that the dragons are less closely related to other lizards than the snakes are, which raises the question 'are they even truly lizards?'

For now though we may restrict our philosophy to respect as we nod and pass by – his species has been on earth at least 20 times as long as ours.

COMMON BIRD ORCHID (*Chiloglottis valida/Simpliglottis valida*)

BRINDABELLAS, NAMADGI NATIONAL PARK. On the bank of the damp shady fern gully is a cluster of paired large, dark green, glossy leaves. Get your eye in and you realise that the numerous leaves extend for a couple of metres along the bank, forming a colony of hundreds of plants. Look even more carefully and something else becomes apparent – many of the plants are in flower, though the flowers are remarkably inconspicuous despite being 35 millimetres across. Part of the reason for their ability to avoid casual detection is their colour, a subtle blend of purple and greens.  Another is the fact that the flowers sit right down on the leaves, on a short stem.

And strange flowers they are too, hooded by a purple cap and a pair of spreading petals, but dominated by a labellum or lip, a large, flat, heart-shaped petal, studded with a few short glossy black stalks known as calli. The labellum nods in the slightest breeze, suggesting to some a baby bird begging – hence the Bird Orchid name. The impression of the calli is vaguely insect-like and astonishingly, this is precisely their purpose. Like many orchids the Bird Orchids are consummate con artists, persuading insects to take their package of pollen in exchange for a promise that the orchid is incapable of delivering.

In this case the sucker is a wasp – the male of a particular species of thinnid wasp who is deceived by the flower in the thing that matters to him above all others. Somehow the orchid gets away with masquerading as his intended and it does this with an almost unimaginable combination of visual and chemical chicanery. Essentially it is taking advantage of the wasp's courtship behaviour, which itself is quite startling. The wingless female wasp, when ready to mate, crawls up a stem and sends chemical signals to the world. The male receives this message from a considerable distance, and races upwind to beat the equally ardent competition. On arrival he seizes her and flies off to a convenient restaurant in a nearby bush, where they sup on nectar while mating. Being a bloke of the new era, the male then gives her a lift home where she burrows in search of scarab beetle larvae in which to lay her eggs.

In this case though, the welcome scent of wasp love is being emitted by the orchid – and the wasp is fooled! Further, in his haste, he mistakes the callus-studded labellum for his would-be mate and in his efforts to sweep her away is thrown by the nodding labellum against the flower's column, where the sticky pollen bundle sticks to him. When he gives up and flies chastened away, he is bearing the precious pollen on his back. He hasn't learnt though, and when he tries again soon afterwards he delivers the pollen to another orchid. After the orchid absorbs the pollen the short stubby flower stem grows dramatically to improve distribution of the minute dust-like seeds.

And all's not bad news for the wasp either. For the trick to work successfully, the flowers have to open just before most of the female wasps emerge and that time is soon. Pretty soon, the male's assignation will be a lot more satisfying.

SUPERB PARROT (*Polytelis swainsonii*)

MULLIGANS FLAT NATURE RESERVE. An early morning walk in the woodlands of Mulligans Flat is always special, and this morning it is particularly so. The first inkling of it comes in a distant musical 'quark'. This is a call not widely heard in the ACT, though it is regular in summer in some northern Belconnen suburbs and around Hall. As the seemingly endless drought proceeds, the call can be heard even deeper into suburbia.

On this occasion it emanates from a scattered flock of a dozen spectacular parrots, feeding in the grass on seeds. They feed quietly for the most part, and we see them as their heads pop up to look around, the purple Chocolate Lilies and white and yellow daisies framing their faces in an unlikely brilliance of colour. The parrots are as big as rosellas, bright grass-green with long pencil-thin tails, a pink bill and blue-edged wings. Among the plain-faced females and youngsters are four even more dramatic adult males, with red-bibbed yellow faces.

These are Superb Parrots; they are summer visitors and the ACT is at the southern edge of their range. In January 2006 a flock of at least 120 of them thrilled Belconnen residents by taking up temporary residence around the Macquarie Ovals. Those birds had finished breeding, in tree hollows just to the north of the ACT, as have the ones we are now watching. A few weeks ago the flock would probably have comprised only adult males, either non-breeding birds or those whose partners were incubating or brooding.

The grassy woodlands, and particularly old Blakely's Red Gums, are critical to their survival. Only when a red gum is over 100 years old can it form the hollows that the Superb Parrots – and many other species – need to breed in. The loss of such trees to old age, with no continuum of younger trees to replace them, to agricultural clearing and, most insidiously, to the firewood industry, has contributed to the decline of the parrots to the point where there are less than 5000 pairs left.

It is a complex story though, because in a few weeks these birds will start to move north to spend winter in warmer climes around the upper Namoi and Gwydir Rivers on the northern slopes of NSW. This is cotton country and it is unclear how much impact that industry's chemicals has had on Superb populations. Their seed-eating habit has also contributed to their decline, with flocks at risk from traffic when feeding on roadside grain from carelessly covered or unsealed grain trucks. Appallingly, there are stories of 20 birds at a time being killed in such situations, but the New South Wales National Parks and Wildlife Service has worked closely with the grain industry to alleviate this quite unnecessary threat. Success has been mixed.

Important work has also been done by communities such as that of Boorowa, both in planting trees for the future and in encouraging landowners to retain essential old breeding trees – dead trees are as valuable as living ones in providing the parrots' nurseries. The people of Boorowa, in conjunction with Greening Australia, have also pioneered the successful use of nesting boxes for Superb Parrots to bridge the considerable gap until the new plantings produce their own hollows.

But now we have approached too closely and the birds swirl into the air and fly in a big circle just above the tree tops, their sharply back-swept wings and slender tails very characteristic. They are a special part of the land and the very existence of reserves like Mulligans Flat and the vision and energy of the people of Boorowa and Greening Australia might just ensure that they remain so.

Note: The Superb Parrot is listed as a threatened species under Commonwealth, ACT, NSW and Victorian legislation.

MACLEAY'S SWALLOWTAIL *(Graphium macleayanus)*

MOUNT GININI, NAMADGI NATIONAL PARK. The top of Mount Ginini provides probably the best drive-in view in the ACT. Today it is at its best; to the south, over the western

shoulder of nearby Mount Gingera, are the Tantangara Plains in Kosciuszko National Park with the waters of Tantangara Reservoir glinting in the sun. Behind it the Main Range is a smudge on the horizon, with the familiar snow drift a slash across Mount Kosciuszko through the binoculars. As we swing round a bit further to admire the off-square hunch of Jagungal, 80 kilometres away but clear and sharp, something closer to hand distracts us.

Two big colourful butterflies are soaring and spiralling round each other just above us. It looks very light and elegant, but in so far as butterflies can be said to be macho, this is seriously aggressive stuff. They are males, of the very handsome Macleay's Swallowtail, and the resident male who has set up a display territory in this prime site has just been challenged by an interloper. The threat dance continues for a few minutes, then with no cue that is obvious to us, the invader suddenly breaks off and retreats, and the resident resumes his conspicuous patrolling above the mountain. He is chocolate and white, with large grass-green patches under his wings and dark narrow tails at their tips.

Now another butterfly approaches, slightly paler and larger, but this time the male's reaction is quite different. She is a female and she is the sole reason for his display flight. She comes up to check the talent; they land, she avails herself of it briefly and flies back down the mountain.

Later, as we drive down the steepish track we are attracted to yet another Macleay's, feeding on the big white flower clusters of Mountain Rose, taking up nectar via her wonderful long hollow proboscis, which she normally keeps coiled out of the way like a clock spring. She is not the same female we have just seen mating. In her case this happened a while ago, quite possibly with the same male, as her body is fat with eggs and soon she will find an Alpine Pepper bush on which to lay her eggs. To our more effete taste this seems a strange choice to offer the children, as the leaves contain fiery chilli-like alkaloids, but the white-spotted green caterpillars will munch and thrive on it. Perhaps in fact the caterpillar gains protection from predators by incorporating the bitter chemicals into its body; certainly it makes no attempt to hide, even when large and conspicuous, though it does not carry any warning colours. It will bluff if threatened, by suddenly producing a foul-smelling forked yellow structure from behind its head to startle the curious.

A caterpillar is little more than an eating machine. When its body is replete it performs a most extraordinary feat. Its skin stiffens as it attaches itself to the underside of a leaf by a sticky silk pad at at its rear end, suspended by a silk sling. The pupa, or chrysalis, survives the rigours of winter while its body constituents break down into a sort of 'soup', which then reorganise into an entirely different form. In late spring the chrysalis case splits open and the adult – the butterfly – emerges, its wings open and stiffen, its body now has three pairs of long legs, it has large eyes and of course it now has sexual organs.

As we descend, we can enjoy other butterflies, but we leave the mountain race of Macleay's Swallowtail behind. Another good reason to visit the Brindies in summer.

HUNTING WASPS

INNER NORTH. It gave me a huge fright the first time it happened. I turned on the tap in the outside laundry and nothing happened – at first. Suddenly there was an explosion of dry mud and water into the sink, plus something else … Closer inspection showed them to be motionless small spiders, including at least a couple of the attractive and hyperactive little Jumping Spiders that often keep me company when I'm sitting at the outside table. It wasn't too hard to work out what had happened. One of the Mud-Dauber Wasps had been at work and I had just undone all its efforts. At least a dozen spiders had died in vain and the same number of wasps were not going to emerge in summer.

I am used to seeing the Mud Daubers' small, elongated, egg-shaped mud nests placed on the back wall or on much less appropriate strata, including the outside umbrella if I've left it folded and leaning against the wall for too long or the inside of my rubber boots. This enterprising but misguided female had found an apparently ideal dark, dry shelter to make her offspring even safer. Oops! She had spent perhaps a couple of days scouring nearby vegetation, pouncing on the hapless spiders – very much the hunters hunted – and carting them to the tap-nest. When she stung them she judged the complex toxin precisely so that the spiders lived, but paralysed, guaranteeing a fresh food supply for her own offspring, which would hatch as larvae from a single egg per spider. Not this time though. Since then I've kept the tap blocked up with a wine cork carved for the purpose, but a couple of times I forgot and the wasp unerringly found me out. She is black with orange highlights and legs and with the famous attenuated wasp waist to an impossible-looking degree.

Despite this, she is actually more closely related to the bees than to other wasps, such as the Paper Wasps which build such exquisite structures under my eaves. They have a bit of a reputation for tetchiness, but I've lived with them for years with no unfriendly interactions. They are small wasps, again black and yellow but with brown wings. Hanging down from the eave, the bell-shaped nest is formed from chewed up plant matter and comprises lots of downward-opening six-sided cells. Within the cells these wasp grubs are fed on caterpillars also gleaned from my garden; I'm a bit ambivalent about having my spiders harvested but I'm afraid I have no qualms about the caterpillars! It is unforgivably self-interested species bias of course, but I do like my Asian greens … Unlike the solitary Mud Daubers the Paper Wasps are colonial, with a queen who lays the eggs. Another difference is that they chew up the caterpillars and feed them to the larvae as they need them, rather than give them a living larder.

Others of their family – the Vespids – make colonial mud nests, but I don't have the pleasure of their company. I do get occasional visits from a much less welcome Vespid, the infamous European Wasp, but fortunately no colonies yet.

Yet another family provides some drama in hot weather too, when the spectacular big solitary Spider Wasps frenetically prowl the garden hunting for a luckless spider, drawing attention with their constantly flicking wings. I have never seen them actually attack the spider – which can be wandering Huntsmen, burrowing Wolf Spiders or web-living Orb Spiders – but have on several occasions watched them dragging the paralysed victims backwards to the pre-excavated burrow. (Some hunters of burrowing spiders very sensibly just use the spider's own burrow.) As with the Mud Daubers, they leave an egg to develop on the 'living dead' spider and very carefully fill in the hole and sweep around the entrance to disguise it. This is essential, as other Pompilids specialise in stealing their relatives' prey. Yet another group of big solitary hunters, this time Mud Dauber family members, behave similarly but specialise in big caterpillars. I have watched in anguish as the wasp rushes around unable to find the prize which she has 'parked' while it searches for the burrow – she always gets there in the end though.

I can only hope 'my' wasps enjoy my company in these lovely warm months as much as I do theirs.

SUPERB FAIRY-WRENS (*Malurus cyaneus*)

AUSTRALIAN NATIONAL BOTANIC GARDENS. It is still 20 minutes to sunrise. There is a faint wash of light across the white eucalypt trunks and pale flowers glow faintly, but it's still too dark to see more than general shapes. A Yellow Robin is piping slowly and sweetly over near the rainforest gully, but most birds are not yet ready to stir.

Some are though. From deep in a dense Brown Pine erupts a short burst of annoyed high-pitched squeaks, then a barely visible small shape darts out of the roost and heads determinedly north, across the rock gardens and the lawn beyond, then across the road and into a shadowy world under some big wattles. The female wren has passed through two other territories to reach here, but her business was not with them. It is now three days before her first egg is due, and she is at peak fertility. The dominant male in her own territory defends a high quality area of food and shelter and he has proved himself an excellent provider for her chicks. But …

There is something about the dominant male in the wattles that she finds irresistible when it comes to mating. Nor is she the only one; she knows she has competition from other errant females, which is why she makes her move so early in the day. Once he has mated he has relatively little fertility left to offer others for the rest of the day. There are a few of these 'super males' in the Gardens and one thing they have in common is that they moult from their drab winter camouflage plumage into the brilliant blue and navy breeding garb earlier than other males. The significance of this is not readily apparent to humans, but that is of no concern to the wrens. She and her philandering colleagues 'know' that these are the best fathers of their eggs and that is sufficient. Sufficient in fact to the point where four of these magnetic males are father to about half the chicks in the entire Gardens! Further, three-quarters of these chicks have fathers who do not care for them – and in each case it is their mother who has actively gone looking for the encounter that produced them. Last year she got confused in the pre-dawn light on one such foray and a helper of the dominant she was seeking got to mate with her instead; indeed, the junior helpers of such über-males father more chicks in this way than most 'ordinary' dominant males do!

The male whose attentions she is now so ardently – and successfully – seeking brought himself to her attention early in the previous winter when he entered her territory, displayed vigorously, and presented her with a Correa flower tube. There was no solicitation then, just letting her know who he was for when the time came … He fathered seven of her 10 eggs (in three clutches) last year, and his genes will be in two of the three eggs of the forthcoming clutch. Her own faithful mate provides the life in the other eggs.

Within 20 minutes she is back in her own territory, just as the sun stains the tree tops pink-gold, and immediately starts foraging across the ground in loose association with her mate and two sons from previous years. These are real homebodies – they will never leave the territory, unless a vacancy arises immediately alongside. Rather they will wait patiently until they can, in order of seniority, inherit from their father. When that happens she will start looking to relocate elsewhere.

Now, she returns to put the finishing touches to her nest – solely her responsibility – near the ground in the same dense pine in which she roosted. It is a side-opening dome of grass, bark and twigs, lined primarily with the abundant Wood Duck feathers that litter the Gardens' lawns. And very soon she will again be laying into it a distant sire's egg.

JANUARY

BOGONG MOTHS (*Agrotis infusa*)

MOUNT GINGERA, NAMADGI NATIONAL PARK. Evening is dimming the mighty granite tors of Mount Gingera, with the distant lights of Canberra twinkling 1300 metres below and 40 kilometres away. The walkers have long left for the lights.

Two months ago the moths which are now emerging like smoke from among the rocks were also distracted by those same lights as they made their way south to here; many could not escape their lure. They are Bogongs, a direct link with colder times of past glaciations, when much of south-eastern Australia resembled the cold sparsely treed high alps. These moths have never been here before – no moth ever makes the journey twice – but deep in the DNA of their cells is an infallible map. This mysterious knowledge guides them from the hot black soil plains of northern NSW and even southern Queensland to the same cool rock crevices used by hundreds of thou-sands of generations of their ancestors. Many head further south, to the peaks of the Kosciuszko Main Range and even the Victorian Alps.

As larvae – known to aggrieved farmers as Cut Worms – they lived underground and emerged at night to feed on the stems and leaves of broad-leaved pasture plants. On emergence as moths they headed south, feeding on eucalypt nectar as they came and flying only at night.

Aside from hordes of waiting predators all along the route, there are now dangers that their foremoths did not have to contend with. The huge wattage of Parliament House which every night bathes long empty corridors and vacant chambers turns the building into a vast moth trap. Tens of thousands of moths are lured in and die. To add further insult to the assault, august members of the House have even committed bizarre libels by accusing them of eating the tapestries. Unfavourable winds sometimes blow them fatally off course; an 1865 Sydney church service was held up when 80 000 off-course Bogongs were counted on the windows. One might query if the need to count them should really have led to the moths being blamed for the interruption ... Others have been carried, very much against the will of their chromosomal compass, across the Tasman to New Zealand.

On arrival at their traditional aestivation grounds (the word is the summer equivalent of hibernation) the first arrivals get the coolest and safest spots in the deepest crevices. Those that follow crawl up after them, tucking their heads under the wings of the moths already there, a tiled wall of moths at a density of over 15 000 animals per square metre. From now on, even though the Snow Gums are flowering, they won't feed until they head north again, relying on the fat stores in their bodies.

Why then this evening flight, these thousands of moths thrumming the air with their wing beats? Only the moths know and they're not saying, but it's a dangerous conceit. Bats, Boobook Owls and Owlet Nightjars flash through the flight, gorging on the rich fat bodies. In the crevices antechinuses and bush rats are taking their share of the bounty; by day Little Ravens and Grey and Pied Currawongs flock around the peaks. In past years people too joined the harvest, using the moth fat to build up body condition after a hard winter. Perhaps the most specialised and insidious moth killers though are two species of mermethids, parasitic worms which over-winter as eggs in the moth debris on the cave floor. In spring they swim up the walls against the tide of melting snow trickling down to reinfect the arriving moths as they drink the water. Now, in January, they are already leaving the dying hosts to return to the floor, rich in moth bodies and debris, to mature, mate and leave eggs to await next year's moths.

It seems amazing that the Bogong population can sustain such depletion, day after day, but while there are fewer moths than in past years, there are probably still tens of millions of them. When autumn cools the mountain air, the survivors will start to head north again to the breeding grounds. Restored with a final feed of nectar, the females will lay up to 2000 eggs into the ground and the entire generation dies. But their Ulyssean journey will be re-enacted every summer, while the map-bearing chromosomes live in those tiny eggs.

EASTERN BEARDED DRAGON (*Pogona barbata*)

WANNIASSA HILLS, CANBERRA NATURE PARK. On the lower slopes of Mount Wanniassa, just off Long Gully Lane, we're playing hide-and-seek with a lizard. She is pressed upright against the furrowed trunk of an old Apple Box, slipping sideways as we circle. As she peers round the tree at us, we can admire the curious false 'eyelashes' of long scales on her lower eyelids which protect her eyes.

A Bearded Dragon nearly 40 centimetres long. She has seen a few summers come and go and we're not the first annoying humans she's encountered. Accordingly, she's not particularly fazed by our next tactic. If I keep circling while Lou stands still, she at least should get a good look. When the lizard realises what's happening her first response is bluff. She suddenly puffs up her throat so that an alarmingly spiky beard envelopes her gnarled head, which opens with an intimidatory 'huff' to show her bright yellow mouth and characteristic triangular dragon teeth. Her body suddenly seems bigger too, as she flattens it so that it appears almost circular. I know this performance, however, from many past Beardy encounters and the next move is also predictable. Sure enough, she abruptly leaps back from the tree, turning in the air and scattering leaf litter as she scuttles away at shimmering speed.

When we first disturbed her she was perched up on a stump, waiting patiently for a passing beetle or grasshopper to stray too close. In other circumstances she will even eat mice and is fond of flowers and berries. By afternoon it will be too hot for her in the sun and she will move to the shade to keep her temperature steady.

From what we know of Bearded Dragons I can speculate as to her recent doings. Last month she would quite likely have laid a second clutch of 20–30 eggs for the season, some six weeks after the first clutch and before the first clutch even hatched, though that could happen soon. Both lots of eggs will be buried in moist soil, where the eggs can take up water from their surrounds. When the youngsters emerge they dig their way to the surface and are on their own from then on. This egg production is prodigious for such a large lizard, so we can assume that predation on the youngsters is severe. Snakes, kookaburras, currawongs, butcherbirds and perhaps even big dragons all take their toll; in an urban reserve like this, cats, dogs and foxes will also be a threat.

Their father will be a big male, over half a metre long, who lords it over several female territories scattered around the mount. He can tolerate smaller males, as long as they observe the niceties and wave a foreleg slowly and obsequiously when he comes into view. Young males in fact will wave even when no-one's around, just to be on the safe side!

'Our' female's duties are now done for this season. Her only remaining responsibility is to feed up in preparation for the long winter snooze in a burrow deep under a rock or log. And while she waits for her next meal, not far away there are stirrings in some buried dragon eggs …

LARGE FOREST BAT (*Vespadelus darlingtoni*)

INNER CANBERRA. A remarkable and deadly hi-tech aerial display is being presented directly over the heads of a backyard dinner party, but no-one notices. Even if the glasses stopped clinking and conversation ceased, the most they would hear would be quick soft clicks – if their ears were still young enough … A bat is hunting insects attracted to the candles of the party. Her delicate wings comprise thin skin stretched over immensely long finger bones, extending down the sides of her body and anchored to her ankles. Unlike a bird she can flap her wings independently of each other, and can thus perform the most extraordinary tumbling aerobatics.

As she cruises round the yard she is emitting steady pulses of sound which constantly provide her with a startlingly detailed three-dimensional picture of the yard, as the echoes are received through her sensitive ears and processed. Each burst of clicks starts at high frequency and quickly drops to lower frequency. The high frequency, short wavelength bursts are picking up tiny objects such as mosquitoes in the air, while the lower frequency, longer wavelengths are giving the bat a picture of the background and large stationary objects to be avoided – trees, clothesline, people. (There is no way that a bat would ever be so clumsy as to get tangled in anyone's hair!) As she closes in on a mosquito the number of clicks per second increases dramatically from around 10 to well over 100. A wingtip flicks out and conveys the doomed mozzie into the bat's mouth. The revellers will never know what they owe to the unseen pest control system.

Now the bat's attention is attracted to something larger and thus more attractive – a moth. The usual crescendo of clicks ensues, but suddenly the moth vanishes! It has its own sensors which have detected the bat's signals while still at a safe distance, and propelled the moth into a near-vertical dive for the ground. Other moths have developed specially fuzzy wings which

22

don't reflect the bat's sonar – and some bats in turn have refined their sonar so that they can again 'see' the fuzzy wings. Other bats have amended their sonar frequency so that it is beyond the moth's ken.

Some moths taste awful, but the bat can't see warning patterns which a daytime bird would recognise. Instead these moths send out their own pulses, effectively saying, 'well here I am, but you really don't want to eat me!'. Yet other moths wait until the last moment before sending out a burst of clicks of a frequency to 'jam' the bat's incoming sonar. There is a very sophisticated arms race occurring above our unsuspecting heads.

At night's end she will return to her roost with half a dozen females in the roof space of a nearby house, an adequate substitute for now scarce tree hollows. Large Forest Bat males, like those of many insect-eating bats, roost alone. Also awaiting her is a large baby, already over a quarter of her own weight when it was born last month. Such an advanced baby has a short infancy, and he will be independent by the end of the month. Like her he hangs upside down; his legs are effectively part of his wings and he cannot stand up on them. No effort is required, as tendons automatically lock when he sleeps. He must, however, swing right way up to defecate or urinate! As mother approaches he is awake and eager to suckle. In March she will mate again, holding the semen through her winter torpor, before giving birth.

For now though, the revellers have long retired, stars are paling in the east and mother and baby are settling down for the day.

WHITE-THROATED GERYGONE (*Gerygone olivacea*)

CAMPBELL PARK WOODLANDS, MOUNT AINSLIE, CANBERRA NATURE PARK. I am entranced as I watch the White-throated Gerygone, a yellow-breasted scrap of a bird with white throat and red eyes, approaching the nest, slipping through the foliage with a caterpillar in its beak. It is very discreet, not wanting to draw attention to the exquisite nest hanging inside the abundant leaves of a healthy young sapling. I was first drawn to it by its glorious song, one of my favourite Canberra sounds, beautifully described by the doyen of Australian bird writers, the late Graham Pizzey, as a 'silvery thread of sound'. It tumbles down the scales from above, pure and powerful, achingly sweet, over and over, mischievously flicking back up at the end as if to restart, before being allowed to fade away. Indeed the somewhat awkward name, Gerygone, comes from Greek for 'born of sound'. They were long known as the Bush Canary, but to my ear this is selling them well short! From the time he arrives back from his winter sojourn on the Queensland coast, a bit south of Rockhampton, the woodlands and open forests vibrate with the lovely songs. By the time she arrives, a week or so later, the territory is established.

For now though he is quiet near the nest. To my eyes the nest is a work of art, though to the birds aesthetics such a vital matter is irrelevant compared with the need to provide shelter from rain and cold and predators. It is a hanging dome of matted bark bound with spider webs, slung from a slender branch among the leaves. There is a long tail of bark at the bottom and the side entrance is protected by an overhanging hood. Into this entrance he now slips, delivers his offering to the insatiable beaks within, and immediately sets out on another hunt. His mate did all the egg brooding, but now the job of feeding the three fast-growing chicks is a full-time one for both parents. Nonetheless it's a good season, there's plenty of food, they've managed to avoid the attentions of the ever-present bronze-cuckoos and there is every chance that they'll fledge these babies successfully.

Their neighbours and close relatives, the plainer-coloured Western Gerygones, nested earlier and while they are still in the woodland their song, equally sweet but somewhat eccentric with elements of *Pop Goes the Weasel*, has now gone quiet. Unlike the White-throated, this is an essentially inland bird whose range extends through central Australia to the west coast. I have spent many a pleasant but exasperating time searching for the origins of the powerful melodies, as the gerygones can be very elusive among the foliage. Eventually though they appear, often hovering at the leaves to pluck insects and spiders.

The nest is always a hazardous place to be, and the parents are working frantically in order that the chicks may grow and get out into the relative safety of the open, where they can hide or flee if necessary. As a result the entire process, from laying eggs to escorting the wobbly babies away from the nest, takes barely three weeks! Initially still fed by the parents, they must learn to forage for themselves in the three months they have left before they must start the long arduous journey to north of the frosts. And that gives me another three months to enjoy them.

TRIGGER PLANTS (*Stylidium* spp.)

CAMEL BACK TRACK, TIDBINBILLA NATURE RESERVE. I am never too proud to stop and admire the views in the course of a climbing walk and the haul up the Camel Back certainly qualifies! The views out over the land below and the ridges around are breathtaking – but so is the view at my feet in a sheltered gully some 1300 metres above sea level. There is a veritable sea of nodding pink flowers, spikes of them on robust stems, all with apparently two pairs of nearly parallel petals. They are Trigger Plants, always a delight, and always a source of deep fascination, demonstrating one of the most extraordinary pollination mechanisms ever evolved.

If I sit – nothing to do with the fact that I'm puffing a bit more than I'd like! – I've got a good chance of seeing them in action, with the hoverflies swarming around. These striped-bodied little flies are quite extraordinary in their own right. They flash along almost too rapidly to follow, then suddenly stop dead in the air, their wings a diaphanous blur. And even now, one is alighting on a Trigger flower. Whack! With a tiny puff of pollen a pad-tipped 'lever' swings up from below the flower, passes upright between the petals and descends onto the back of the insect who was only after a quick, free, sugar snack, per the flower's nectary gland. But, there's no such thing as a free lunch here either and the whole purpose of a nectary is to offer a pollinator, be it insect, bird or mammal, a reason to visit a flower. The hoverfly, in this case, pays for lunch – actually an invaluable energy hit – by being an inadvertent courier for the flower's pollen. Most flowers simply ensure that the pollinator comes in contact with the pollen, so that it passively sticks. Not the Triggers though, who leave nothing to chance!

One of the wonders of the system is that the padded tip of the column performs quite different functions at different times. If the flower has just opened, the pad will *deliver* pollen onto the insect's back. If it has been opened for a few days though, hairs grow through it to form a tuft, and it now *collects* pollen from the aerial courier.

As for the lever action itself – well! The upper edge of the column is flattened and can buckle in or out. When it is poised, triggering causes sudden tension changes in the tissue, giving a sudden buckling which 'pulls' the whole column inwards suddenly. The tiny triggers which release the dramatic event encircle the top of the flower tube. But … how? In an animal I could readily understand how the firing of nerve synapses can transfer such information almost instantly, but a plant has no such system. Information travels within a plant by hormones, but that can take hours. The only burst of experimentation was in Europe a hundred years ago, which gradually faded out as no definite answers were achieved. I love such mysteries which remind us of the very real limitations of our knowledge.

As I ponder, another hoverfly alights, but as I hold my breath in anticipation of its coming shock – nothing happens … Rather than a malfunction, this actually represents another very clever piece of evolutionary fine-tuning. The plant doesn't want its own load of pollen brought back to it, so while the trigger resets in less than 15 minutes it stays insensitive for long enough for the insect to get well out of the area. In the south-west of Western Australia, where I have been bewildered by the diversity of Triggers growing together, there are even more amazing strategies to ensure that the insect carries each precious load on different parts of its body, and can only deliver to the correct address.

But much as I love watching, I can't really defer the rest of the climb for much longer. I may just pop in again on the way down though.

LAUGHING KOOKABURRA (*Dacelo novaeguineae*)

BLACK MOUNTAIN, CANBERRA NATURE PARK. A child is being systematically beaten to death by her older siblings, while outside her parents are laughing.

Stripped of the anthropomorphism, the facts remain. The doomed baby kookaburra is guilty only of being the third to hatch. Her mother was slightly below peak condition and the third egg was notably smaller than the others. Furthermore the first hatchling, a male, arrived only a day before his older sister (who will be larger than him), then there was a gap of three days, so the last is also by far the smallest. This seals her fate.

The events taking place in the hollow are no aberration. Third kookaburra chicks hardly ever survive; her existence is purely as an insurance, in case the other two eggs don't hatch or the older chicks die young. In this case she's out of luck. So intrinsically is this behaviour a part of kookaburra existence that the chicks are equipped with a temporary 'tooth' on their beak to make it a more efficient offensive weapon. If the insurance isn't required, it makes no sense for the parents to expend energy feeding it after that; more than likely, they will later eat it.

Another way in which the dice rolled against her relates, ironically, to the way in which adult kookaburras are among the most cooperative birds in the world. Kookaburras can and do

breed alone, but when they do so it is very rare for more than one chick to fledge. The parents of this dying chick have helpers, offspring from last year, but sadly for her they are both female. For some reason males are more efficient caterers and carers and her chances would have been better had there been two male helpers. Kookaburra society is complex. One of the helpers, older sister of the nestlings, left home after a year and 'helped' at her own sister's territory on Aranda Ridge. Then her sister's mate fell victim to a speeding car and she returned home and was welcomed back into the territory. When she finally leaves again to set up her own territory she will be well-versed in raising young.

The nesting hollow is high in an old Scribbly Gum on the sunny western slopes of Black Mountain. The Cauliflower Bush is white with flowers and beneath it a 1.5 metre Eastern Brown Snake is hunting lizards. While kookaburras will certainly take snakes on occasions, this one is safe by virtue of its size. The traffic noise is a constant background hum, but generations of these kookaburras have lived with that as part of life. One of the helpers is now arriving at the nest with a grasshopper in its bill and the two large chicks defer their assault and jostle for position to receive it. The other adults are sitting watchfully on perches near to the nest tree, waiting for movement in the dry litter, of insect, reptile, or even mouse. All kingfishers have superb eyesight and these, the world's largest, are no exception. Now the father sets off in a straight shallow glide, landing momentarily alongside a skink and seizing it in a crushing grip of his huge bill. He flies up to a branch and systematically batters it into softness before heading to the nest, the skink now dangling limply.

Suddenly hunting is put on hold as all four adult birds fly hard and direct to where a burst of kookaburra taunt is still hanging in the hot air. They range on the invisible boundary, which is as plain to them as a line on the ground, facing the offending neighbours, bursting into a concerted roar of defiant and territory-affirming 'kok kok kok wook-wook-wook!'. One takes to the air and performs a brief angry display flight, but the other clan had never seriously intended a take-over – it's just worth testing the defences sometimes. This clan has a small dam in their territory and their chicks get frogs, dragonfly larvae and even the occasional small fish. As they retreat the residents restate their boundary with a slow conspicuous flight along it.

The smallest chick is dead. As a result her older siblings though will fledge and thrive and grow, as kookaburras do.

LITTLE MARBLED SCORPION (*Lychas marmoreus*)

DOWNSTREAM OF PINE ISLAND, MURRUMBIDGEE RIVER CORRIDOR. I can't help it. If a rock looks movable without damaging anything which might be under it, I can't resist having a peep. You never know what you might miss by not doing so. On this occasion a truly ancient creature is my reward. The small scorpion backs, startled, away from the sudden wash of light.

Scorpions have attracted much more than their share of misinformed hyperbole over the years. Certainly this little fellow is deadly – but not to me. But if I were a small beetle or especially a termite (a favourite food of this species), it would be a different story. In fact this superbly evolved little creature would be a pretty terrifying hunter if I were of its scale. At night it leaves its shelter and on its eight legs roams the surrounding countryside looking for prey, its sting, a strangely attenuated extension of the abdomen, carried high above its back. A victim is seized with the powerful pincers, which are wonderfully modified mouth parts. Immediately the sting whips down and injects venom into any vulnerable parts of the prey's body. The amount of venom used depends on the size of the prey, and is moderated by muscle control; this venom, a cocktail of nerve poisons, is valuable stuff, and not to be wasted! Death is pretty well immediate and the scorpion's pincers tear the body apart and 'juice' the segments into its mouth. Other, larger, species tackle tough prey such as spiders, centipedes, millipedes and even small vertebrates such as skinks.

A meal can last for months. Such a prey also provides the scorpion's water needs, and its cuticle is so waterproof that it may never need to drink, even in the desert. If you think I'm waxing lyrical on such an unlikely topic, you'd be right. I am a huge fan of scorpions, and have been ever since I was taken to see Walt Disney's classic *Living Desert* at an Adelaide drive-in. I well remember the mating dance (though I'm sure I didn't realise what was happening, and I'm pretty certain that Disney was non-specific on the details). The pair clasp claws, and he leads her backwards until he finds a suitable piece of ground on which to deposit a package of sperm; as she passes over it, she takes it up. It seems extraordinary, but the scorpion's gestation time is between two and 18 months, depending on the species! The forty or so live youngsters are carried around on mum's back, at first soft, helpless and stingless, living on food reserves for the first few weeks until their first moult, when they become independent. If they survive predation – especially from other scorpions – they will live for up to 20 years. In fact they may not even become mature for six years or so.

Scorpions didn't always have to skulk under rocks. In times long gone there were scorpions up to a metre long, which would have been well worthy of respect! Even today there are very formidable 30-centimetre-long scorpions which can indeed threaten human life, but not in Australia. As a dynasty their glory days have passed, but scorpions are still a successful group; there are some 700 species worldwide, but only 30 or so in Australia. One important measure of this success is that there has been no need for them to make 'improvements' to their basic structure in the past 420 million years! The first scorpions were marine hunters; they were apparently among the first predators ashore, following the first millipede-like grazers. In other words they predate the dinosaurs by 230 million years, coexisted with them for 130 million, and 60 million years later are still going strong! I would be willing to bet that their kind will be around long after mine is forgotten, but it's not a bet I'd be able to collect on.

One odd characteristic of scorpions is that their shell fluoresces under ultraviolet light, a phenomenon that is used by those who study scorpions as they go about their nocturnal business. Hopefully you can make use of that piece of information …

For now though I carefully replace the rock, ensuring that the little survivor is safely in a crevice.

MOUNTAIN PLUM PINE (*Podocarpus lawrencei*)

MOUNT TIDBINBILLA, TIDBINBILLA NATURE RESERVE. Even in summer there is a hint of ice in the early morning wind that probes hurriedly among the tumbled granite tors on the brooding hump of Mount Tidbinbilla. Small animals – searching ants, a skink trying to bask, an inquisitive antechinus – can't afford to lose body heat so they seek to avoid the chilling breeze. And in this they have two important and unconscious allies.

The rocks themselves are a wonderful heat sink and still retain some of the sun's heat that poured into them yesterday and throughout summer. Equally important though is the dense mat of leafy branches which clambers over the rocks, providing a still-warm air layer even in winter when snow lies on top of the foliage. The leaves are dark green, dense and small, giving no clue as to the plant's relationship. Often I ask people to rub and sniff these leaves when we come across them. If they are able to trust their nose rather than their eyes they have no difficulty in realising that this sprawling shrub is a pine.

At least 190 million years ago the family of pines we call Podocarps arose in Gondwana, one of the two large truly southern pine families. (The other family, the Araucarians, includes such well-known trees as Bunya, Hoop, Monkey Puzzle and Norfolk Island Pines.) The podocarps are perhaps less familiar, though the Tasmanian Huon Pine is famous. At the peak of their reign they formed great forests across what is now Africa, Australia, South America and Antarctica; southern dinosaurs roamed beneath them, rubbed itches against them and gobbled their leaves. At this time there were no birds, no mammals and no plants with flowers.

When flowering plants did evolve some 120 million years ago, also in Gondwana, their revolutionary new system for using animals to distribute pollen and seeds efficiently brought them rapid dominance over the ancient pine families which relied on chance and the wind to distribute their pollen. The cone-bearing pines – thus called conifers – maintain their dominance only near the poles and on mountain heights where the animal pollinators are scarce. They survived though in other places, and the podocarps are still an important part of rainforests in Africa, New Zealand and South America, supporting major timber industries. There are species in eastern Australian rainforests too. They are conservative, these podocarps, still growing in the rainforest habitats in which their immensely distant ancestors arose. Unlike some other rainforest plants none of the Australian podocarps have adapted to the arid lands which began to dominate some five million years ago. But …

This 'but' concerns just one species which has adapted to a particular type of dryness – that found in very cold conditions where mountain ice and frosts rip the moisture from plants. The Mountain Plum Pine grows above the tree line up to the summit of Mount Kosciuszko and throughout the Victorian Alps, as well as in the high Tidbinbillas and Brindabellas. No sensible plant except the rugged Snow Gum sticks its head up in such conditions, so the Mountain Plum Pine lies flat to the ground, pressed to the granite boulders. As did its ancient ancestors, it has separate male and female plants; males have small purple cones and females have bare seeds on a swollen red fruit-like stem whose purpose is to attract animals to distribute the seed.

The pine grows terribly slowly, branches of just 25 millimetre diameter being perhaps 100 years old. It is vulnerable to fires, such as those formerly set by high country graziers, and in NSW and Victoria has been often removed in the construction of ski runs. Here in the ACT, however, the Mountain Plum Pine lives only in national parks, so its future seems more secure – as much as any high country organism can be secure in this fast-warming world.

REGENT HONEYEATER (*Anthochaera phrygia*)

MOUNT MAJURA, CANBERRA NATURE PARK. There! It has taken me half an hour, but I've finally tracked down one of Australia's rarest birds, alongside suburbia and only kilometres from Civic. Regent Honeyeaters tend to stay quiet when feeding like this in the nectar-rich Yellow Box flowers and I've been following the quiet little bubbling 'plip' calls for a while. I have been sent astray a couple of times too by this bird's apparent mimicry of the raucous Red Wattlebirds which are also revelling in the nectar bonanza, and chivvying the Regent when they encounter it. Perhaps the richer more confident musical calls described in the books are reserved for when the Regents are in the majority, but this doesn't happen much these days.

This is a most striking bird, black with yellow wing and tail flashes, mottled below and with a bare warty pink face. (It got its name from its colour similarity to the Regent Bowerbird, which in turn was named for the regent George IV, though that naming was a bit of colonial sycophancy and there is no suggestion that these were George's colours. A hundred years after its discovery people wanted a more 'proper' name than Warty-faced Honeyeater!)

Back in January 1996 four pairs of Regent Honeyeaters bred on the edge of Watson near where I'm watching this bird, but since then the few ACT records have been of single birds around northern Canberra, including in the ANU and inner Belconnen. We know far too little, but these birds have probably wandered up and down the eastern seaboard from northern NSW (where atypically they sometimes feed in coastal heathlands) down to the ironbark forests of central Victoria. A stronghold is the Capertee Valley west of the northern Blue Mountains, where a huge effort has gone into restorative plantings and public education about the value of the woodlands. At least two of the birds which bred here in 1996 and were colour-banded later turned up at Capertee.

The nest is a delightful structure of bark bound with spider webs and usually tucked into a tree fork. In fact my first encounter with Regents was many years ago at Wyangala Dam near Cowra, when I watched enthralled as a pair assiduously collected spider webs from the deep black crevices of the trunk of Mugga Ironbark.

Sadly there are probably less than 1500 individuals of this fascinating bird left. This is particularly depressing given that only a hundred years ago flocks of thousands were still being reported in the Sydney hinterlands. Even as recently as 1964 the redoubtable Brigadier Officer (it's true!) could write that it has 'stood up successfully to the encroachments of settlement' and told us that it was still found in inner Melbourne suburbs. Not now though. They, like too many Australian birds, are victims of the ongoing loss of the rich grassy box woodlands and ironbark forests of the inland slopes.

How I'd love to see a flock of Regent Honeyeaters moving confidently through the blossoming Yellow Box. As if to underline the unlikelihood of this happening, this bird is suddenly discovered and harangued by a small group of Red Wattlebirds and in the way of its kind flies high, fast and far. Now, as I do so often, I am left to muse on what was and what might have been.

Note: Listed as a threatened species under Commonwealth, ACT, NSW, Victorian, Queensland and South Australian legislation.

PEA FLOWERS (Family Fabaceae)

MOUNT GININI, NAMADGI NATIONAL PARK. The top of Mount Ginini is a pretty good place to start the New Year; I reckon it's the best drive-in view in the ACT. I resent the intrusive presence of the Air Navigation Facility, but must acknowledge that it has to go somewhere … Looking back to the east where the road climbs up I'm looking out over Stockyard Spur; this was the site of one of the five lightning strikes in the ACT that led, in combination with NSW fires, to the horrific events of 18 January 2003. Behind it is hidden Corin Dam and then across the plain are the rugged granites of the Tinderries. In the other direction is Kosciuszko National Park, with the jagged Bogong Peaks on the horizon to the west. Further round to the south and even further away is the square lump of Jagungal and nearer to hand are the open lands of the Tantangara Plain and the gleam of water that is Tantangara Reservoir. Then, looking due south along the line of the Brindabellas is great Gingera, looming above Mount Little Ginini. But something's odd about Gingera today – it's stained yellow.

I have seen this before and know that it's a solid mass of flowering Leafy Bossiaea, whose flowering began a bit late this summer after a cold spring. There is more of it under the Snow Gums just below us and along the road on the way up, though the lower ones are mostly finished now. We wander down towards them now to admire the tiny bright green leaves and clear yellow pea flowers. As is often the case, the foliage is covered with glossy green cockchafer beetles, *Diphucephala*.

Anyone who's gardened will know a pea flower when they see it – whether it's a Broad Bean or Sweet Pea flower or any of the 1100 native species (or indeed any of the 12 000 different peas throughout the world) the essential shape remains the same. There is a big petal, the standard, across the back of the flower. Pointing forward are two more, the wings, and beneath them two more, fused like the keel of a ship and called – yes, the keel! In times not so long ago, when romanticism was allowed a freer rein, the family was called Papilionaceae for the butterfly resemblance of the flowers.

These Bossiaeas, and other high Brindies pea shrubs – like the two species of Shaggy Peas, and the abundant Narrow-leaf Bitter-pea and small spiny Gorse Bitter-pea – are performing a wonderful and essential task. With the help of bacterial colonies in their roots they are steadily replacing vital nitrogen that was burnt from the soil during the fires and storing it in the soil in a form that is accessible to other plants.

Some of the Bossiaeas are already forming pods from the fertilised flowers. In this case they are small, round and flat, unlike the long cylindrical ones that we think of as food; the bitter-peas have triangular pods. And people have been eating pea seeds for a long time – Broad Beans and Lentils were grown at least 9000 years ago in the Middle East. The so-called French Bean is actually from America and has been found in ancient Peruvian graves. Green Peas have been excavated from 5000 year-old German pottery deposits. Peanuts arrived in Africa from Brazil in the 16th century to become a food staple; the underground pods grow when the plant sticks its head in the ground after the flowers are fertilised. Liquorice comes from the root of a pea. The organic pesticide Derris also comes from a pea's roots, while the valuable dye indigo was first extracted from pea leaves at least 2000 years ago.

My companions' smiles are becoming a little fixed. Time to descend the mountain and perhaps mollify them with a New Year champagne. Or two.

FEBRUARY

STRIPED LEGLESS LIZARD (*Delma impar*)

MULANGGARI GRASSLAND RESERVE. A small, dark, beady-eyed head is peeping out of a clump of Spear Grass.

It shouldn't be here. This was intended to be part of a major shopping centre complex; the legless lizard's grass clump is pretty much in the middle of a car park which, fortunately, never came to be. On this occasion knowledge and a recognition of the responsibility to protect tiny precious native grassland remnants took rare precedence over convenience and plans already committed to paper. After a period of inevitable but increasingly tedious cracks about 'legless lizards, mouthless moths, earless dragons' etc., responsible governance won out and the Gungahlin Town Centre now stands a little to the north of its originally intended location.

The rest of the lizard – some 20 centimetres of black stripes along a pale brown body – emerges. She is sinuous and superficially snake-like, but there are several clues to her true nature. As she cocks her head the ear opening is obvious; no snake has this. Now she cleans a fleck of dust from the transparent scale protecting her eye using her broad lizardly tongue, not at all slender or forked. Turning back on herself she shows clearly the little flap on her flank which is all that remains of her distant ancestors' hind legs. And behind that is a tail which is noticeably longer than all the rest of her body, far longer than the short tails of snakes.

She hatched very close to here nearly 10 years ago, quite oblivious to the fact that her fate and that of the Mulanggari Grassland had recently been determined and reprieve granted. Philosophising is a human conceit and the lizard's issues are much more direct and pragmatic. A sudden looming shape hurls her into frenzied twisting action, her whole body writhing up and back through the grass. The kestrel, now only a metre from the ground, spreads wings and tail in confusion and briefly stops her plunge. Recovering, it snatches at the now disappearing lizard and seizes its tail – half of which promptly detaches from the lizard's body. The little falcon takes to the air, carrying a still-squirming meal, while the lizard slips safely down between the tussocks. Several of her tail vertebrae carry a weak plane of cartilage; she has just contracted muscles around one of these vertebrae, setting a series of events in train. The tail shears as if cut, and other muscles squeeze the blood vessels shut so she doesn't bleed. Over the next few weeks the tail will regrow, though the effort costs valuable energy. The tail bones won't regrow but the new tail will contain cartilage, perfectly functional but not as flexible as a jointed skeleton. In future emergencies she will only be able to drop the tail above this break.

A lizard has short attention spans, and perhaps too some deep instinct tells her that she'll need extra nutrition now, because soon she re-emerges to hunt spiders, crickets, caterpillars and cockroaches. Fortunately she laid her two parchment eggs back in December, hidden under the litter. In autumn they will hatch and the babies will feed up before burrowing down into the base of a tussock and going into a torpor for winter.

Here, just metres from a busy shopping centre, ancient grassland cycles spin on. Great place, Canberra.

Note: The Striped Legless Lizard is listed as a threatened species under Commonwealth, ACT, NSW, Victorian and South Australian legislation.

MEAT ANTS (*Iridomyrmex purpureus*)

CALLUM BRAE WOODLAND, CANBERRA NATURE PARK. The distant 'toodle-oo' of Peaceful Doves is leading me through the delightful, if somewhat weedy, woodlands of one of our most recent nature reserves. I am distracted (my perennial condition, I sometimes think) by a broad and well-beaten track through the dry grass. An animal track certainly, but the sheep have been removed and this one was not made by the ubiquitous roos. In fact the constructors are even now pounding along it, keeping it clear and open. The number of ant feet-hours required to achieve this is beyond my imaginings. These are Meat Ants, a particularly narrow name since all is grist to their mill (though it originally referred to their appreciation of bush meat safes). Bending down close I can see the constant stream of supplies being ferried back to the nest. Meat certainly – grasshoppers are popular at the moment, small grubs, unidentifiable bits of tiny butchered carcasses – but also large numbers of seeds. The many who appear to be empty jawed are probably carrying nectar and honeydew inside, to be regurgitated within the nest.

Following the track in the direction of the apparent cornucopia I am led to a big eucalypt; the ant parade marches straight up it. Aside from some ants so minute that they are barely visible, no other ant species are visible. The Meat Ants own this tree and if any other ant wishes to harvest it, it must do so at night when the owners are resting. Back the other way I come to the nest, which in this case is something of a surprise. The distinctive low, wide gravel mound surrounds a higher mud termite mound. Meat ants are ruthless enemies of termites and if they can find an entry will invade the termite citadel, remove the larvae and eggs to their own larder, and take over the living space. No termites will survive here, though the mound was impregnable to the ants until it was breached by a wandering echidna.

Around the nest are drifts of straw, discarded from grass seeds, but among the winnow are many other seeds. These are from plants, including wattles, grevilleas and hibbertias, which bribe the ants to carry their seed away, by means of a nutritious bribe attached to it. This elaiosome is more attractive to the ants than the hard seed, which is stripped off and discarded before the elaiosome is taken inside. The seed is now far from the shade of the parent plant, and the seedling probably even gains protection from growing near the ant nest.

Other ant tracks radiate out from the nest too. Some of these lead not to food supplies but to other nests, extensions of this great colony which sprawls for half a kilometre. But now I've trodden too closely to the nest and a swarm of workers emerge to defend it, jaws raised. Meat Ants have no sting, but their bite, their sheer numbers and a chemical secretion all make for a formidable nest defence and I readily back off. They also regularly patrol the well-defined boundaries of their territory against raids by neighbouring Meat Ant colonies. In a strange ritual the rival worker armies line up against each other for hours or days, pushing and kicking but not using their jaws. Only an ant could know when the ritual is complete and the workers may go back to their business, without a single life being taken.

All the workers (including the 'soldiers') are sisters. Ants rarely have any use for mere males, except when it's time to start a new colony. Then winged males and females hatch and form mating swarms, after which the males – who can't actually do anything else – die, leaving the females to get on with it again. One of the sisters, the 'queen', tends the eggs until workers hatch to take over the role. She spends the rest of her life pumping out eggs; the type of egg she lays is geared precisely to the needs of the colony at the time.

As I resume my pursuit of the elusive dove, I find myself dodging a nest of very aggressive Bull Ants, ancient primitive stingers. The more modern Meat Ants have done away with such weaponry; is there a lesson here?

VARIED SITTELLA (*Daphoenositta chrysoptera*)

MULLIGANS FLAT NATURE RESERVE. The sight of a flock of Sittellas working the branches of a Red Stringybark always makes me smile. They are so busy. It is almost impossible to follow one as they scurry jerkily along the branches towards the centre of the tree and spiral down the trunk, flitting to another branch before they've had a chance to check this one properly, or so it would seem. Suddenly the entire flock hurtles to the canopy of another tree to create chaos there too. As they fly they seem all wing; their broad orange wing bars flashing 'sittella!' to all who can read. The flocks, especially in winter, often drag with them other insect-eaters such as pardalotes and thornbills. Sittellas have black caps, staring yellow-ringed eyes, up-pointing yellow-based chisel bills and big strong yellow feet. The big bills are used to prise off pieces of bark to seize unfortunate insects and spiders cowering beneath, and to probe into crevices and hollows. As they work and fly their splintery little contact calls are as busy as their owners.

As I'd expect from nature, however, apparent chaos is actually well-ordered. Though it's not obvious from a distance, the white-throated males have larger bills than the dark-throated females and this enables the group to divide up the tree's resources more efficiently. He probes more deeply into the rough bark lower on the trunk. She tends to concentrate higher up in the tree on the smoother bark of the outer limbs.

This group is a tight-knit clan, mostly related, comprising a dominant pair, probably past years' offspring and two or three of this season's now semi-independent chicks. (They can feed themselves perfectly well, but don't mind begging freebies when they think they can get away with it.) The group will have cooperated in building the nest and feeding the chicks, though their mother, the dominant female, will trust no-one else to incubate the eggs or brood the babies in the nest. She is happy for the helpers to feed her as she sits on the nest though. A Sittella's nest is a beautiful structure, superbly disguised in the bottom of an erect eucalypt fork. Clad in bark and lichens and bound with spider web, it is almost impossible to recognise unless we've seen the birds approach it. Even this clue is not always given; I've watched a Sittella working down the trunk and as it passed the nest, surreptitiously slipping food to the waiting chick without a pause in its descent.

In the past it has been assumed that Sittellas were related to the Australian Treecreepers or even the northern hemisphere nuthatches, but we now know that these resemblances are due solely to similar lifestyles and the Sittellas are old Australians with no close relatives. Like other woodland birds they seem to have declined in numbers in recent years, but Mulligans Flat is one place where they can reliably be found. I am very glad of that.

Note: The Varied Sittella is listed as a threatened species under ACT and NSW legislation.

DRAGONFLIES (Order Odontata)

INNER NORTH SUBURBIA. I am sitting in my leafy backyard in the gloaming, watching a chillingly efficient hunt taking place above my head. The hunters are swift, remorseless and efficient, with few of their prey seeming to escape their darting attacks. The hunt is eerily silent and apparently bloodless. This is not surprising as I'm not watching birds or even bats. No bird or bat could hover motionless, manoeuvre into position, then dart almost too quickly for my eye to follow to seize the helpless victim. I haven't yet seen a missed attack. The assassins are dragonflies and the prey are ant alates, 'flying ants' heading out to start a new nest. As light fades, so do the images of the hunt. The ants will found their new nest of course – sheer numbers will see to that and the dragonflies will retreat with the fading light.

It is warm and my glass is not yet empty so I continue to sit musing that it is as well that dragonflies are no bigger. And yet, they once were, in a far off world that was still

Black-headed Skimmer

earth – the earth of 270 million years ago, before ants, before flowers, before even dinosaurs. Then there were dragonflies with wings 70 centimetres across, terrorising lesser creatures. The dinosaurs arose, dominated the world for vast aeons of time – and vanished. The descendants of the great dragonflies remain however, with some 2000 species of dragonflies and damselflies an active part of the world. Three hundred of them are Australian. All are voracious aerial hunters of mosquitoes, bees, butterflies and indeed any large flying insects. Old names reflecting this include 'bee butcher' and 'mosquito hawk'. Others though were quite inaccurate, including 'devil's darning needle' and 'horse stinger'; they can't sting and never attack mammals.

Damselflies are an integral part of the dragonfly group, but are distinct and distinctive. They are slenderer, at rest they hold their wings erect like a butterfly (dragonflies hold theirs flat), and they have smaller eyes at the sides of their heads; a dragonfly's eyes are large and almost meet on top of the head.

Mating often occurs on the wing, after spectacular displays involving coordinated or even linked flights. I have enjoyed watching these love flights many times, including from the hides at

Jerrabomberra. Some species drop eggs straight into the water, others cut slits into reeds and lay elongated eggs into them. Dragonfly offspring are as voracious as their parents, and while adults only live a season, the nymphs may grow in the water for several years. They have not the speed and grace of the adult, but they do have stealth and strength, and an extraordinary nightmarish appendage called a mask attached to the lower lip. This triangular plate hinges below the jaw, tipped with sharp spines. When the victim is close enough the mask swings forward and impales it. 'It' may be mosquito larva, small fish or tadpole – or one of its own kind. When the nymphs are ready to transform into an adult they crawl out of the water onto a reed, rock or tree trunk.

Even the most consummate hunters may also be the hunted, and dragonfly nymphs and adults are eaten by larger fish, frogs, birds and snakes. Adults are also taken by birds like the Rainbow Bee-eater or are trapped in spider webs.

Enough musing for now though. The hunters have gone and the mosquitoes have ventured forth. Tonight though I'll dream of 50 kilometres-per-hour ruthless flashes of red or blue, from a time before even the dinosaurs dreamt.

HOBBY (*Falco longipennis*)

TUGGERANONG. Evening near the Tuggeranong Town Centre, with streamers of starlings coming in to roost, silhouetted against the orange clouds. Suddenly a larger sharp-winged rusty shape explodes amongst them, coming from behind at unnerving speed. A cloud of feathers erupts and the Hobby, working hard now as he carries the dead starling which is a third of his own weight, flies with it to a window ledge on the nearest building. Here he settles down to dismember and eat his hard-won prey at leisure. A forensic examination would show that among the fatal injuries suffered by the starling is a broken neck from a bite by the hooked 'tooth' in the Hobby's bill.

In the distance he can see his daughter hunting flying insects, her large eyes enabling her to hunt in dimmer light than most local birds of prey. While she is not yet skilled enough to catch early-flying bats, she is quite capable of snatching a moth from the air and while still in flight, bringing it up to her beak, snipping off the wings and swallowing the body. She is doing well; a few weeks ago she'd have been harassing dad for a share of starling.

His mate, considerably bigger than him, is perched quietly in a high dead eucalypt down by the Murrumbidgee, waiting for the Red-rumped Parrots to come in to drink. Nearby are the remains of an old Australian Raven nest; it was also the nest that produced her own two chicks. Hobbies, like other falcons, do not build a nest of their own. Other falcons use building or cliff ledges or tree hollows, but Hobbies find that old crow or raven nests are just perfect for them. They are probably the most familiar bird of prey in Canberra and February is their month. The sight of a Hobby scything above the rooftops, streaked rufous below with black cap, is a common one this month if we're quick enough to see it. The apparent rise in numbers now is due to the scattering of newly independent youngsters. Next month many Hobbies will start to leave Canberra, heading up the coast towards Queensland where the winter is warmer. This Tuggeranong pair will follow the migrating honeyeaters along the Murrumbidgee and beyond, picking off stragglers as they go.

Other local falcons stay here through winter. Out in the open country the little rusty Kestrels hover while working the paddocks for grasshoppers, mice and lizards, while the big Brown Falcons soar or hover heavily seeking rabbits, snakes and ground birds. Downstream the pair of powerful Peregrine Falcons stays near their cliff-front nest site, preying on galahs and pigeons. While the Hobby and Peregrine are the archetypal falcons, swift long-winged pursuit hunters, all four species share ancestors which broke away from the main bird of prey line some 36 million years ago, hurtling after the ancestral starlings.

Tonight the starling descendants sleep uneasy in their leafy roost, dreaming perhaps of flashing rusty death.

NORTHERN CORROBOREE FROG (*Pseudophryne pengilleyi*)

GININI FLAT, NAMADGI NATIONAL PARK. In a remote corner of the great sphagnum moss expanses of Ginini Flat, far from human ears, a sound startlingly like a wet finger being rubbed on a balloon is emanating from the moss. Most of the bog was savagely burnt in January 2003 but with a lot of help from determined and dedicated ACT Parks staff and wildlife officers it is beginning the slow recovery process. This corner escaped the fire though. The hummock of moss emitting the squeak appears greenish-yellow, but under the top growing layer is a 70 centimetres deep, dead pile of compacted moss which we know as peat. The living moss grows at the rate of less than a millimetre a year and the mound is over 3000 years old. This may well represent the time since the previous big fire in the flats.

The caller is a tiny porcelain-perfect frog, less than 30 millimetres long, glossy greenish-yellow with swirling broad black stripes. He pauses briefly to snap up a passing tiny black ant, his staple diet, and resumes calling. He is calling for a mate – in fact he is calling for another mate, because already beneath him in a mossy chamber is a fertilised clutch of 23 large eggs. Rapidly absorbing water from the damp moss, they swelled to seven millimetres in diameter. Their mother came on a dark overcast afternoon a few days ago. In the way of her kind she dithered for some time, hesitantly approaching the male who by now was aware of her and had come to the surface, calling with increasing urgency. Eventually she pushed down into

the moss, he clasped her from behind in typical frog manner and fertilised her eggs as she laid them. What is definitely not frog-like though is the site – most other frogs lay into water. These eggs are laid on land, though insulated and kept moist by the moss. Not until the winter will the cavity flood and allow the eggs to hatch.

Meantime they grow rapidly, forming embryos with large nourishing yolks in just six days. Three weeks later the embryos hatch, still within the egg, into tiny tadpoles. Not until the first major winter rains flood the nest site can the tadpoles hatch safely. If the snows come before the rains do, the tadpoles remain trapped in the eggs beneath the snow until the spring melt frees them. Even if they have managed to hatch early, the tadpoles are trapped in the moss burrow under the snow, torpid and scarcely growing in the intense cold. Any other tadpole would be excreting ammonia, fatal in the burrow confines, but remarkably evolution has found the solution to this problem by allowing Corroboree tadpoles to absorb their waste nitrogen directly and turn it into protein. Not until nearly a year has passed, when they will still be less than a centimetre long, will they grow back legs and crawl for the first time onto land.

Their father meantime goes on calling, but he will not get another taker this summer. Corroboree Frogs, abundant not so long ago, are now scarce. It is hard to pinpoint the precise cause, but it seems that a combination of increased drought induced by rising global temperatures, habitat loss and the advent of the deadly Chytrid Fungus is responsible. Our male cannot know it, but the future of his kind may lie in massive captive breeding programs such as are being carried out below his mountainous ancestral home at Tidbinbilla Nature Reserve.

Next month he will haul out of the bog and make his way into the surrounding Snow Gum woodlands where he will spend winter deep under a log. It was under such a log that this year's mate survived the 2003 fires; females only visit the bogs to breed. Meantime though he goes on squeaking in the vast silence of the mountains. The future of his line depends on it.

Note: *The Northern Corroboree Frog is listed as a threatened species under Commonwealth, ACT and NSW legislation.*

MOUNTAIN GRASSHOPPERS

MOUNT FRANKLIN, NAMADGI NATIONAL PARK. In my lifetime, the top of Mount Franklin will never look the same as it did before 2003, simply because the ancient Snow Gums will not regain their former grandeur in such a brief span. In other ways though things are pretty much business as usual. In particular there is a plethora of grasshoppers fleeing from my feet as I walk. We are used to this in the high country, but it's really a bit odd, as grasshoppers are essentially a heat-loving group of insects characteristic of low hot grasslands and deserts. In fact the mountains are not rich in the number of grasshopper species, but in sheer numbers they may be the dominant insects. On the way up I had to drive around several of the big and dramatically blue  and red flightless female Mountain Grasshoppers, out searching for their slimmer flying mates. A peek under a rock by the roadside at such a stop revealed a big, robust, burrowing Mole Cricket.

A quick snatch now and I can admire a handsome brown grasshopper, spangled with creamy spots, in my hand. The powerful great hind legs are a feature common to the 3000 species of Australian grasshoppers and crickets. These legs can hurl some species two metres through the air. In many species a leathery pair of wings protects another, filmy pair, but this one is flightless, with only little wing flaps. While it is understandably quiet, around me I can hear males calling. Doubtless there are others calling too which are too high-pitched for me to hear, but that's of no concern to the insect, whose targets are the abundant females. The sound is produced by rubbing a 'file' on one wing against a 'scraper' on the other. The one I'm holding is one of the many 'short-horned' grasshoppers; other groups include long-horned grasshoppers and various crickets, but the terms don't mean much. The little black Bog Crickets scurrying through the grass and the green katydids pheeping sadly in the Snow Gums are just grasshoppers by another name.

The one in my hand is one of the Mountain Spotted Grasshoppers. A close relative has found an extraordinary way to survive in conditions very different from those experienced by its desert relatives. Many of its cohabitants simply die at the end of summer, leaving eggs to survive the winter, but the Alpine Spotted Grasshopper is made of sterner stuff. Not unexpectedly, normal activity ceases when temperatures drop below 10°C, and they can only manage to crawl slowly when it gets to 0°C. Colder than that and they cease moving altogether, but it makes no attempt to dig in as other grasshopper species do. In fact it can survive 'normal' winter alpine conditions perfectly well. It does this by a marvellous trick; at low temperatures it synthesises sorbitol in its blood. In a car we would call it antifreeze!

Releasing the spotty hopper, I am immediately attracted to a big green long-horned grasshopper which, improbably, is munching on a small blue-green flightless one. This is *Austrodectes monticola*, a common predatory mountain grasshopper. Its victim is of the *Kosciuscola* group, mountain specialists. Among them – possibly even this one, but it is no longer readily identifiable – is the wonderful Alpine Thermocolour (or Chameleon) Grasshopper. As the day warms up its body changes from dark, glossy blue-black to pale blue-green; at lower temperatures it is absorbing maximum solar radiation, but starts to reflect it as it becomes more intense.

In this way it can develop at maximum speed. It must do this, as it has to start its season later than its low country relatives do, hatching, maturing and laying eggs all at least two weeks before the soil freezes in autumn to allow the embryos to develop sufficiently to survive the winter. Other species compress their cycle by reducing the number of immature stages. The Mountain Spotted Grasshopper has allowed itself a more leisurely existence by surviving the winter. Yet others overwinter in the frozen ground as immatures, and continue development next summer.

For now I leave the big green long-horn to its lunch and find a spot for my own. I will be sharing the spot with grasshoppers though.

COMMON BLUEBELL (*Wahlenbergia communis*)

TIDBINBILLA NATURE RESERVE. The Tidbinbilla roadsides – along with roadsides throughout the lower ACT – are a mass of blue. I love the hardy native bluebells, which go on flowering long after many other flowers have given a heat-stressed gasp and finished their display. This is one of the reasons that these Common Bluebells, along with the very similar Tall Bluebell, are perhaps my favourites among the group. They can grow profusely out of hard, gravelly ground which scarcely seems to warrant the word 'soil' and are perhaps the most widely known and recognised local wildflowers. Indeed they are often mistaken for their alpine relative on which has been bestowed the lofty accolade of the ACT's floral emblem.

Funny things, emblems. It seems to me that the criteria for selecting a regional emblem should be that the plant or animal is either one with which most people are familiar and with which they have an empathy, or (preferably and!) which is unique to the region. Our selected emblem, the Royal Bluebell, is truly a very beautiful flower indeed, but it meets neither of those criteria. Growing high in mountain bogs and wet banks, it is never seen by most Canberrans. Moreover it is widespread throughout the alps of NSW and Victoria. It is also nearly impossible to keep the Royal Bluebell alive through the hot, dry Canberra summer, as very many loyal emblem supporters have found to their cost, while the Common Bluebells flourish untended on the nature strip. I have always been of the opinion that the more humbly named and knock-about Canberra bluebells were better suited to the role and I'm amused that so many people assign it to them anyway!

Not that the plants care of course. Nor do they care that their allotted name *Wahlenbergia* comes from a Swedish botanist and medical professor called Goran Wahlenberg who lived from 1780 to 1850. He explored thoroughly in the icy expanses of Lapland and northern Norway, and wrote floras of both Lapland and Sweden, as well as treatises on vegetation and climate in southern Switzerland and papers on mosses, lichens, tree structure and fossils. He never saw the massed roadside Common Bluebells though, nor they him.

Aside from the 26 Australian species of *Wahlenbergia*, there are some 200 species elsewhere in the world, mostly in the southern hemisphere. Their large family, Campanulaceae, also includes the Scottish Bluebells, known as Harebells in England. (The unrelated English Bluebell is in fact a lily.) Wahlenbergias have developed a curious pollination method whereby the young flower produces sticky liquid on the style (the female part of the flower), which catches the anthers and pulls them out of the flower, thus presenting the pollen to passing insects. Later the female role of the style takes over.

Aboriginal people are known to have eaten the flowers raw and they are reputed to go well in a salad, but I prefer to enjoy feasting on them with my eyes.

GLOSSY BLACK-COCKATOO (*Calyptorhynchus lathami*)

MOUNT MAJURA. On a hot late afternoon among the Drooping She-oak groves on the mid slopes of Mount Majura, the breeze through the hanging foliage has a whispering quality produced by no other leaves. It has been likened to the sound of an aeolian harp. That and the heat is all – but stand still for a moment. Up the slope a little is another odd noise, a soft grating creak, almost mechanical. Follow it and yet another subtle sound emerges, a gentle pattering like light rain on the ground; no rain has fallen here though for many days now.

Suddenly an uneasy shuffle pulls our gaze up from the ground, crunch-dry and littered with broken cones, to a large dark bird surprisingly close by in a she-oak. Then another and another come into focus; this bird often feeds in threes. These are Glossy Black-cockatoos, which arrive periodically when the Casuarinas are bearing seed, stay for some weeks and then vanish again. They may be back next year, or we may not see them again for years. Meantime though they work steadily. The seeds they're extracting are not much larger than dust motes, so most of the day must be committed to their harvest. First the bird must find a good tree, on which the cones contain a high proportion of seeds; it tests a few and if the cones are not up to scratch another tree is tried. When the rewards are good, the cocky settles in and may work methodically in the same tree for hours. It bites off a cone and holds it, base upwards, in its left foot. The huge beak works like a precision tool, stripping the woody material in layers and extracting the essential seeds, rotating the cone until it is empty, then immediately starting another one.

The bird we are watching is a female, with blotchy yellow head. The male's head is plain dull brown; both sexes have red tail panels. The young bird with them hatched six months ago in a hollow in a tall dead tree in wet coastal forest. The loss of such hollows, which can only form in a tree at least 150 years old, is one reason that the Glossies are now a threatened species. The youngster's skills are still developing and it feeds more slowly than its parents, dropping cones while manipulating them.

As the sun drops low the birds suddenly hurl forwards out of the trees, heading for the dam on the lower slopes behind the houses. Here they sit for a while, glowing in the horizontal light on the branches above the water, waiting for a gap in the parade of walkers and dogs before coming down to the water's edge to drink then going to roost somewhere on the mount. And tomorrow they'll find another seed-rich grove and do it all again. Or maybe they'll be gone …

RIVER OAK (*Casuarina cunninghamiana*)

URIARRA CROSSING, MURRUMBIDGEE RIVER CORRIDOR. From the Mount Majura Drooping She-oaks we have driven to Uriarra Crossing for a picnic under yet another she-oak – the taller, finer-foliaged, small-fruited River Oaks, which never seem to grow away from streamsides. I love she-oaks, I love the whisper of wind in their branches and I love their essential 'Australian-ness', 65 species of them from tropical seashores to red central Australian dunes, tall trees and sprawling shrubby heaths.

They superficially resemble pines, but are in fact one of the oldest of flowering plant families. It is a bit early in the season yet, but lying back and looking up I can pick out a few precocious flowers. The single-stamened male flowers are tiny and brown, in simple spikes at the end of the upper branchlets. The female flowers are always on a separate plant, a crowd of red filamentous heads at the end of short branches. Though their ancestors were pollinated by insects, the Casuarinas are now wind-pollinated.

They appear leafless, but a close look with my trusty magnifying lens reveals rings of tiny triangular leaflets about a centimetre apart around the cylindrical branchlet. Such leaf reduction is usually a strategy to conserve water. The problem of course is that leaves are necessary to produce essential energy for the plant through photosynthesis, so to compensate for that loss the branchlets themselves are green, containing chlorophyll to enable photosynthesis. This is most unusual in plants; another example of the strategy of dispensing with water-losing leaves and letting the stem do the work is the American cactus family.

It seems to me that Casuarinas probably evolved on sea-shores, which pre-adapted them to an arid lifestyle. Even with plenty of rain, sea-shore plants grow in a perpetual drought situation, through having to compete for water with salt in the soil. From here they spread into the drylands as Australia's rainforests shrank. As we saw while watching the Glossy Black-cockatoos on Mount Majura, the fruits are tiny seeds, held in a woody cone.

Not much grows here under the River Oaks and it seems that at least some Casuarina species reduce competition from other plants either by antibiotics produced by the bacteria in the root nodules, or by compounds in the shed branchlets. All have nitrogen-fixing bacteria associated with their roots, so they have a key role to play in enriching low nutrient soils.

She-oak timber was used by Aboriginal people, and also by Europeans. This is always given as the source of 'she-oak' i.e. an inferior timber to European oak, but I'm not convinced at all by that. For one thing Casuarina timber was in fact well regarded by early settlers. There are two other pieces of circumstantial evidence for my belief that the name is of Aboriginal origin, later anglicised for convenience. One is the occasionally met alternative 'shiock'; the other is in the name of the Western Plains species Buloke. As for *Casuarina*, the great biologist Linnaeus, borne on flights of fancy stimulated by I know not what, thought that the foliage resembled the hairy plumage of the Cassowary! (Recently some botanists have seen fit to split the species with larger and rougher fruits off from *Casuarina*, calling them *Allocasuarina*.)

High in the River Oak are clumps of foliage-mimicking She-oak Mistletoe. Around them flit small butterflies which flash brilliant blue when seen through my binoculars. These are Satin Azures which rely entirely on the mistletoes, feeding on the nectar as adults and on the leaves as larvae. The females are looking for small black ants, whose presence stimulates her to lay eggs on the mistletoe. When the caterpillars hatch, the ants accompany them as they feed, taking secretions of sugar and amino acids with which the caterpillars 'pay' for their protection from an array of insect predators and parasites.

Our own picnic calls and the light is fading, but above the River Oaks whisper on.

AUTUMN

AUTUMN IS A TIME OF MOVEMENT, OF PREPARATION FOR THE HARD
TIMES COMING, OF YOUNGSTERS FINDING THAT THEY HAVE TO MAKE
THEIR OWN WAY IN THE WORLD.

In the mountains the last fledglings are urged from the nest and into flying lessons, to join the flocks making their way down the slopes, often following forested stream lines, drifting along and feeding as they go. In some cases they are following older siblings who hatched earlier in summer and have already moved to the warmer safer lowlands. Beneath them, but less obviously, kangaroos and wallabies are making similar journeys. Some of the flocks will simply spend winter in valleys and plains below, or in the cornucopia of Canberra gardens. Suburbia is being made raucous by flocks of Pied Currawongs, King Parrots, Crimson Rosellas and Gang-gangs arriving from the ranges.

In part they are filling gaps created as huge numbers of other species – including honeyeaters, cuckoos, kingfishers, dollarbirds, martins, cuckoo-shrikes, fantails, flycatchers, reed warblers and orioles – start their much longer journeys north, as far as tropical Queensland and even beyond, across the Torres Strait. Overhead flocks of swifts ride the storm fronts, feeding up prior to a far greater journey to their breeding grounds at the northern ends of the world. Only in autumn do Canberra householders see mountain species such as Rufous Fantails and Rose Robins as they pass through on their way north.

Grown-up young Pied Currawongs, Magpies, Sulphur-crested Cockatoos and Galahs still beg noisily, and increasingly in vain, to be fed. At night even noisier altercations are taking place across the suburbs as young Brush-tailed Possums are evicted from their mothers' sleeping quarters.

As breeding ends, male birds such as grebes and Superb Fairy-wrens are undergoing one of their twice-yearly moults into drabber garb, less conspicuous to hungry eyes now that they don't have to impress mates and rivals.

A second, though lesser, flowering is taking place. Some species which flowered in spring now do so for a second time, but others, such as some eucalypts (Ribbon Gum, Brittle Gum and Apple Box), Silver Banksia and orchids, mostly inconspicuous ones including several greenhoods and midge orchids, set flower now when there is less competition for pollinators. Many other orchids are producing leaves from their underground tubers, and will be ready to flower when spring comes.

Many fungi put up their fruiting bodies in autumn, following the rains. In the lowland woodlands and grasslands some of the native grasses produce their seeds, attracting flocks of finches and parrots – though far fewer than in former times. In the less heavily grazed areas the Kangaroo Grasses are turning purple with new growth, below their now empty rusty flower heads.

Among the grasses and hillside shrubs lizards are building up their fat reserves in the last sunny days. Insects are laying eggs to survive the winter that they themselves will not see.

The quiet, cold days are coming.

Grey Fantail on Pomaderris aspera, *see page 84*

MARCH

GREENHOOD ORCHIDS (*Pterostylis* spp.)

GIBRALTAR CREEK, WOODS RESERVE. I am indulging myself. I should be at my desk writing this story, but instead I'm taking a break to look for orchids, a favourite pastime of mine. I am an unrepentant orchidophile – though sometimes I suspect 'orchoholic' might be more accurate. This is a delightful short walk, leading out of the southern end of the Woods Reserve car park and following moist banks along the side of Gibraltar Creek, crossing and recrossing the creek en route to the base of the most impressive Gibraltar Falls.

In autumn, orchids often mean greenhoods, a very special group of often cryptic orchids, and this sheltered track is a good place for them. At the moment I am kneeling in front of a Summer Greenhood (which despite its name flowers well into March). It is not particularly flower-like at first glance, not least because we're not used to seeing green flowers. Further it is utterly unlike any familiar flower shape, a strange white-banded, green bulbous apparition with a long down-pointing 'nose' and long erect filamentous 'ears'. The defining hood is comprised of three flower parts (a sepal and two petals to be precise) tightly overlapping; in

Summer Greenhood

this species the hood is upright but in many other greenhoods it is held horizontally. The extended tips of the hood forms the 'nose'; the 'ears' represent the other two sepals. If I get down – and I always prostrate myself in front of orchids! – I can see a short black tongue protruding from the front of the flower. But now, my perspective distorted by peering through a magnifying lens, I've bumped the flower and the tongue has vanished inside.

What I've inadvertently done is to imitate an insect, a fungus gnat or mosquito, which is attracted to the flower's scents which mimic those of his own female. We know too little about the details of who pollinates which greenhood, not least because we still don't really know a great deal about the family tree of the tiny fungus gnats. Like many other orchids, the greenhoods are consummate confidence tricksters – once attracted, the unfortunate insects are not offered any nectar compensation. As the little fly enters the flower it too triggers the tongue which snaps shut, locking it in. To escape it must force its way out through the overlapping sections of the hood, a path which also involves pushing past the pollen sacs.

Up the bank among the snow grasses is a small colony of startling red and white striped Scarlet Greenhoods. This is the fourth greenhood species I've seen on the walk. Single plants of Fisch's Greenhood, with a single narrow very 'long-nosed' flower, have been scattered through the grass. There was also a colony of the white and green-brown striped fat-flowered Dainty Greenhoods. In spring on the same track I could easily see another four or so, including the big head-hanging Nodding Greenhoods and crowds of erect little Maroonhoods. (I can see another 20 or so throughout the ACT.) Once I've got my eye in I can detect the characteristic ground-hugging rosettes of leaves of these spring flowerers already. The same late summer rains that triggered the Scarlet Greenhoods to put up a flower stem also encouraged the tubers of the others to sprout the rosettes, which will be ready at the end of winter to produce their own flowers.

I will be back for them too.

Note: Recent work divides this genus into several new ones, but most current authorities still use Pterostylis. *Additionally the new proposal retains* Pterostylis *for several species, including a couple of those seen on this walk.*

WHITE-THROATED NEEDLETAILS (*Hirundapis caudacutus*)

COOLEMAN RIDGE RESERVE, CANBERRA NATURE PARK. I have only stood among the swifts a few times before in my life, and it's always a thrilling experience. I am walking along the low, long Cooleman Ridge, which forms the south-western border of the Weston Creeks suburbs, looking out over the Murrumbidgee Valley and the Bullen Range to the Tidbinbilla Range beyond. Today is classic swift weather. The grey-purple storm clouds are boiling, rumbling and flickering over the Tidbinbillas in the middle distance, and the wind coming ahead  of the front brings the swifts, with smaller numbers of swallows, martins and woodswallows. These other birds are superb aerialists, but alongside the swifts they look pedestrian.

All are harvesting the unimaginable numbers of flying insects, especially winged termites and ants, which swarm in such conditions. They, and numerous beetles, flies, moths, bees and grasshoppers are swirled high into the air by the turbulent conditions. The swifts ride the edges of the rolling cold front, plunging through the insect swarms again and again, like sharks through shoals of fish.

Often they fly so high that they appear as mere dots against the clouds, but today they have come down almost to ground level. White-throated Needletails (until recently known, and probably more usefully, as Spine-tailed Swifts) are startlingly big when seen close up like this. Half a metre of back-scythed wings, dominating the stub-tailed body, swoops low along the ridge, swings around me not much above head level, then is halfway to Mount Taylor before I can properly register what's just happened. Loud in my ears though is still the tearing swish of its passing wings. And suddenly they are all around me as the front arrives, screaming wildly as they stoop, soar up and sweep down and around.

These super-long narrow wings are not actually the ideal shape for high-speed flight – they are too long to flap very quickly – but are perfect for soaring. Much of the breathtaking speed of this flock is driven by the energy in the storm front winds, soaring into them and riding them down again. In fact, one of the things these wings do best is allowing the swifts to fly below what would normally be stalling speed, making it easier to home in on prey in calm conditions. The huge wings also carry them on an incredible round trip twice a year; within the next couple of weeks they will start out for their breeding grounds in eastern Siberia and Japan. Here they alight on solid ground for perhaps the first time in nine months, when they nest in tree hollows. The harsh winters of their breeding grounds produce a bonanza of insect food in summer but can't supply them in winter, so they head south again as soon as the chicks are independent.

One of the downsides of the immense wingspan is that the wings are too long to allow them to take off from a flat surface, so they must land on the side of the trunk and climb into the nest, and later must launch into the air from the hollow. In fact they have little use for feet, except for clinging to a vertical surface, and they are tiny and weak. (Their family name means 'without feet', but that's a bit of poetic licence.) Even mating takes place in the air and to drink they simply skim the water surface. We used to believe that while in Australia, White-throated Needletails don't land at all, but we now know that they roost in groups inside eucalypt foliage, from which they can simply drop into space in the morning.

Soon this breathtaking harvest will be over and the swifts will be gone, from Weston, from the ACT and from Australia. But not from my mind's eye.

WHITE-FACED HERON (*Egretta novaehollandiae*)

O'CONNOR WETLANDS, BY O'CONNOR SHOPS. These wetlands are 'new', the initiative of a community organisation (the Sullivans Creek Catchment Group, which started with just five people) collaborating with government and industry. An ephemeral woodland stream had been turned into a sterile concrete drain, but now this section at least lives again, flourishing as birds, turtles, frogs and aquatic insects find and colonise it. Along the bank stalks a White-faced Heron, eyeing the water's edge.

A ripple causes him to stop, wait briefly, then hurl his head forward to grab a dragonfly larva. The larva, in turn, had been stalking a tadpole, who will now live long enough to become a frog – which next year will be

eaten by another heron ... When the heron reaches the reed beds he slips in and settles to wait, with the sun behind him, for unwary frog or fish to come within range.

He belongs to one of the least fussy heron species in the world, in terms of what he eats and where he forages for it. He himself spent last winter at the coast, driven down from the tablelands by drying dams. While there he learnt to hunt crabs on the rock platforms. Returning inland at the beginning of spring he stopped along the way at farm dams to catch yabbies, hunted crickets in open paddocks and even picked larvae from a roadside kangaroo carcass. This morning he was distracted from his early morning flight over the suburbs by a backyard pond. Alighting in the yard he helped himself to four plump goldfish and was gone, leaving the puzzled and aggrieved owners to argue about whether to blame the local kookaburras or the neighbour's annoyingly free-ranging cat.

He has only recently become a single bird again, his two surviving chicks having fledged and gone their own ways. The nest, one of the few in Canberra suburbia, was a big untidy stick platform on a flat fork high in a tree by the North Lyneham shops. Mostly he brought the sticks and his mate placed them. When it was complete she laid four palest blue eggs, spread over a six day interval. One, the third to be laid, was taken by an opportunistic Australian Raven during a changeover of brooding responsibilities. When the last egg hatched, three and a half weeks later, the chick was notably smaller than both its siblings and was unable to compete successfully for food; it never flew. The other two fed on the usual White-faced Heron smorgasbord, first regurgitated into the nest alongside them, then taken directly from the parent's bill. As soon as the meal-bearer arrived the nearest chick seized the very top of the adult's bill in its own, holding it crosswise, frantically coaxing the parent to produce. This continued for nearly another four weeks, by when the supply of food began to dwindle and the youngsters were ready to leave the nest. The chicks would still harass their parents for food in nearby trees, but were starting to forage for themselves.

Focused on the water at his feet, he doesn't notice the elegant, pure white Great Egret flap heavily over, heading for Jerrabomberra Wetlands. White herons are called egrets, but there are no meaningful differences. In fact the little White-faced Heron is more closely related to the Little and Reef Egrets than he is to other Australian 'herons'. Still less is he related to the stately cranes (represented in Australia by Brolgas and Sarus Cranes), despite his widespread folk name of Blue Crane, immortalised in Hesba Brinsmead's 1964 *Pastures of the Blue Crane*.

But these things are concerns for humans, not herons. Frogs matter more.

CENTIPEDE (*Scolopendra morsitans*)

RED ROCKS GORGE, MURRUMBIDGEE RIVER CORRIDOR. She is in her prime at three years old, nearly 10 yellow centimetres long, and one of the top predators in her world. Not quite the top predator though, so she shows caution as she emerges from her log crevice for an evening's hunting. In fact it is many decades since quolls also hunted along the banks of the Murrumbidgee, but avoidance mechanisms developed by millions of years of evolution do not fade quickly. If she ventured out in the light the temptation of her several grams of protein would be quite enough to overcome fear of her defences in bird or large lizard. And even at night Antechinuses, small quoll relatives, are still around, though scarce, and must be avoided.

Were she capable of musing, she might envy some of her tropical relatives which are 30 centimetres long, big enough to turn the tables and prey on mice and lizards themselves. In fact one such formidable creature from South America, the Amazonian Giant Centipede, is powerful enough to drag small bats from the air as it clings to the walls of their roost caves. Even this magnificent animal though would, 300 million years ago, have been merely a moderate snack for her distant ancestor Euphoberia armigera, *fully a metre long, though it is not clear that Euphoberia was in fact a hunter.*

As her flat, jointed body with 21 pairs of legs slips among the river stones her hard cuticle rasps audibly, but the hunting Wolf Spider does not hear. The centipede's eight simple eyes are quite good enough to detect light and movement and her antennae are also conveying information about the world, in particular the big juicy spider moving slowly ahead of her. She pauses, judging distance and angles with computer-like precision. Then a quick burst of acceleration over the gravel, scattering sand with her legs swinging wide, and she swarms over the spider, pinning it with her body, curling around it and gripping with the long, back-pointing hind legs. She bites once with the big venom fangs under her head. Unlike the doomed spider's own fangs, hers are actually modified walking legs. The spider's own attempt at biting is thwarted by her cuticle and very soon the centipede's venom has stopped any such attempts. Already the centipede's mandibles are dismembering the spider, taking precious protein and liquid. A worm or snail or even a grasshopper or cockroach would have been easier, but she cannot afford to bypass potential nourishment. If a human were careless enough to provoke her into biting, they would suffer pain and swelling but no lasting harm.

A little later she is again attracted by movement in the litter, but backs off when she realises that it is a Geophilomorph, an Earth Centipede, smaller than herself and very slender with many more body segments. She has no compunction about eating other centipedes but the Geophilomorphs emit noxious chemicals when threatened. They share this characteristic with more distant relatives that the huntress regularly encounters, the slow and otherwise harmless millipedes. These are grazers, usually black with cylindrical bodies and two pairs of legs per segment. Similar and probably related animals were among the very first animals to leave the sea some 450 million years ago, munching on the algal meadows that had also recently come ashore.

Her own recently scattered offspring are certainly now at risk if she encounters them, even though she guarded their early weeks fiercely and tenderly, curling her body around the egg cluster and then the babies themselves through the first couple of stages of their lives. They will not need to fear her for much longer though. Sharper eyes and stronger claws than hers are out tonight and even now fatal claws are relinquishing their grip on a eucalypt perch to lead the Boobook's deadly descent.

GALAH (*Cacatua roseicapilla*)

COTTER ROAD FARMLAND. We have pulled up by the road to wonder at a flock of at least 300 Galahs picking their way across the paddock. Galahs suffer from over-familiarity but they are truly beautiful birds, coloured like a sunset through clouds. The remarkable thing about this gathering is that just 50 or so years ago it would not have happened. Had I been driving along the Cotter Road in the mid-1950s and seen even a single Galah, I'd have stopped in surprise and made sure I reported the phenomenon. Today we are, sadly, more likely to respond 'just Galahs'. They are truly birds of the inland plains, but we opened broad Galah highways to the south and east with permanent water points and swathes of cleared pasture and croplands replacing forested land and the Galahs came, starting in the 1940s. So too, a couple of decades later, came the Crested Pigeons, and more recently, the Little Corellas.

The flock we are now admiring has come together after the breeding and there are many rasping demands from hopeful youngsters, really too old to be fed and mainly being quite properly ignored. The mated pairs stay together as long as they both live; this is not the pattern for most birds and is almost unknown among other animals. It is only likely to be found among long-lived birds and Galahs, like other cockatoos, are certainly that. Caged cockatoos have been known to live for well over 50 years and it seems likely that once a wild Galah has sur-

vived the hazardous first year of its life, it will live for at least 20 years or so. These birds are gleaning the ground for seeds and digging in the soil for fleshy roots and tubers.

Most probably bred within 10 kilometres or so of here; Galahs for the most part are home bodies, despite their great diaspora of the last century. From where we can sit we can actually see a nesting tree across the paddock. Galahs habitually and systematically strip bark from around the hollow and the white patch gleams against the fawn-coloured bark of the old Yellow Box. It is probably this visibility that they are intending – 'this hollow is occupied, so don't bother to come investigating'. The pair would have renewed their partnership back in early spring, initiated by him swaggering along a branch towards her with crest raised and murmuring endearments. She then led him in a wild chase through the trees until they landed and repeated the performance, ending with mutual preening. Both parents worked on the hollow, clearing it out and lining it with eucalypt leaves which repel parasites. Anything from two to five white eggs would have been laid and both birds brooded and later fed the incessantly wheezing, grating begging babies. Galah chicks spend a long time in the nest – around two months – and then the parents, doubtless desperate for some peace, deposit them in a huge deafening tree-top creche of baby Galahs while they forage. They haven't lost a sense of responsibility though, as they will often deem that creche unsuitable and transfer their offspring to another.

But our musing and enjoyment is interrupted suddenly as the whole flock explodes into a frantic screeching pink and grey whirl. The reason is high overhead; a Peregrine Falcon, one of the pair which breeds on nearby Murrumbidgee cliffs. Galahs fear Peregrines like nothing else, and with good reason. Australian Peregrines specialise in hunting Galahs and as a result are bigger and stronger than their overseas relations; evolution in action. The show is over for now, and it's time to resume our trip. I renew a vow I've made many times before – when I get sick of Galahs, it's time to hang up my binoculars.

KANGAROO GRASS (*Themeda australis*)

MULLIGANS FLAT NATURE RESERVE. The native grasses are always a delight to the eyes, but Kangaroo Grasses in autumn are particularly fine. This is prime growing season and the nodding rusty brown flower heads, now empty of seed, hang above the purple-tinged fresh green growth. By the time winter comes the leaves will be frost-burnt to a warm brown.

With an explosion of noise a plump covey of Brown Quail explodes from nearby and hurtles 50 metres away before diving back head first into cover. No matter how often it happens my stomach always lurches at the sheer unexpectedness of it. It is still warm enough for skinks to be flicking through the tussocks, moths flutter looking for a site to lay eggs, beetles, grasshoppers, wasps and spiders work the stems all looking for different resources. The grasslands are extraordinarily rich, which of course is why there is so little of them left.

When the first European settlers arrived in south-eastern Australia, vast swathes of grasslands swept across the plains, tens of thousands of square kilometres from northern NSW to Melbourne and west to Adelaide. In the southern tablelands alone there were at least a quarter of a million hectares of pure treeless grassland. There are accounts of riders travelling through grasslands up to horses' bellies, with flowers to the horizons and quail constantly bursting ahead. Not much more than a hundred years ago flocks of Emus, Bustards and Brolgas roamed the Canberra plains. Bandicoots and bettongs were abundant. But the sheep and cattle, the new burning patterns, the ploughing and the weeds, and more recently the spread of housing, have reduced the grasslands to less than 1% of that.

To add to their problems, they look to the untrained eye much like any other paddock, with none of the grandeur of the tall coastal range eucalypt forests, or the mystique of the rainforests, which led to at least partial protection of those habitats. Further, grassland inhabitants tend to be small and inconspicuous, prickly and scaly; not much here that is cuddly or brightly coloured or charismatic, characteristics which sadly we have often tended to favour when scarce conservation resources and passion are being allocated.

Kangaroo Grass does not tolerate heavy long-term grazing, so its prevalence here at Mulligans Flat is an indicator that the property was well-managed for its century and a half of European stewardship, which of course is why it was declared a nature reserve in 1994.

These Mulligans Flat grasslands are secondary grasslands – that is, they originally grew as an understorey to eucalypt woodland, before many of the trees were cleared – but this does not reduce their value and interest. In fact the very presence of Kangaroo Grass is an indication of low disturbance levels (ploughing or heavy grazing soon eliminate it) and otherwise scarce plant species are often found with it. In late spring and early summer the grasslands produce a superb flower display equal to anything in the region. The low, well-drained ridges of Mulligans Flat are ideal Kangaroo Grass habitat, though it may also dominate in boggy situations. Up here we can also find patches of the white tufts of flowering Wallaby Grasses and the long slender heads of Spear Grasses.

When asked if I'd rather be able to see into the past or future, I have no hesitation in choosing the past; among other things I'd give a lot to see the grasslands sweeping to the horizon again and have the quail giving me palpitations with every step I take.

Some botanical authorities retain the name Themeda triandra, *a species whose range extends from Africa to southern Asia. Others believe that the Australian Kangaroo Grass represents a separate species; that is the approach taken here.*

GARDEN SPIDER (*Eriophora* sp.)

INNER NORTH BACKYARD. Silk is truly a most wonderful invention, though last night, en route to the compost heap, I copped a face full of it and for a moment my appreciation was not unalloyed. Despite my momentary panic I knew I was safe, as a Garden Spider's first reaction is to scramble up out of the way or to drop to the ground. Even if I'd threatened her enough to make her bite me, the effect would have been minimal and temporary.

Tonight I've come back with a torch, confident that she'll have rebuilt in the same spot – and she has, strung between the shed and the big eucalypt. Already she's slipping away across the surface of the web to gain the safety of the tree trunk. Her heavy, hunch-shouldered body is some 30 millimetres long, so she isn't hard to see at the moment; when she reaches the trunk though she will tuck her solid legs in and her mottled body will effectively disappear against it. The web is an infinitely complex and subtle structure which she rebuilds every evening and dismantles before dawn, eating the material so as not to waste it. I can see now the strong, multi-threaded 'bridge' line running horizontally across the top of it from which it all hangs. Fortunately this one is well above my head level, because she will leave that in place as a starting point tomorrow night. From each end of this a line runs down to the ground where they meet to form an upside-down triangle, which frames and supports the wheel of the web. In the centre of the spiral of the web, where all the radius lines meet, is a space where the spider sits and waits (when I'm not disturbing her).

Silk has freed her. The ancestral spiders were aquatic hunters, which followed the first nibbling millipede look-alikes onto the new tiny green pastures on the shore at least 400 million years ago. The most ancient living spiders – the funnel-webs and trapdoors – still bear the mark of this ancestry in their two pairs of gill-like lungs which mean that they are substantially confined to cool, moist silk-lined burrows. The much more numerous and diverse modern spiders have freed themselves from this constraint by evolving a more insect-like breathing system which enables them to take in more oxygen, and so follow their prey wherever it may lead them. Some, such as the Wolf Spiders and Huntsmen, run their prey down, but the most modern and numerically successful spiders are sit-and-wait ambushers, saving huge amounts of energy courtesy of the wondrous web.

A bundle of silk hanging near the top of this web has wings protruding – a moth that didn't concentrate hard enough. As soon as the spider felt the vibration in the web she'd have rushed out and wrapped the struggling moth in a shroud, both as a safety measure in case it was a victim which may cause damage to her and to avoid further damage to the web. Then, a quick bite and the moth stopped struggling. She may have already finished feeding or I may have disturbed her.

Silk, as I said, is a most wonderful product, far stronger than steel for its diameter and a lot more flexible. I have read that a pencil-thickness of it could stop an airliner in flight … It is a protein produced by glands (spinnerets) at the rear of her body and played out by her back legs. Different spinnerets produce different types of silk for different purposes, such as the sticky spiral studded with drops of glue, the dry radius threads along which she can safely run, the sheet in which the moth is wrapped and silk in which she will shortly wrap her eggs. A few days ago, after a complex and prolonged courtship which the male initiated by plucking the web with a very specific tune, she allowed him to mate; whether she allowed him to escape uneaten this time depended on whether she was already full of beetle or moth! Very soon she will lay up to 300 eggs, wrap them in silk – of course – and hide them in a curl of bark where they will spend winter before hatching in spring and dispersing, many by silk parachute threads. She however will probably be dead in a week, her task done. My path to the compost heap will be clear – but I'll miss her.

GREY TEAL (*Anas gibbosa*)

KELLY'S SWAMP, JERRABOMBERRA WETLANDS. Kelly's Swamp has been atypically dry for nearly six weeks and it's taken two days of steady rain to put a few centimetres of water across the basin. During the rain the opportunistic Purple Swamphens trotted purposefully across the road from the sewage ponds to find seeds and insects washed in with the waters, and to seek tubers in the softened mud. But within a day of the rain ending these colonisers were joined by a small party of Grey Teal, perhaps the greatest water opportunists in Australia. Four of the group had only recently joined the flock, up near Crookwell at Pejar Dam whose waters were also dropping dangerously. The other pair though had been on a remarkable odyssey.

They had both hatched three autumns ago when the Riverina was flooded. As water poured into the Red Gum and Black Box channels and overflow pans dense with sheltering Lignum, something remarkable happened. Drawn by magnets that no mere human could understand, uncountable thousands of Grey Teal had arrived and immediately begun a raucous mass courtship. The billabongs boiled with flapping, whistling, grunting ducks and pairs flew along every waterway and around every tree large enough to contain a nesting hollow. The frenzy was triggered by the sight of rising water; this alone can start the Grey Teal's hormones racing, as only water across the land can produce the level of food required to produce young. In less than a fortnight every limb spout and tree trunk hollow had up to a dozen eggs in it. As soon as the hollows were all taken the less fortunate birds began to commandeer the tops of tree stumps and even fence posts. After that, eggs were laid on the ground, under Lignum or grass clumps, among reeds or in rabbit burrows.

The predators came to feed off the bonanza. Tiger Snakes, Australian Ravens, Whistling Kites, Lace Monitors, Water Rats, Foxes and many others feasted on eggs and ducklings. A pair was doing well to get two ducklings to the 'flapping' stage, but this was enough to make it worthwhile. Eventually the waters started to fall and huge numbers of ducklings became trapped on drying lagoons. The youngest of these perished on the smaller ponds. But untold thousands did not, including the pair now on Kelly's, and as the waters fell still further, they began to scatter. A waterbird in the land of El Niño must use the water when it comes, then move or die.

Flocks moved in literally all directions. Some headed south-west and ended up on the Coorong in South Australia. Others went east until they hit the coast; many of these continued north along it. And some flocks headed due north, billabong-hopping until they eventually reached the great flood plains of Kakadu. These included the pair now dabbling upside down, eating seed and green matter from the muddy bottom of Kelly's Swamp, in sight of Parliament House. For a rich summer and a winter they stayed in a tropical cornucopia, then next summer the rains failed and the flocks again scattered. Some followed the coast, either east to Queensland, or west where a few eventually reached the coastal lagoons south of Perth. This pair though moved south again and have now reached Canberra.

They won't stay though. Grey Teal don't.

GREY-HEADED FRUIT BAT (*Pteropus poliocephalus*)

HALL, OUTER NORTH CANBERRA. She is working the fig tree methodically, testing each fruit for ripeness and taking the softest and most redolent, crushing it in her mouth, swallowing the energy-rich juice and letting the skin and fibrous material drop to the ground below. She scrambles nimbly through the branches, skilfully using her elongated thumbs, as well as her powerfully clawed feet. Suddenly, from the dark sky, another bat flaps noisily into the branches, attracted by the smell of the fruit. She reacts angrily to him, screeching hissily, but he is not going to be deterred so she resumes her meal, chittering a running warning lest he gets too close. Inside the nearby house, other mammals are also responding to the disturbance, cursing and pulling pillows over their heads; 4 o'clock in the morning means something very different to them than it does to a fruit bat.

This lovely big bat, dense ashy grey fur on body and head, with rich, rusty gold scarf, was born a decade earlier in a huge camp on Bellingen Island in northern NSW. Her earliest memories were of the constant squabbling cacophony, and powerful fruity musky scent, of over 100 000 of her kind in the branches of rainforest remnants by the river. During her life she

has been drifting steadily southward, in part pushed along by the encroaching big Black Fruit
Bats from the north. In the past 80 years the black bats have extended the southern limit of
their range well over 1000 kilometres south, from central Queensland to as far as Sydney.
Most fruit bat habitat in NSW is fragmented and scattered, and the incursion of tens of thou-
sands of newcomers has put more and more pressure on the food supplies provided by remnant
rainforest and eucalypt patches, swamp tea-tree stands and of course fruit orchards. Some of
the orchardists have invested in netting to protect their crop, but others continue with an older
and more brutal approach, shotguns shattering the night and bones. Others even set up elabo-
rate and lethal wiring systems to electrocute hungry bats. Such persecution has kept this female
moving, ever southward. She spent a year in the Royal Botanic Gardens, Sydney, then drifted
even further southward. (A wise move, though she didn't know it – plans are afoot to rupture
daytime sleep there with loud noises, to encourage the colony to move elsewhere.)

Soon she will have had her fill and will head back towards the busy camp in trees near the
lake in Commonwealth Park, within a few metres of an equally busy café and visitor information centre, and an outdoor entertainment venue. Here her son, now too big to hitch a ride
with her, clinging to fur and nipples with claws and teeth, is left in a creche to await her return.
The 15 kilometre flight is nothing to her – in the north there were nights when she would
cover twice that distance from a camp to a rainforest patch when the wild figs were abundant.
When she starts for home soon she will still have a last fig in her mouth, and won't drop it until
she's flown nearly five kilometres. On this occasion it will merely provide a source of utter puz-
zlement in the morning to the suburbanite whose car it lands on; in a wilder environment,
however, she provides an invaluable service to rainforest trees, spreading their seeds far across
the countryside between isolated rainforest patches.

Surprisingly few of the daytime strollers, joggers and cyclists look up at the remarkable sight
of upwards of a thousand big bats hanging upside down, wrapped in their superb fine leathery
wings stretched out over four hugely elongated fingers. From a distance they could resemble big
hanging fruit, if it were not for the eternal restlessness of a fruit bat camp, where someone is
always scratching, stretching their wings, abusing their neighbour or seeking a more peaceful
branch to escape such a tirade.

Four years ago the flowering in the coastal forests north of Batemans Bay was poor, and
desperate for new sources of pollen, nectar and fruit, she joined a small cohort of bats that
moved inland in summer seeking better rewards. They ascended the escarpment and, following

the Tallaganda range and the forests of the Queanbeyan scarp, found their way to Canberra, where that year the street ironbarks were in full flower, providing a cornucopia of pollen and nectar. Backyard fruit trees only added to the bounty they enjoyed, and the camp at Regatta Point was founded. When the frosts started to bite they descended the range again to the milder coastal forests, but fruit bats are intelligent and quite capable of remembering. The following year they made the same trek, this time bringing more animals with them; every year since the numbers have increased, and a tradition has been established.

The world is changing; individual Little Red Fruit Bats in particular have always visited Canberra sporadically, but a major camp of Grey-headed Fruit Bats as an apparently permanent annual fixture is novel. Canberrans no longer have to travel north to thrill at the evening spectacle of hundreds of big fruit bats streaming out against the glowing evening sky, heading for feeding trees throughout the suburbs. Their pleasure is of no significance of course to the female now flapping powerfully back to Commonwealth Park; she does appreciate their figs however.

Note: The Grey-headed Fruit Bat is listed as a threatened species under Commonwealth and NSW legislation.

AUSTRALASIAN GREBE (*Tachybaptus novaehollandiae*)

YERRABI POND, AMAROO. Yerrabi Pond has quickly developed a healthy ecosystem and the cranky chittering of the Australasian Grebes cuts across the fluting honks of the swans, the whiney 'wow!' of the Wood Ducks and the hard screeching of the numerous Coots. We have stopped by for a look on the way home from the nearby Mulligans Flat and are struck by the numbers of grebes present. Such gatherings are not unusual as breeding comes to an end – the Fyshwick sewage ponds are another reliable magnet for them.

Among these are some still wearing their handsome breeding plumage, with broad stripe of quickly-applied creamy lipstick and rich rufous neck patch. Indeed one pair is still accompanied by a couple of youngsters whose fading baby stripes are still visible. Now that we've become aware of them, we can also see the abandoned nest behind them, a pile of floating green vegetation at the edge of the bulrushes. In this their mother would have laid up to five pale blue eggs and the cooling dampness of the nest was offset both by the parents' incubation and the heat of the composting material. When disturbed the parents would have quickly arranged some of the vegetation over the eggs and slipped quietly away. The chicks could swim almost as soon as they hatched, but initially usually rode on their parents' backs, even being carried down as they dived.

I am always somewhat awed by the vast age of the grebe dynasty. *Neogaeornis* dived in Chilean waters 80 million years ago. Fifteen million years later its distant descendants survived the cataclysmic explosion of the asteroid strike that took out all the dinosaurs, the remaining toothed birds and indeed 85% of all animal species on earth. Somehow the grebes lived through the biting cold under the choking dust cloud that followed. Grebes in 'Australia' watched as the very land tore apart and they became forever isolated from their South American heritage. Perhaps only the emu lineage has lived here longer than the grebes.

The Australasian Grebes that we now watch diving for snails, small fish and aquatic insect larvae are not the descendants of the earliest Australian grebes. Their genus is a worldwide one and they are very closely related to the near ubiquitous Little Grebe, so presumably their ancestors arrived in the not so distant past. If descendants of the old Australian grebes live, they are the superficially similar Hoary-headed Grebes which are scattered thickly among the grebe raft in front of us. A closer look reveals that a few of these too are still in breeding plumage, with their apparently whiskered grizzled cheeks and crown. Their genus is confined to Australia and New Zealand and apparently arose in one of these places and found its way to the other, as grebes periodically still do today. Tellingly too, their closest relatives are still in South America. The handsome, big Great Crested Grebe that we were admiring last week at Acacia Inlet at the western end of Lake Burley Griffin is a real newcomer; the same species is found through much of the world.

In their evolutionary quest to be consummate divers grebes have reversed the trend of flying birds everywhere which sacrifice every skerrick of surplus weight, and they have developed heavier bones – they are even known to swallow pebbles to help them stay under. Their 'flight' – mostly pattering across the water when disturbed – is a bit pathetic but that doesn't stop Australasian Grebes in particular from colonising every farm dam across the countryside. They fly at night to avoid predators who would find them very easy pickings indeed. Once on the water though they simply dive to safety.

This diving is pretty slick, involving a little leap into the air to gain momentum. Nonetheless, the old shooters' story of a grebe being able to see the flash of the gun muzzle and dive before the bullet arrives has just a whiff of hyperbole about it.

Time to do some market shopping, but the grebes will still be here for next time – and for long after we're gone and forgotten.

APRIL

YELLOW-FACED HONEYEATER (*Lichenostomus chrysops*)

KAMBAH POOL, MURRUMBIDGEE RIVER CORRIDOR. A party of 30 Yellow-faced Honeyeaters is dithering. They are fluttering nervously in and around a big Yellow Box on the ridge. Every now and then a small group starts out to cross the hundred metres of open space to the denser cover of the corridor along the river, but each time they panic and flee back to the shelter of the tree and the flock. Their apprehension is soundly based. Two hundred metres away in the top of a dead tree a Collared Sparrowhawk sits in a flurry of feathers, methodically plucking one of their number. Sparrowhawks, Brown Goshawks, Hobbies and Peregrine Falcons regularly follow the migrating flocks, taking a steady toll.

Their numbers are now swelling. They have been joined by a dozen little White-naped Honeyeaters, who start moving a couple of weeks after the first Yellow-faced and will still be coming after the bigger birds have gone, and the same number of big Noisy Friarbirds. The drive to move is strong and perhaps the presence of the rough, tough friarbirds emboldens them, for now they suddenly all stream out, flying fast and low for the trees at the top of the gorge. The sparrowhawk is busy eating now, and her mate, circling high above, is also sated. If the gap of dangerous open country was bigger, it might take an accumulation of hundreds of birds before they'll risk taking the plunge – that way the danger to any individual is low. One way or another, however, they will eventually go; the imperative to move is on them and they cannot ignore the commands of their hormones.

The first cold mountain breaths that are harbingers of the coming winter have prompted them to start moving now, but for weeks they have been getting increasingly restless, with irresistible hormonal changes triggered by the shortening hours of daylight. Next spring, when days again reach a key length, they will return from the north to breed in the forested ranges of the south-east.

Among the safety of the riverside trees the birds move more slowly now, feeding as they go, but heading steadily upstream, to the south-east. This seems to be the wrong direction for them, but a safe indirect route is preferable to a hazardous straight line. South of Angle Crossing on the NSW border they will leave the Murrumbidgee and start to head east, across the Shoalhaven and into the coastal ranges. The young birds doing the trip for the first time would be able to find their way to their northern winter destination using a magnetic compass in their head, but they lack the certainty that experience will bring. Sometimes groups of juveniles travelling alone will cast about uncertainly, trying to match what their compass is telling them with the unfamiliar landscape. Older experienced birds though can fine-tune the route, using maps developed on previous migrations to avoid dangerous sections and to make sure of a constant food supply. Migrants of other species which travel over the sea have to feed up very seriously before the journey. The honeyeaters have the luxury of being able to eat as they go – in fact it is a very leisurely trip. They normally only travel on nice clear sunny mornings, with no uncomfortably early starts. Not for them either non-stop long hours over lethal oceans, battling through storms if necessary. Nor do they take the option, as many migrants do, of moving in the safety of night – perhaps the reduced stress afforded by spending early mornings and afternoons feeding compensates for the dangers.

Many won't survive the journey, but very many more will, to bring spring back to our gardens and forests when the urge to move is on them again.

BRUSH-TAILED POSSUM (*Trichosurus vulpecula*)

SOUTH-EAST BELCONNEN. Stand-off! The two cats, one arched and rangy, the other short-legged and stocky, snarl and hiss, tails bristling, as the lean one circles. A strangely rolling rush from the heavyweight and the other backs down and retreats, screeching furiously. A beam of light from the opening kitchen door shows that the victor is no cat though, but an angry, muttering Brush-tailed Possum. A quick scurry now and he's up into the wattle where he watches, with little evident concern, from a branch three metres up. His kind have been urban animals in Canberra, and indeed in Australia, for as long as the cat's ancestors have. If he thought about such things he might even lay claim to being the most urban-adapted large mammal in the world, having had far less time to adjust than northern hemisphere squirrels, foxes and raccoons. Also well outside his ken is the fact that these days most mainland brushtails live in suburbia; outside towns they are no longer a common animal at all.

This is the second time this evening that his peace – and that of the householders – has been disturbed. Earlier a young possum, evicted by his mother from the hollow in the old Yellow

Box in the park, had wandered into the territory of the old bloke, been intimidated by the sitting threat posture with hiss-growling and finally scruffed and sent on his way. They are father and son, but the fact is of no relevance to either. The youngster will spend a couple more uncomfortable days exposed in a tree fork, harassed by birds, before finding much more desirable accommodation in a custom-built possum box on a house wall. His dad has choice digs behind a cupboard in the householders' garage.

For such a quintessential Australian, it is perhaps ironic that we refer to him by a name that had its origin in an indigenous American word for an entirely different marsupial. The essentially American opossums have none but the most distant relationship with their vegetarian Australian namesakes, but from the time of Captain Cook we have used the American name here. Indeed it was only a few decades ago that the initial 'o' mostly disappeared in Australia.

Many tens of millions of years ago the ancestral possum, a small ground-dwelling rainforest marsupial, took to the trees. Much later one group of possums came to the grounds again; we refer to these ground-dwelling possums as kangaroos. Indeed, our Brush-tailed Possum is as closely related to the Eastern Grey Kangaroo grazing in the adjacent park as he is to the quiet little Ring-tailed Possum which has emerged from nearby Black Mountain to investigate the neighbour's roses cautiously.

Meantime the scrapper has moved higher into the wattle and across into the adjacent eucalypt to chew on young leaves. Eucalypt leaves are appalling food – low nutrient, high fibre, and full of toxins – but there is a near infinite supply of them. Only four large Australian mammals eat lots of them, and the Brushie is one. To cope it has a large hind-gut chamber full of bacteria to help break the chewed leaves down, taking up to three days to do so. The tree has some pretty heavy-duty chemical defences, including tannins which combine with proteins and deny the possum the essential proteins, and terpenes which are more directly toxic, especially to the necessary gut bacteria. Brush-tailed Possums are able, to at least some extent, to digest the protein-tannin compounds and to avoid the trees and individual leaves which are highest in terpenes and associated nasties. Nonetheless, unlike Koalas and Greater Gliders, Brushies don't attempt to survive solely on gum leaves. After an hour or so in the eucalypt, this one descends and picks hopefully through the vegetable garden, but there's not much there at the moment (not that he should complain, having taken the last of the tomatoes last month). He chews a bit on the cabbage seedlings, but there's not much protein there either. The exception to this is the unlucky overnighting grasshopper on the cabbage leaf, but while the possum has no objection to this, he doesn't go out of his way for it.

The female who shares his garage, albeit living in the far corner from him, has just given birth to his joey, still a tiny embryonic creature in her pouch. It will start to travel on her back in early spring, be weaned in late spring and evicted in time for the whole cycle to start again.

Meantime his oblivious father has swaggered off along the top of the fence, looking for the next course of his night-long progressive supper.

ANEMONE FUNGUS (*Aseroe rubra*)

HANGING ROCK TRACK, TIDBINBILLA NATURE RESERVE. There are lots of good reasons to do this short easy walk, the key of course being the superb vast overhanging granite tor that dominates it and the surrounding wet forest. Another, especially in autumn, is the plethora of fungi that can be found here (as well as pretty well anywhere else). Just now I'm delighted to have found one that I regard as among the more remarkable of them, though not everyone shares my enthusiasm. The Anemone or Starfish Fungus is one of the stinkhorns – both levels of name tell us a fair bit about it! It is shaped like a red starfish on a short stem, with eight fleshy forked 'arms' around a green-purple slimy centre. And yes, it does stink if you get close enough, unpleasantly like rotting meat. This is no coincidence and the flies crawling over it are good evidence of its virtuosity in this regard. Even to my eyes the overall impression is of a badly infected wound and this is what the flies are investigating; in the process they will pick up the spores and transport them far from the parent fungus. I am separated by well over 200 years from the first non-indigenous Australian to be interested in them though – back in

1792 the splendidly titled Jacques-Julien Houtou de La Billardière, naturalist to Admiral Bruny D'Entrecastaux's scientific expedition, made it the first Australian fungus to be collected and named.

I am using the term 'fungus' very carelessly here and in fact the actual organism is entirely out of sight underground. Fungi are not plants at all – they form an entire kingdom of their own, alongside plants and animals – but I can best understand the relationship of the 'starfish' to the fungus by a plant analogy. Under the ground is a spreading net of fine hairs called hyphae; the net is a mycelium, equivalent to a shrub which is present all year round. Seasonally, fruit appears on the shrub, producing seeds which must be dispersed to ensure the survival of the shrub's genetic line. The starfish, toadstool or mushroom is like the fruit, arising in response to rain and warmth to produce spores which must be carried away to form new mycelia. The mycelium absorbs organic nutrients from its surrounds, in this case the soil. As the mycelium of grassland fungi expands more or less evenly, when the fruiting bodies appear they form the familiar mushroom ring around the perimeter of the mycelium.

But there are very many types of organic material, and I can be quite sure that somewhere a fungus is taking advantage of every single one of them. The big woody bracket fungi on the tree trunk are digesting the dead wood of the tree; these fruiting bodies are unusual in that they are hard and remain after the spores are dropped. At my feet is a small pile of characteristically cube-shaped wombat droppings; from them are growing tiny orange fungi which, along with many other fungi, specialise in this environment. A dead log is a veritable garden of mosses, lichens, tiny plants – and fungi. Others devour living insects.

Yet other fungal fruiting bodies are produced entirely underground. In southern Australian forests these – the truffles – apparently rely on small mammals such as potoroos to distribute the spores. The little puffballs growing out of the brutally hard roadside ground await the pressure of raindrops, or my foot, to blow the spores out. Yet others, including the mushrooms, simply drop the minute spores and rely on breezes to carry them.

Here is a little colony of greenhood orchids. Like all other orchids they rely entirely on fungi growing in association with their roots to get them established; their tiny dust-mote seeds have not enough room to provide nutrient for the embryo. Even the eucalypts are in an association with fungal hyphae, exchanging water and nutrients – both tree and fungus have access to nutrients that the other cannot itself produce.

Fungi are an entire world and I've only been looking at a few of the bigger ones. The bread I had for lunch and the beer I'm looking forward to later on rely on yeast fungi. But that's a whole other story.

FLAME ROBIN (*Petroica phoenicea*)

GOOROOYARROO NATURE RESERVE, CANBERRA NATURE PARK. An early season frost is shining as it retreats before the sun, now starting to break through the rising mist. Along the fence line is a scattering of orange sparks. As the mist continues to clear the sparks are resolved as male Flame Robins, among a larger number of soft brown females and youngsters. They are flying down from the fence to prey on insects and spiders made torpid by the cold. Just yesterday morning the wires were bare and colourless, but during the afternoon they lit up as the flock arrived, fresh from the post-fire flourishing of the high Brindabellas' Snow Gums. The breezes carried their measured high-pitched cheerfulness across the landscape.

Three youngsters sit together, still following their parents though now independent of their care. In fact the parents have now stopped spending time together and within a few days the immatures will just be individual members of the group, though all the young birds will tend to seek each others' company. They hatched in December in a cup nest of snow grass stems bound with spider web and disguised with scraps of bark and lichen. This was placed in a cavity in a cutting in the Mount Franklin Road a thousand metres higher up, hidden by a hanging screen of Prickly Star-wort. In the rich summer bounty of the high country they grew quickly on a diet of caterpillars, grasshoppers and beetles. By the time the cool fingers of winter were probing through the evenings and early mornings, they were ready to join the loose flocks making their way down the slopes to spend the winter in the open country of the valleys and plains around Canberra.

They have other robins as neighbours in the rich remnant Goorooyarroo woodlands. In the adjacent open forest of Red Stringybark and Brittle Gums is a pair of Scarlet Robins. The male differs from the Flames in his letter-box red chest and black chin; his mate has a rusty-washed breast. They bred here, though they are also joined by a few of their species moving down from the lower mountain forests. Also in this forest patch is currently a lovely, rich mauve-breasted male Rose Robin, drawing attention by his characteristic wing fluttering display. He is just passing through, on his way from the wet Brindabella gullies to his wintering grounds in the open forests of the Pilliga, hundreds of kilometres to the north.

Other Goorooyarroo robins are not red, a fact which is only odd to the humans who named the group for the confiding red-breasted birds they met in the new Botany Bay colony over 200 years ago. These birds reminded them of their beloved Robin Redbreasts from distant England, though they were not very similar and not in the least related. In the gully a little to the north of the Flame fence is a pair of Eastern Yellow Robins, who also live here all year round, perching sideways on tree trunks to pounce on insects. Unlike the Flames, male and female Yellows are identical. Their sweet insistent piping will wake the newcomers throughout the coming winter. Further down the fence is a pair of actively insect-chasing brown Jacky Winters, whose persistent 'teepa-teepa-teepa' has now gone quiet until spring. And deeper into the open woodland is a family of Hooded Robins, sombrely brown except for the superbly pied male.

All will share the resources of the woodland bounty until the warming days of distant spring again lure the Flame Robin flocks away and up again into the Snow Gums.

CRESTED PIGEON (*Ochyphaps lophotes*)

GOLF COURSE, WESTON PARK. Many have come to Canberra to live over the years, including quite a few refugees from crisis in their homeland. Among them is the group of quietly dressed individuals with extravagantly plumed head ornamentation who are taking advantage of the facilities provided by the golf club's greens. Their recent ancestors came though, not from another hemisphere, but from just a few hundred kilometres to the west.

Until 1980 Crested Pigeons were essentially unknown in Canberra. In drought years in the late 1930s and 1960s some arrived here from their western heartland,

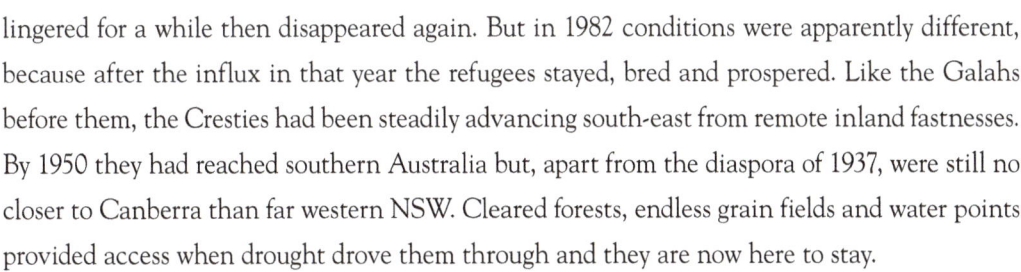

lingered for a while then disappeared again. But in 1982 conditions were apparently different, because after the influx in that year the refugees stayed, bred and prospered. Like the Galahs before them, the Cresties had been steadily advancing south-east from remote inland fastnesses. By 1950 they had reached southern Australia but, apart from the diaspora of 1937, were still no closer to Canberra than far western NSW. Cleared forests, endless grain fields and water points provided access when drought drove them through and they are now here to stay.

This group is picking up seeds from the range of exotic grasses that cover the golf course, taking the odd clover leaf and caterpillar as they present themselves. They are keeping an eye on the approaching party of golfers, but familiarity prevents any particular alarm. Nonetheless they start walking away, accelerating until they are as close to running as decorum will allow. The sudden appearance of a golf ball finally propels them into the air with the distinctive whistling whirr that characterises their flight. It is not chance, but an alignment of a single flight feather, which enables a bird to warn others of potential danger simply by the act of taking off. As they land in a nearby tree they all tip forwards, swinging their tails into the air.

One pigeon is already perched higher in the same tree, on a branch chosen for its clear view of the bush within which his mate is sitting on the typical pigeon nest, a sparse stick platform seemingly barely solid enough to hold the two shiny white eggs. Nights are getting cool but Cresties seem to be willing to breed at any time of the year, as the mood strikes them. When the chicks hatch they will be fed by a trick shared only by flamingoes, on a cottage cheese-like secretion from the crop, rich in protein and fats. It is referred to as crop (or pigeon) milk, but doesn't contain the sugars of mammalian milk and tellingly is produced by both parents. (Male Emperor Penguins produce an emergency secretion for their chicks if their mate doesn't bring the fish home in time, but they don't have a crop.)

The golfers scarcely notice them – Crested Pigeons have truly become the new Galahs – and the flock flutters down to resume feeding. They are neither the first nor the last refugees to make good here and enrich the Canberra landscape.

SUNDEWS (*Drosera peltata*)

NURSERY SWAMP, NAMADGI NATIONAL PARK. It is a killing field. Thousands a year who stray in, or are lured in, don't come out again. All are attracted by the promise of a free energy hit, but the promise is lethal. The unsuspecting confidently make the climb to the prize, gleaming in the sun and smelling of sugar. The prize though is held by a terrible circle of sticky fibres which entangle and close in, trapping the victim in a cage. The very liquid which attracted the doomed individual to start with now begins the slow process of digesting its soft tissues. Eventually the cage opens and the indigestible remains blow away.

From a human perspective the killing field is almost invisible, scattered through the grass around the moist edges of the bog. Each Sundew plant is only a few centimetres high, with each deadly leaf supported by a stem in the centre and surrounded by a circle of glandular hairs. The sticky tip of each hair sparkles with a drop of the fatal attractor. A close look reveals black dots in the middle of many of the leaves. These dots have legs and sometimes wings – they are the corpses or still-living bodies of ants and flies and wasps which are providing the plant with essential nutrients in this nitrogen-poor soil. Other sundews form rosettes of rounded leaves lying on the ground or long straps; all digest large numbers of small insects.

In spring they produce attractive white or pink five-petalled flowers which also attract insects with a sweet smell and another sugary bribe. This time, however, they definitely don't want the insects to be eaten – or at least not until they have performed their essential task of pollination. To this end they hold the flowers high above the deadly leaves.

The idea of animal-eating plants is a rather horrifying one for us – our world view tells us firmly that the natural order of things is the other way round. At least five Australian plant families practise the habit though. Best-known are perhaps the vines of the pitcher-plant family, found in Australia in Cape York rainforests. In these the central vein of the leaf extends as a tendril beyond the leaf tip, then the pitcher grows from it as a swelling shaped by the up-turning tip of the tendril. It inflates with air, and glands on the inner wall exude digestive fluid – perhaps a few litres in the biggest ones. The lid keeps rain out, and is coloured to attract prey to the nectar it produces. Above the liquid level is a waxy zone, and above it is a series of down-pointing teeth just below the rim. As the insect follows more nectaries downwards, it slips on the wax, and falls into the liquid. The wax and teeth make escape impossible. When it has decomposed the plant absorbs its nitrogen. In south-east Asian species, even lizards, birds and small monkeys are known to be trapped by them. The great pioneer evolutionary biologist Alfred Wallace spoke of drinking the water in Borneo, unaware of its soupy nature!

The unrelated Albany Pitcher-plant has a similar approach to the pitcher plants, while the bladderworts are aquatic plants with tiny hollow 'traps' on the roots. When small organisms are washed by the current near to the trap, sensitive hairs swing the opening inwards, and the adjacent water, plus the animal, is swept in, the door snaps shut and the water pumped out again, after which the prey is digested. The bladderwort known as Fairy's Aprons can also be found in Nursery Swamp.

A lot of animals are being devoured here by plants every single day. The world is rarely as we think it should seem.

CRIMSON ROSELLA (*Platycercus elegans*)

WESTON CREEK. They are truly a cacophonous, squabbling, motley crew, jostling for precedence at the backyard bird feeder. These olive-green youngsters are gradually moulting into adult plumage, red blotches appearing on the duller background of their bodies. Like their parents, who tend to avoid these unseemly juvenile rucks, their wings and cheeks are blue. These cheerful larrikins have finally accepted that their parents are no longer going to feed them and have moved in from the bushland reserves in which they were bred to take advantage of the suburban cornucopia. They will spill through the suburbs, scrounging handouts where available, until spring comes around when they will take on their own parenting responsibilities. Almost any vegetable matter is grist to their mill; seeds from the ground or in trees, native and exotic, fruit, flowers and buds. Some of this lot spent a day or so in the rainforest gully at the Australian National Botanic Gardens, carefully stripping the spore capsules from the back of the leaves of tree ferns, removing much of the foliage in the process. Nor are they committed vegetarians; they will spend hours chewing gall capsules from trees and shrubs, especially wattles, to extract the psyllid larvae supposedly safe within.

If they had childhood memories, they would be of a dark space with wood walls and wood chips on the floor, with an opening high above them. Their earliest memories might be of their mother, continuing to brood them for a few days after incubating the eggs, and their father feeding her at regular intervals. They might recall, as they grew bigger and stronger, jostling and screaming for attention when their parents came with food, thrusting their heads into their parents' bills and urgently receiving the regurgitated mush. Such memories would not appreciate the complexities of this feeding though. For instance, unlike the situation in many other birds where only the strongest chicks make it, Crimson Rosella parents carefully ensure that all chicks get the same amount of food, regardless of their size and strength. Or at least their mother does, while dad tends to favour the bigger ones. The overall outcome is that all female chicks get equal chances, while in a poor year young brothers are at risk, so that if food is short females are favoured.

These noisy birds currently rampaging through Duffy may well have later memories of leaving the nest hollow and harassing their parents for food until mum and dad simply flew away.

Right now their largely forgotten parents are foraging quietly together in other yards and reserves round Canberra, seemingly enjoying their hard-won privacy. Each night they roost close together and will do so until one dies, apart from the time that she is on eggs and young chicks when he sleeps close by outside.

Breeding hollows are the most crucial of resources, the shortage exacerbated by clearing of old trees and by the advent of aggressive hollow thieves such as starlings and mynas. Such is the pressure that the greatest cause of Crimson Rosella nesting failures is the attempts by other rosellas to take over the hollow.

In the park over the fence from where the crimson ruckus continues, a small group of much more demure Eastern Rosellas feeds quietly on the ground. Children of the open spaces of the woodlands, they tend to give way to the more rumbustious Crimsons, which were originally primarily birds of the mountain forests but have eagerly taken advantage of the opportunities offered by suburbia. It was the Eastern Rosellas which first came to the attention of English-speaking settlers, out on the plains where Parramatta now sprawls. It was Rose Hill then, and the lovely parrots became Rose Hill Parrakeets, then with commendable Aussie terseness, just Rosehillers and finally Rosellas. It's true! Even less apparently plausible is the fact that well into the 20th century they were also known as Nonpareil Parrot, to acknowledge their beauty; at least that one didn't stick.

One of the many ways in which Canberra is interesting to anyone who loves nature is the unusual juxtaposition of two rosella species. Not that the rowdy Crimson gang cares as it suddenly swirls up and out of the yard, looking for somewhere to roost and preen until it's time to bring afternoon colour and chaos to another yard.

TWO-SPINED BLACKFISH (*Gadopsis bispinosus*)

UPPER COTTER RIVER, NAMADGI NATIONAL PARK. The Cotter here, upstream of Corin Dam, is deep and quiet, flowing quietly under a dense overhang of tea-tree. Through the glint of sun on water the pool initially seems empty of anything larger than the water beetles skating across the surface. In the shadow cast by a nearby Black Sallee though is a hint of something not quite right about the pebbly bottom. Then a patch of the marbled pattern moves slightly, and is outlined as a 20-centimetre-long fish. He is a Two-spined Blackfish, at home in one of his kind's last refuges and quietly hunting insect larvae. The reddish bloodworms, larvae of midges, small non-biting flies, are relatively easy. Other prey are more cryptic and require great patience. Mayfly larvae nymphs crawl under bottom litter or hide in crevices and he must wait for them to make a rare move out of cover. Caddisfly larvae are even trickier, as they disguise themselves to a remarkable degree, with portable cases festooned with pieces of stick, sand and other debris to break their outline. The blackfish is patient.

Sometimes, however, he doesn't need to be and these can be the most rewarding times. A large green katydid, or short-horned grasshopper, has tumbled from the tea-tree in an attempt to evade a bois-terous foraging family of Suberb Fairy-wrens. In this she has succeeded, but it's definitely a case of exchanging one fate for another. A sudden lunge

and the mouth of the blackfish opens beneath her, engulfing her in a splash and a swirl. He is competing these days with voracious newcomers too. The exotic trout are now everywhere in these upland streams, excluded only by dam walls, waterfalls and swamps – except where humans help them to leapfrog even these obstacles. Once the blackfish would have shared this pool with the little native Mountain Galaxias, but they have retreated everywhere before the trout onslaught.

He is now big enough not to be threatened by them directly, though he has only recently grown to that size, but he must guard his eggs vigilantly. Last November the female had laid a couple of hundred of them, each over three millimetres in diameter, among the stones on the stream bed. Immediately afterwards he fertilised them then stood guard. Not only trout, but dragonfly larvae and crayfish were among the threats to them that he had to see off. Even after they hatched, 16 days later, his task was not yet half over. The babies relied on the yolk reserves stuck to the egg membrane and not until that was all gone after another three weeks were they ready to make their own way and he was free to resume his own life.

Not that he has places to go or things, other than eating, to do. He hatched four years ago in this same pool and in his whole life will never move more than 15 metres from the stone beneath which he devoured his own egg yolk while his father did sentry duty.

And now the wrens have dislodged another panicked insect across the pool and he must hurry to beat the trout to it.

Note: The Two-spined Blackfish is listed as a threatened species under ACT legislation.

WILLIE WAGTAIL (*Rhipidura leucophrys*)

GUNGAHLIN HILL, CANBERRA NATURE PARK. I like to stop in at Gungahlin Hill Nature Reserve if I have some time while coming or going along the Barton Highway between Hall and Gungahlin Drive. I am especially assiduous in this regard in spring, when it's excellent
for orchids, but it's worth a look any time. And
today I'm in for a real treat; Rhipidura means
fantail, and this is their morning here.

There is a mob of Eastern Grey Kangaroos in the open country to the east, where
the Gungaderra Grasslands roll away and
join with the other very special Gungahlin
native grassland reserves. A family of four Willie
Wagtails is using them as insect harvesters. They ride the

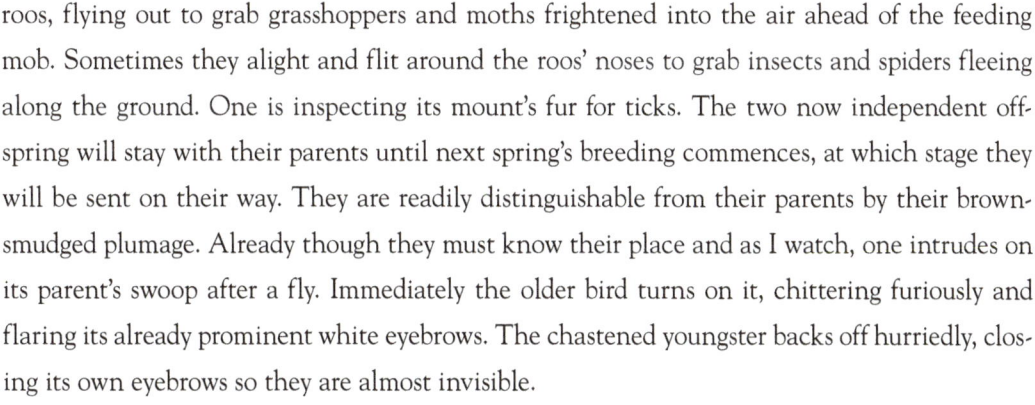

roos, flying out to grab grasshoppers and moths frightened into the air ahead of the feeding mob. Sometimes they alight and flit around the roos' noses to grab insects and spiders fleeing along the ground. One is inspecting its mount's fur for ticks. The two now independent off-spring will stay with their parents until next spring's breeding commences, at which stage they will be sent on their way. They are readily distinguishable from their parents by their brown-smudged plumage. Already though they must know their place and as I watch, one intrudes on its parent's swoop after a fly. Immediately the older bird turns on it, chittering furiously and flaring its already prominent white eyebrows. The chastened youngster backs off hurriedly, clos-ing its own eyebrows so they are almost invisible.

It is quite likely that they bred in the Red Stringybark forest remnant of Gungahlin Hill, but it's also possible that they have come down for the mountains for winter. Either way they will have constructed a beautiful little grass and bark nest bound with that most utilitarian of glues, spider webs, which they may collect by flying into the web of the long-suffering architect and taking it away entirely. It is placed on a branch, often over water. Willies seem to be follow-ing me today. Last night one serenaded the full moon for much of the night outside my window, with its sweet but incessant 'wheat-witty-wheat-wheat' call. Now a truck horn startles the roos – why do so many people feel the need to toot at bird-watchers? As they flee, the birds fly back to the shelter of the trees and I follow. They continue to work close to the ground, flushing the insects with wing flicks and the ever-wagging tail.

Above them now appears a pair of their small busy relations, the Grey Fantails, flying out from the branches to catch insects higher up. In this way they and the Willies can share the forest without competing for resources. Their scratching reeling song earned them the name of Cranky Fan from early settlers. These too may have bred here or may have moved down from higher elevations. Unlike the Willies though, which will definitely spend winter here, there is uncertainty about their intentions. They may stay on or they may move on to the lower country out west, returning in spring. Grey Fans build one of the most exquisite nests, like a small version of the Willies' but with a long tapering tail.

My time's up and I head for the exit gate, but my Rhipidura morning is not done. A sudden flash of rusty red catches my attention and there, to my surprise, is the third of the south-east Australian trio of this group, the larger and very beautiful Rufous Fantail. This bird is definitely just passing through. It has spent the warm months breeding in the wet gullies of the Brindabellas or Tidbinbilla Range and is now escaping the coming winter, heading north to tropical Queensland or even across the Bass Strait to New Guinea.

A good morning, but just what I expect of one spent in the bush capital.

TERMITES (*Nasutitermes exitiosus*)

BLACK MOUNTAIN, CANBERRA NATURE PARK. The citadel has been breached. An Echidna is ripping through the hard clay walls of the termite mound, utterly indifferent to the desperate attempts of the soldiers to rebuff him. Galleries are exposed to the hated light and drying air and his huge, deadly sticky tongue flickers along them and withdraws, each time dragging hundreds of workers, juicy eggs and plump larvae into his mouth. A pair of matching tough pads at the back of his palate and tongue grind them all into a sticky, muddy mass which he swallows. The carnage continues for some 20 minutes, by when he is temporarily sated and wanders off, leaving havoc behind. The colony's ordeal is not yet over, as the ever-present Meat Ants have already begun investigating the damage. In some ways they are the bigger threat, because once inside they can remove all the eggs and larvae, destroying the entire colony.

This time though the termite soldiers can hold their own. Though blind, like all termite workers, they stand shoulder to shoulder, hard black funnel-shaped heads facing the threatening ants. From these funnels they exude a sticky white material which both repels the invaders and entangles their legs. Behind them the surviving workers are labouring frantically to seal the gaps, with jaws instead of the soldiers' snouts. By nightfall they succeed, the soldiers having held their line. The humidity inside rises again to a comfortable 95% and with a population of over two million the business of the colony has not been greatly disrupted.

Deep under the 30 centimetre high dome the huge bloated body of the queen has continued pumping out eggs, over 2000 of them a day, so that the colony will soon be back to pre-echidna strength. She can live for decades, so her output of termites is extraordinary. She is attended by a king; this is one way in which the caste system of termites differs from that of their deadly enemies, the ants, which belong to a completely separate order of insects. Termite workers differ from ants in their soft pale bodies, lack of eyes, straight (not kinked) antennae and lack of a narrow waist. The term 'white ants' is not only totally incorrect, it is a fearful termite insult!

As eggs are laid, workers move them into a nursery where they tend them until – and after – they hatch into larvae, which over time develop into workers or soldiers or winged 'alates', according to the colony's needs. The alates develop in spring, fly from the nest and start a new colony in a sheltered moist area alongside a dead stump or log. The toll taken on these dispersers is huge – bats, dragonflies, spiders, frogs, lizards and birds take great numbers of them. The surviving pioneers form mated pairs which become the king and queen of the new colony.

Meantime in the repaired nest the workers' tasks continue – in fact for many of them it didn't cease. Along sheltered dark tunnels through the soil or in runways of chewed soil across the surface of ground or tree trunk they march ceaselessly, bringing back particles of dead wood, leaves and twigs. Bacteria in their gut breaks it down into food that they can utilise; they feed this, with the essential bacteria, to soldiers, alates, king, queen and larvae.

Their neighbours, *Coptotermes lacteus*, build a hard-walled castle two metres high; their soldiers defend it with huge crushing mandibles, as well the repellent chemicals. Most of Australia's 350-odd termite species though live underground or inside logs; the majority of them are grass harvesters. Less than 20 species are problems in buildings – the rest play a crucial role in recycling forest litter. Without their assistance most bushfires would be a lot more intense.

A world without termites would be poorer and more dangerous.

MAY

PIED CURRAWONG (*Strepera graculina*)

RED HILL, CANBERRA NATURE PARK. As the sun vanishes behind Red Hill the currawongs are gathering to roost. To roost, but not yet to rest. This is a wild, whooping, yodelling reunion of large birds, bursting with confidence in their own power and ability to dominate nearly all other birds in their world. In small parties they come with their brash direct swooping flight, all black but for their staring yellow eyes, white wing patches, rumps and tail tips. 'Woop woop ….. po wow!' they declaim to each other and the world.

They are successful because they have adapted wholeheartedly to the opportunities provided by urbanisation. Cities have offered them the chance of burgeoning populations and Pied Currawongs have seized the chance. In a very few generations they have altered patterns developed over the course of 10 000 years since the last glaciation, and established long before that during the current Ice Age. Less than 30 years ago all Currawongs in Canberra in May would have recently come down from their mountain breeding grounds in the high forests. Some currawongs still make the yearly odyssey to their traditional summer haunts and these Red Hill birds have indeed recently come back down to avoid the tough times of winter and swell the ranks of the currawong urban push. A few hardy individuals even remain in the high country through the season of frosts and snows, as their forebears have always done. Many more now stay down in suburbia all year round, however, breeding where no currawong would have dreamt of breeding a few scant years back, feasting on the suburban cornucopia.

Pied Currawongs are essentially fruit eaters and winter gardens, especially exotic ones, are a better source of fruit than the hill and riverside native forests used to be. Many of this lot have spent the day foraging on the innumerable berries of Pyracantha and Cotoneaster shrubs that still line many of the streets, parks and gardens of old inner Canberra. Tonight hundreds of seeds that they have eaten with the fruit, but not digested, will be dropped in the reserve to add to the weed load that already threatens it. Others of the flock have been prowling lawns and ovals, probing for larvae such as fat scarab grubs which are eating the grass roots. All have at times searched foliage for insects lurking there. Elsewhere on the tablelands they take a huge toll of the big stick insects that can defoliate areas of forest if unchecked; for preference they prey on the egg-swollen bodies of the females, thus increasing the efficacy of their control.

For a time in spring, while feeding their own chicks, they switch to bigger prey to keep the protein intake up, and nestlings of smaller species are a convenient food source. Unlike their mountain-breeding colleagues, the urban currawongs are taking large numbers of exotic birds, but certainly many small native birds' nesting attempts are curtailed too, and currawong numbers are probably increasing.

And while we continue to offer them exotic gardens and lawns to maintain their numbers through winter the annual spring harvest of Canberra Silvereye, honeyeater and Willie Wagtail chicks will continue.

FRESHWATER CRAYFISH (*Euastacus armatus*)

GIGERLINE NATURE RESERVE, MURRUMBIDGEE RIVER CORRIDOR. She is a beautiful animal, and perhaps the oldest non-human animal for many kilometres around. She is over 30 years old, 30 centimetres long and well over two kilograms in weight. This makes her an anomaly these days, as most of her kind are taken from the water by humans long before that. Fortuitously this stretch of the Murrumbidgee is protected by a short section of cliffs and by chance was not fished in the last few decades before it was reserved. Her body is a lustrous deep blue-green, covered with short creamy rose-like thorns. A pair of huge white claws is held defensively out in front as she backs into a bank crevice, threatened by a sharp-eyed Water Rat. He has eaten many crayfish in his life and makes a lunge, but it is an uncertain one as he realises he is out of his league here – this beauty is no mere Yabby and he backs off, seeking an easier meal. After a while she emerges on four long pairs of spindly walking legs and resumes grazing the bottom of the cool, deep, fast-flowing channel, picking vegetable matter and transmitting it to her mandibles. She is searching for the carp carcass on which she had been dining before being interrupted, but unfortunately for her this has become the easy meal the rat went off to find.

In all the wide freshwater crayfish world only the Giant Tasmanian Crayfish is bigger, but this female's universe is no bigger than this stretch of river channel. She is carrying beneath her body nearly a thousand tiny eggs anchored to hairs on her swimmerets, which are short, broad appendages attached to her abdominal segments. Throughout the cold winter she will continue to feed and to carry the eggs until they hatch in spring. Even then the babies will cling to her for a while longer before going off to take their chances in a dangerous life among dragonfly larvae, fish, birds and rats. This time next year, if they survive, they will still weigh only 10 grams and in three years only 40 grams. They will not mature until perhaps another nine years, when they will still weigh only 250 grams. If allowed though they will go on living and growing long after that.

She has close relatives – well outside her ken – in the high, cold streams of Namadgi National Park in the ranges to the west but only her kind extend into the slower, warmer reaches of the lower Murray and Murrumbidgee. They have come a long way since their ancestor moved upstream from the ocean perhaps 150 million years ago – nowhere in the world have freshwater crays evolved and diverged as much as they have in Australia.

Now she encounters a slightly more distant relative. The Yabby is big and near the prime of her life too, but is a mere 250 gram slight youth compared with the old crayfish. The uniformly dark green Yabby is probably at no risk from her giant neighbour, but she hasn't got to her age without learning caution and with a flick of her tail scurries backwards out of potential harm's way. She is six years old but already very near the end of her life. Everything about the lifestyle of her kind must be done at frantic pace compared with that of the Murray Cray. For instance she breeds twice each year; the babies grow bigger in their first year than the cray manages in three and they will start breeding next year. Despite this she will soon go into a winter torpor in a warmer shallow side pool in the same bank burrow where she has spent her whole life. Yabbiekind has benefited greatly from dams and pondages and other human interferences with its world, while the big slow-developing Murray Cray has not coped with the changes and heavy, often illegal, fishing.

This one though is living much as her ancestors did and she will still be doing so when the Yabby's offspring have died of old age.

Note: The Freshwater Crayfish (also known as Murray River Crayfish) is listed as a threatened species under ACT and Victorian legislation.

YELLOW-TAILED BLACK-COCKATOO (Calyptorhynchus funereus)

WALKING TRACKS CAR PARK, TIDBINBILLA NATURE RESERVE. The walking tracks have only recently reopened after the 2003 fires, but the forest round the car park is recovering well, and today is a good day – the black cockies are in. We have followed their evocative wailing to here and now they are all around. Some are sitting high in the trees, preening and loafing, but some are low down, ripping great chunks out of the Silver Wattle trunks. They are after the big succulent moth grubs that favour the soft wattle timber. A couple of experimental bites of the trunk to see whether it's hollow, then a powerful downward ripping to remove sections of trunk to reveal the tunnel and the luckless cat-

erpillar is hauled out, grasped in the foot and devoured like a sausage. One bird, however, is investigating the trunk of a smooth white Ribbon Gum, moving awkwardly backwards down the tree, using its spread tail as a prop. We realise that it is looking for the tell-tale frass holes where the grub has entered and through which it voids its sawdust droppings. Suddenly it stops and carefully bites into the trunk and seems to ponder. Then, satisfied it seems with what it's found, it digs its great tool of a bill deep into the timber, and straining, hauls off a long strip of wood until it's at about 45° to the tree. It then uses this as a perch to start serious work on the trunk. The eucalypt wood is much harder than that of the wattles, and this is going to take some time.

Our attention is distracted by the hoarse insistent begging of a young bird who'd like just one more feed from its parents, no matter that they've laid down the law to it on this matter before! It would be nice to think that it had been bred in the nearby mountains, but such youngsters can follow the flock for hundreds of kilometres and this one may have come from the north coast of NSW or from Victoria. Either way it saw its first glimpse of daylight from the bottom of a deep hollow high in a forest tree some 200 years old – only such an old tree can provide the size of hollow required for such a big bird. These very old trees are getting scarcer and we have some concern that we are watching an ageing population of cockies – at least some of the birds around us could well be 50 years old.

A newcomer has arrived in the group, bringing a snack. She – her white bill, bright yellow cheek patch and inconspicuous eye-ring distinguish her from a male, who has black bill, dark-smudged cheek patch and red eye-ring – is carrying a chewed pine cone and now continues to extract the seeds with her bill tip. She may have carried this for kilometres and as we watch she decides she's finished with it and carelessly drops it. It bounces in the bushes nearby and we retrieve it – there are still seeds in it and pines are one of the most aggressive weeds of bushland. My suspicion is that the cockies have seized on pine cones as a substitute for banksia cones which are now harder for them to find; we have certainly watched them avidly gnawing on banksias at the coast.

The bird hanging on the Ribbon Gum trunk is flying up to a solider perch, clutching the prize in his foot, but the flock is starting to move now, streaming and wailing away down the valley. They will be spending winter at low altitudes though and we'll catch up with them again.

KURRAJONG (*Brachychiton populneus*)

MOUNT MAJURA, CANBERRA NATURE PARK. The groves of Kurrajongs along the saddle of Mount Majura were founded last century. In 1919 and 1920 Thomas Weston, Canberra's first official 'gardener', planted over 20 000 of them on the denuded slopes. I am not sure whether he was replanting trees that he knew had previously been there, but their prior presence is quite plausible. In the past I would come up here regularly as part of my fruitless attempts to add Painted Button-quail to my ACT list. Now I've caught up to them locally – in my suburban backyard, *inter alia*! – but it's still a delightful walk and view. In particular I very much enjoy being among the Kurrajongs.

A Kurrajong is a truly lovely tree, with beautifully rounded smooth pale trunk and soft glossy bright green leaves. I can see here both older and younger leaves. The mature foliage is heart-shaped, the young ones being three-pronged, like a kangaroo's foot. I find it interesting to see them here with the foliage drooping down towards the ground, because in most of the places where I enjoy them, out on the western slopes grazing lands, they seem inevitably to have been browsed as high up as the sheep and cattle can reach. This palatability to stock is a two-edged sword for Kurrajongs – while they are still lopped in droughts to provide valuable stock fodder, their very preservation in areas where all other trees have been removed is due solely to this.

I grew up with the classics, which most certainly included May Gibbs' *Cuddlepot and Snugglepie*. So it is a certain childhood nostalgia that prevents me from passing a Kurrajong without picking up a black, hard canoe-shaped seed pod and thinking of its use as a boat in those long ago times. Another piece of mythology also makes me smile. I have been told on several occasions by geologists that Kurrajongs are a sign of limestone. I am perplexed by this; while they do grow on limestone hills they also grow on virtually any soil type, including granite slopes, on volcanic bases like Mount Majura, and deep soils like those of the western slopes.

Kurrajongs have been regarded as of economic importance for many thousands of years before pastoralists discovered their drought value. Aboriginal people winnowed the seeds from the pods, carefully avoiding the stinging hairs, and ate them. Even more important to the First People were the valuable fibres of the under-bark, particularly that of the roots, which were woven into cords and nets. Our misunderstanding of what we were told – we seem to have too often failed to listen to what we were, and even are, being told by Indigenous Australians – led to our naming of the tree. 'Kurrajong' (in what language, I'm ashamed to say, I don't know) referred to the fibre, not only of this tree but of some of the totally unrelated and dissimilar Pimeleas or Rice Flowers, which are also sometimes called Kurrajong.

It may or may not be coincidence that as I wander down I pull some chocolate from my backpack – cocoa is a family relation of kurrajongs, as are, closer to home, the spectacular Illawarra Flame Tree and the wonderful Bottle Trees of central Queensland (though not the Baobabs of the far north-west). And in my hand is still the gumnut babies' boat. I'll leave it in the grove, but not just yet …

BLACK-SHOULDERED KITE (*Elanus axillaris*)

POINT HUT CROSSING, MURRUMBIDGEE RIVER CORRIDOR. In the late sun the bird looks golden as it hangs in the sky, seemingly standing almost erect in the air, its wings high above it. This hovering is an remarkable performance, with the wings rotating in a figure eight so that its forward movement is just countered by pushing back; at the same time it is precisely opposing gravity, but no more than that. And in all this its head is rock-steady as it scans the ground for prey. Now it parachutes down and as its wings fan out just above the ground, its foot snatches out and the little hunter swoops to a willow by the river carrying a limp mouse in its left foot. As soon as it seized the squirming rodent it began to squeeze its claws in and out, crushing the mouse's chest. Perched, the kite suddenly appears white and surprisingly seagull-like, though with frowning red-eyed ferocity that a gull cannot muster.

His slightly larger mate is now approaching swiftly across the paddocks with a swooping soaring flight, bringing another mouse, her black wing-tips in strong contrast to her pale grey back and white undersides. The soft wheezy whistles they exchange seem quite incongruous, belying their fierce demeanour. Together they fly up to a tall pine near the picnic ground where, less than a month from winter, they have a nest with two chicks. Both the use of exotic trees for nesting where eucalypts are absent and a second, minor, autumn breeding season distinguishes Black-shouldered Kites from all other local birds of prey. They both land on the compact stick nest, less than 40 centimetres across and lined with eucalypt leaves which repel parasites, some of which can survive in the nest over summer from the last breeding attempt. The leaves are changed regularly to maintain optimum hygiene. The chicks are well-developed and will be taking their first wobbly flaps soon. Unlike their parents they are rusty red on the head and breast and dark on the back, which will fade over their first year of life.

Black-shouldered Kites focus almost exclusively on mice and when the supply starts to dwindle they will move on, finding a new mouse resource. In pre-European times they fed on native rodents and made the switch quite seamlessly when advancing agriculture eliminated their traditional prey and replaced native grasslands with exotic ones. So reliant on rodents are they that their ancestors only became established here a few million years ago as Australia drifted close enough to Asia for the rats to raft ashore.

The two surviving chicks – their youngest sibling did not survive a soaking during a sudden storm not long after hatching a month ago – will soon be making brief forays from the nest. For another month though they will rely on their parents for decreasing amounts of their food, after which they will go their own way. One will stay in the area, following the river upstream towards the looming Mount Tennent. The other will wander far to the west, ending its days hunting mice in the Riverina cotton fields.

For now though the sun is setting and the family settles down to huddle against the chill of the coming night.

SPHAGNUM MOSS (*Sphagnum cristatum*)

GININI FLAT, NAMADGI NATIONAL PARK. The frosts are already becoming harsh and are lingering long into the mornings, among the mountains a kilometre above Canberra. Most animals have descended the range to kinder climes, have left eggs or larvae in frozen soil and died, or are entering a torpor until spring. One of the few exceptions is the solitary wombat ambling across the flat, each breath a puff of white mist. Plants have produced seeds to ensure their presence next spring, and have died back or have shut down all but the most essential of their systems. Not quite all plants though – they too have their wombats. The rich and very special world of these high country bogs, and the waterways that they feed, rely heavily on a very modest plant which goes right on growing and functioning in the chill clasp of winter's claw. Perhaps the modesty of mosses is too often taken at face value.

The sphagnum, which literally underlies the whole bog, looks like a yellowish-green carpet, though its thickness becomes obvious along streamlines, where the hummocks may be 70 centimetres high and 3000 years old, the lower layers of dead moss being compacted as peat. Close up it has leaves and stems and roots, though 'it' is actually a mat of hundreds of thousands of tiny moss plants. The thread-like roots do not conduct water, as do those of the now somnolent shrubs growing through it, but simply anchor the moss. Above it waves a forest of little pennants, each of them a hard, spore-bearing capsule on a stem. Not only does the life of the streams below rely on the extraordinary water-holding properties of the sphagnum, but the obliviously teeming masses of the suburbs of Canberra do too. The great moss carpet can hold up to 20 times its own mass of water and releases it gradually so that the streams below it do not swing from spate to dry, but run steadily in wet times or drought. It does this by way of a most unusual structural trick. Among the normal, living energy-fixing green cells are interspersed large dead hollow cells which absorb the water.

Humans have long known and valued sphagnum. In the Celtic lands of Britain, people rely on dried peat for fuel as their ancestors have done for hundreds of generations. Still in the Celtic lands, peat smoke has long been used as a key ingredient in many Scotch whiskies, by flavouring the malted barley – another thing I'm grateful to my father for having taught me. Countless armies have tended their soldiers' wounds with the wonderfully absorbent moss, even until the First World War. There are tales of Ginini sphagnum being harvested for gas mask filters. And of course on a negative note sphagnum bogs the world over are still shamefully mined for the garden potting trade, also for their water-holding qualities.

They are not harvested here in Namadgi though, and year round the waters tumble out of the bog and over Ginini Falls to join Stockyard Creek below. In this shaded course more moss species grow on rocks and along the banks, their rootlets anchoring them firmly. Every now and then a fragment is washed off but, far from being lost, it will settle on a rock or the bank downstream and form a new moss cushion. Even if the levels fell and the moss dried to a crisp, the first rain or water rise would bring them instantly back to life – the 'higher plants' around them could not do that. The mosses went their separate way from nearly all the other plants around them not too long after the first algae left the safety of the oceans and began the colonisation of the vast, empty and indescribably harsh dry land. The bryophytes – mosses and liverworts – did not develop the water-conducting vessels that characterise other plants. They have managed very well without them, but it has severely restricted any size ambitions they may have had.

Liverworts grow on the banks here too, like flattened green flakes, though others resemble mosses. On a boulder near where Stockyard Creek runs into the Cotter River, both mosses and liverworts grow thickly. Soil has accumulated and other plants have taken root in them – as they so often do, the bryophytes have enabled the start of a new ecosystem on a bare surface. And, like any other plant, they can do what no animal has ever managed; that is, to fix the sun's energy by photosynthesis and store it in sugars, like batteries, for later use – if an animal doesn't first pinch it by eating it.

No, we ought not let ourselves be fooled by the inherent humility of mosses.

EASTERN SPINEBILL (*Acanthorhynchus tenuirostris*)

AUSTRALIAN NATIONAL BOTANIC GARDENS. I am sitting on a favourite bench in the Proteaceae section of the Gardens enjoying, as ever, the frantic business of the spinebills scrambling over the grevilleas and probing the flowers for nectar. Where the flowers are within the bush the spinebills cling to the stem and probe the tube with their remarkably attenuated bill, but where the flower is outside the foliage they hover at it. This is an extraordinary trick and I wish my eyes had about a hundredfold the time acuity that they actually do, so I could watch their wings working. I know roughly what I'd see; though our understanding of hovering is based largely on studies of the doyen of hoverers, the mostly South American hummingbirds, spinebills and other Australian practitioners of the art must use similar strategies.

From side on I would see the blur of the wings emerge into a consistent vertical figure eight beating pattern, pushing alternatively forwards and backwards so that it maintains a stationary position in the air. Only a very small bird can do this, and only one which is taking a very high energy intake – e.g. nectar – to fuel the huge energy output. Relative to its body the spinebill must carry breast muscles weighing up to twice as much as the birds around it which have a more leisurely lifestyle.

The flower's tube has evolved so that only a bird with a long bill can reach the nectary in the bottom of the flower and in the process collect on its forehead the pollen attached to the sides of the tube. Even if I could see through the tube wall I wouldn't be able to see what's going on (unless I could keep my super-speed vision while adding X-ray powers), as the bird's tongue is flicking in and out at the rate of 10 times a second. Its tip is divided into four and each filament is like a paint brush, to take up the nectar by the same capillary action utilised by the wielder of a paint brush.

Such an active bird, flashing black and white and rusty red, could never be discreet anyway, but it is noisy as well. There is a constant high-speed, hard brassy piping from all around me, underlined by bursts of snapping 'prrrrrp' generated by their wings. Presumably both are messages to other spinebills that 'I'm using this bush, find your own'. In fact right in front of me now another male has entered an occupied shrub. The incumbent goes into a piping fury, hops through the branches to the interloper, then when close he turns side on, bristles out his head and throat feathers and fans his tail to look as big and intimidating as possible. It evidently works as the other bird retreats to an unoccupied food source. On the other hand the bigger, doughty black, white and yellow New Holland Honeyeater is pragmatically tolerated and avoided.

Back in summer I watched them working the kangaroo paw beds, just as enthusiastically. There is a small irony in this, in that these wonderful flowers evolved in Western Australia in association with a very close relation of these spinebills, the Western Spinebill. For a long time the climate was kinder and spinebills lived right across southern Australia. Then the drying came and the moist south-east and south-west corners became isolated as the drylands came right to the sea across the Great Australian Bight. The spinebill populations, isolated now from each other, diverged until two species resulted.

There are some spinebills present in the Australian National Botanic Gardens all year round – why on earth would they leave this cornucopia after all? – but most Canberra spinebills move across the Murrumbidgee in spring to breed in the mountain forests. The Gardens' population has recently been greatly augmented by their return. So has my pleasure.

CHERRY BALLART (*Exocarpus cupressiformis*)

BENDORA DAM ROAD, NAMADGI NATIONAL PARK. This is a fascinating road, taking us through so many different habitats, starting in the Snow Gums at Bull's Head

Survival Shelter, descending through the Alpine Ash forests, through wet gullies and exposed dry peppermint and gum forests and finally down to the Ribbon Gums and fern beds along the Cotter River. Today I've stopped in the dry forest to see how the recovery of the Cherry Ballarts is coming. I wasn't the only one to have been surprised when many of them resprouted after the fires – they weren't 'supposed' to do that! This one is doing well, covered in pine-like slightly yellowish foliage. It also has a few remaining small fruits on it. At least they look superficially like little red fruits and popped into the mouth they taste good. But something's not quite right.

There appears to be a hard green seed sitting on the end of the fruit. But only non-flowering plants, like pines, have exposed seeds, and they don't have fruit, so what's going on here? In fact the green 'seed' is the true fruit, and the seed is inside it. The red 'fruit' is actually the flower stem, swollen, coloured and filled with sugar to be attractive to the birds which distribute the real seed. The hard little fruit and seed are eaten accidentally with the stem, and deposited somewhere else with the bird's droppings, to grow far from the parent tree. The tree's scientific name reflects this; *Exocarpus* means 'outside seed', referring to the extraordinary arrangement of true and artificial fruit. *Cupressiformis* incidentally means 'cypress-like', a reference to the surprisingly pine-like form of the tree. Both leaves and flowers are tiny, green and inconspicuous.

I am not convinced about the Cherry part of the common name; I reckon the fruit (it's easier to refer to them as a fruit) look and taste more like the individual portions of a pomegranate.

This tree has more surprises though. It is a semi-parasite, attached to the roots of the surrounding plants and pinching water and soluble minerals from them. It does do its own photosynthesis, as the green of its leaves tells us. The family to which it belongs is closely related to the aerial parasites, the mistletoes; all have a common parasitic ancestor and have taken different parasitic paths. This family, Santalaceae, contains a couple of other familiar Australian trees. Not far to the west of here, in dry woodlands, grows the Quandong, which produces large, red edible fruit containing big pitted seeds. The fruit were commonly used to make jam and the seeds were used to make cheap Chinese checkers sets – I still have my grandmother's old set. A couple of species of sandalwood were harvested in vast numbers in Indonesia, the Pacific Islands and Western Australia for use in Asia as incense, for making sacred carvings, and for the distillation of sandalwood oil for medicines and perfumes. Many of the islands were brutally plundered, and Australian Sandalwood is still very uncommon in Western Australia. At times in the 19th century sandalwood provided up to half of Western Australia's revenue. Much closer to here in the Brindabellas another *Exocarpus* grows, the shrubby Dwarf Ballart, with equally edible attractive mauve fruits.

I love musing on nature – wherever we start there are so many stories flowing from it. And the ballarts are as good a start as any.

DIAMOND FIRETAIL (*Stagonopleura guttata*)

TUGGERANONG HILL, CANBERRA NATURE PARK. We are wandering up the slopes of Tuggeranong Hill east of Theodore and above the Monaro Highway, heading to those humblingly ancient Scribbly Gums on the unfortunately named Poverty Point. These trees, some of them six metres in diameter at the base, were old when Europeans settled on the Limestone Plains. High on some of the trunks are the old nails and rail remnants that remind us how these first British settlers used the convenient big trees as property boundary markers. We have already paid a quiet visit on the way up to signs of an even older culture. In the native grasslands on the gentle lower slopes are some 80 axe-grinding grooves in the sandstone, where many generations of people sat with bark water containers from the creek below to work on the edges of weapons and tools.

But now our attention is distracted totally by a flight of brilliant red and black butterflies from almost at our feet. No, hang on, not butterflies at all, but finches – the glorious and sadly declining Diamond Firetails, children of the once-vast grassy woodlands that carpeted the land west of the divide from Queensland to South Australia. These wanderers still follow the seeding of the native grasses, apparently unable to adapt to the coarser seeds of the exotic replacements. As they fly to the fence their reddest rumps shine like lights; perched in a row the adults are a delight, red bills and eye, a broad black breast band on a white background and a row of big white diamonds down the black sides. With them are several much more demurely costumed youngsters from last spring.

Leaving them to resume feeding, we go on to admire the trees – and are again distracted. In branch forks and foliage is a series of big grass nests each with a bottleneck spout to the side.

Some are nicely decorated with yellow Clustered Everlasting flower stems woven into them. These are the firetails' nests, built for the spring breeding but recently repaired for use as cosy communal roost shelters over winter.

Back when these nests were being built in early spring there was a lot of romance associated – at least from the perspective of those of us privileged enough to watch the display dance. I love seeing the male present a ridiculously long stem of grass to his intended. High on a branch he grips it by the tip and bounces up and down, singing through a full beak and twisting his head to display his trophy from different angles.

Diamond Firetails are not ancient Australians, but they are venerable by finch standards. Their ancestors apparently arose in the great developing grasslands of Africa as the forests retreated with climate change some six million years ago. Spreading across the world they represented the first of three waves of finches to enter Australia, adapting to the evolving drying landscape of coastal heathlands, inland woodlands and even the arid interior. (Later came the Zebra Finch and Double-bar ancestors, which spread similarly. The most recent arrivals have largely remained in tropical grasslands.)

Old trees, old Australian birds. The day too is ageing and it's time for us to descend.

Note: The Diamond Firetail is listed as a threatened species under NSW and Victorian legislation.

BLACKWOOD WATTLE (*Acacia melanoxylon*)

BULLS HEAD, NAMADGI NATIONAL PARK. I have wandered across the road to where the Blackwoods and Silver Wattles grow among the Snow Gums, having used the non-freezable toilets at Bulls Head – carefully placed across the border in NSW and thus out of the Cotter catchment in case of accidents … It always seems a bit odd to see Blackwood growing up here, when they are generally much happier in sheltered wet gullies. Blackwood is, to my eye, one of the handsomest of the coastal and hinterland wattles and I've enjoyed it from the Adelaide hills to tropical Queensland. While these Brindabella specimens are undoubtedly lovely, with their glossy dark green foliage, they are pretty modest in stature compared with the magnificently towering giant I remember from near Strahan in south-west Tasmania. I would never have recognised it had it not been labelled.

It seems to me that, over the past couple of hundred years, wattles must have had the widest range of uses by non-indigenous Australians of any native plant group. Many other groups have been used for timber, and eucalypts have also been the basis of an oil industry, but wattles have been employed much more widely. Pretty much from the time the First Fleet landed, wattles were cut and used for building, using the abundant whippy shrubs and small trees which awaited them. The overwhelmed settlers knew nothing of these plants, but they still knew the old ways of building, including driving stakes into the ground and weaving supple branches between them. This 'wattling' was so old that the word itself had been in the language for at least a thousand years. ('Daubing' it with mud to make it weatherproof was part of the same process.) Used as a noun, the term became applied here to the plants so used, but more than one group of plants was employed and the builders were not botanists. Hence Sydney's Black Wattle Bay is named, not for an *Acacia*, but a totally unrelated near relative of the familiar NSW Christmas Bush. Throughout Australia though the numerous *Acacia* species became known uniquely as Wattles, rather than Mimosas, which is the word the Romans used for them in north Africa and which is used elsewhere in the world.

The next big wattle industry followed soon after, using tannins from wattle bark in the leather tanning industry; the first tannery opened in 1801. The value of the bark was such that in many areas settlers went into supposedly virgin areas and found large areas of dead wattles with the bark stripped off. Tens of thousands of tonnes of bark were exported, western Victoria being a major source; indeed at one time Portland was being called Barkopolis! Today most of our wattle bark products are imported from South Africa and Brazil.

Timber, particularly from Blackwood, also became significant early in the history of the colony, with sawmills established in Tasmania and eastern Victoria by 1830. Blackwood was used throughout Old Parliament House as wall panelling and for the doors and frames, including the massive external front door. Today it is still sought by artisans for products ranging from furniture to stringed instruments.

Wattle seed has become part of the burgeoning and very trendy 'bush food' industry, and more significantly some Australian species are proving to be a valuable food source in east Africa. Not something to try at home with one of the backyard wattles though – many of them have seeds that are very bad for us indeed! As a chill mist climbs the range and reminds me that winter is nearing I retreat, but can't help another wattle-inspired grin.

This silly grin comes unbidden whenever I think of the recent extraordinary furore and political machinations that ensued when it looked as though we were going to have to change the name of most of our *Acacia* species to the admittedly awkward *Racosperma*. We had known for ages that *Acacia* is a very broad and loose grouping of at least five genera around the world and that one day these would be described and named – and that *Acacia* would stay with the group of the first one described. Sadly for us, that one happened to be African (though most species are found in Australia). Very aggravating for us, though not of course for the Africans. To pre-empt this inconvenience, frantic lobbying took place to change the rules to make an exemption where 'unnecessary disruption to nomenclature' would result from applying the universally accepted rules. It worked too and I can't help but wonder what interesting precedents have now been set.

It does seem somehow appropriate in the light of the achievements of these latter-day world-class Machiavellians that Blackwood adorns the old constitutional home of national plotting and scheming. Home time.

Brush-tailed Possum, see page 73

Yellow-tailed Black-cockatoo, see page 89

WINTER

WINTER IS A TIME OF SURVIVAL, BUT ALSO ONE OF PREPARATION FOR THE BUSY TIMES AHEAD; AS SOON AS DAYS GET LONGER AND NIGHTS GET WARMER EVERYTHING MUST BE READY TO BEGIN THE CRUCIAL BUSINESS OF BREEDING.

Up in the mountains only a few hardy animals remain active, ranging in size from Common Wombats to White-browed Scrub-wrens. Many others, reptiles, frogs and invertebrates, survive in torpor, near-frozen under rocks and logs. Yet others have died, having left eggs or even immature animals to survive in the frozen soil. Most larger animals, however, both mammals and birds, have left the high country to overwinter in the milder plains and valleys below, or have even travelled far to the north.

Larger plants, trees and shrubs, simply survive, slowing down essential processes. Many herbs either die back to ground level, to regrow from underground tubers in spring, or die altogether having left a seed bank in the cold soil.

Lower down however things are more active. A winter phenomenon common to both bushland and gardens is that of the mixed feeding flock, wherein dozens of small birds of several different species move together in a busy wave, collectively seeking food and avoiding predators. The bush may be apparently lifeless one moment, then be bursting with activity.

Suburban gardens may even be livelier than in summer, with feathered refugees from the ranges, plus some which have bred in the surrounding woodlands, over-wintering and finding food and shelter. In addition to commoner species such as Pied Currawongs, King Parrots, Crimson Rosellas, Gang-gang Cockatoos, Sulphur-crested Cockatoos and Eastern Spinebills, gardens of lucky Canberrans are visited by many more Golden Whistlers, Satin Bowerbirds, Red-browed and Double-barred Finches and Spotted Pardalotes than are present in the warmer months. Birds such as magpies and White-winged Choughs, normally insect eaters, feel the pinch of food shortages and come to backyard feeders to eat seeds.

A perhaps surprising number of birds begin breeding while the morning frosts are still deep on the ground. Wedge-tailed Eagles, Black Swans, Australian Ravens, Masked Lapwings and even the tiny Yellow-rumped Thornbills are courting and laying eggs in and near the chilly suburbs. In the even colder ranges Superb Lyrebirds are doing the same thing and the mountain gullies are splendid with their performances ringing through the mists.

And before winter has fully come to a close many more species have launched the breeding cycle. Echidnas are forming mating trains and Wood Ducks and parrots are squabbling over nesting hollows; leaving it any later means a very real risk of not having an essential hollow at all.

And the busiest days of the year are yet to come.

White-throated Treecreeper, see page 170

JUNE

GANG-GANG COCKATOO (*Callocephalon fimbriatum*)

AUSTRALIAN NATIONAL UNIVERSITY. I am having a working lunch in perfect winter sunshine on the verandah of an old wooden building converted into a restaurant. Unfortunately I'm having some trouble concentrating on the undoubtedly interesting topic because of the small flock of Gang-gangs feeding and loafing in the old Apple Box almost alongside us. It is just as well that my companions are not only aware of my foibles, but have some empathy with them.

I can't imagine who could not be smitten with these growly little cockatoos, the demurely ashy females and the males seemingly unselfconscious of their outré wispy red coiffure. Many of them are crunching on the seed capsules of the Box which flowered in autumn, so is a good winter food supply. Their use of their feet is very deft. A cluster of gumnuts is held in the left claw while the stem is bitten through, then they turn it in the foot as they delicately extract the seeds. There is a steady pattering of the fragments to the ground. In a nearby wattle an immature male, with creamy-edged breast feathers and touches of red blush on his cheeks, is cracking open green galls and extracting the white grubs. In summer we could have watched them delicately harvesting spitfire larvae, carefully extracting the sac of eucalypt-derived toxins from the back and discarding it before munching on the caterpillar like a long eucalyptus lolly. Very few birds have learnt that trick.

A pair is sitting quietly and close together as she assiduously nibbles, preening behind his neck. The continuous quiet creaking with which they all stay in contact is reminiscent of distant farm gates swinging in the breeze – or perhaps a multitude of corks being lovingly eased from wine bottles …

Some of this group could well have bred in hollows of the ancient woodland remnant trees right here on campus, or across the road in the Australian National Botanic Gardens. Most though are likely to have spent the summer in the high mountain forests above Canberra and come down with their offspring as the frosts took charge.

Truly Gang-gangs are part of the essence of my Canberra – in no other city in Australia (or indeed the world) can they be found throughout the urban area, even in the commercial centre.

Part of their success is their easy acceptance of humans at close quarters, as we are currently experiencing and enjoying. They are also very adaptable and have accepted exotic food such as Hawthorn and Cotoneaster berries and cypress pine seeds in lieu of their traditional diet.

We don't know the language from which their name comes, but it could be that Gang-gang is the only Ngunnawal word in regular English usage.

Suddenly, as we muse on these things (our agenda briefly deferred) the whole group of birds, for no evident reason, takes off with much hoarse screeching, finally attracting the attention of hitherto oblivious diners. With their deep driving wingbeats they whirl above and through the foliage, then as suddenly as they left they settle and resume their various activities as if nothing had happened.

'Are we agreed then?' Hmm. On Gang-gangs, probably. Otherwise … what was the proposal again?

Note: The Gang-gang Cockatoo is listed as a threatened species under NSW legislation.

SOFT TREE-FERN (*Dicksonia antarctica*)

BLUE RANGE, NAMADGI NATIONAL PARK. The all-encompassing fires of early 2003 jumped this gully at the northern end of the Brindabellas, and of Namadgi National Park, merely scorching the tree-fern crowns. It remains deep and lush and green. The tree-ferns are three metres high, entirely shading the little creek trickling beneath them. A rare Spotted-tailed Quoll appears from the bracken and disappears into the shadow. From up the hill a Lyrebird is calling, pure silver bolts of sound piercing the mist. The scene could have been set 300 years ago.

Take away the eucalypts and herbs, remove the lyrebird and replace it with an ancestor, an erect running carnivorous theropod dinosaur insulated with feathers, and the scene could have been set 150 million years ago. Remove the dinosaur, replace the quoll with one of its distant lizard ancestors, a shambling big sail-backed pelycosaur – no dinosaurs had yet evolved – and the gully could have been thus 300 million years ago. The ferns were well established by then and didn't look very different from their current form. The pelycosaurs arose, chewed on them, and died out, leaving their mostly tiny mammalian descendants to scurry in their shade. The dinosaurs appeared, dined on ferns for a 160 million years, and died in the fire of a titanic meteor strike and the vicious endless winter which followed it. The ferns remained.

Like the softly luminous pale Ribbon Gums above them, they have a complex array of vessels, an intricate plumbing system constantly moving water and dissolved nutrients up from the

roots, and sugars, the products of photosynthesis, down from the leaves. These essentials are delivered by the network of vessels (visible as 'veins' in a leaf seen against the sky) to every cell in the plants.

The enormous leaves of these tree ferns are well over three metres long; from the centre of the crown new fronds are delicately uncurling. They are emerging from a solid pithy brown trunk, formed not of wood but of the bases of old fronds which have been shaded out and subsequently died back. Each frond is complex, divided into leaflets, each of which is divided again.

Unlike the Ribbon Gums though, the ferns have neither flowers nor seeds. On the backs of some fronds are rows of little brown cups, the sporangia, which will open to release millions of dust-like spores to be carried by the wind. Each spore carries a cloned genetic blueprint of its parent plant. On the moist sheltered creek banks are tiny rounded green discs, the fern prothallus. These plants, entirely unrecognisable as ferns, grow from the spores and produce swimming sperm and eggs in a surprisingly animal-like fashion. When the sperm fertilises the egg of another prothallus, a new fern plant grows from beneath the tiny leaf. This system of alternating sexual and asexual generations is very ancient and very complex.

Masses of dark green leathery Fishbone Ferns fill the gully and spill up onto the shady hillside. Delicate Coral Ferns grow along the bank. Higher up the slopes of Mount Coree, among the Snow Gums, tough resilient big Mother Shield-ferns grow among the rocks. In fact most of the ACT's 50 species of ferns grow in the Blue Range. Australia, the dry continent, has some 350 species of the world's 10 000, many of which are confined to the tropical rainforests.

A cold misty rain rolls down the slope from the west. The Lyrebird falls silent, the quoll slips away to a rock den. The ferns remain.

SILVEREYE (Zosterops lateralis)

GUNGAHLIN. The yard is bursting with activity. Yellow-rumped Thornbills, Striated and Spotted Pardalotes flutter at the foliage to glean insects, a pair of over-wintering Grey Fantails is making regular forays out from a perch, White-plumed Honeyeaters hop through the bushes. And the Silvereyes, grey backs and olive green heads with distinctive white eye-rings, are swarming everywhere. These mixed feeding flocks move like waves through the bush and through gardens in winter, taking advantage of many eyes to avoid predators, sharing the resource and ensuring they are not searching where others have just been.

Most of these are birds which stay in the ACT all year round. The thornbills are locally resident, as the fantails have chosen to be this year, both the pardalote species move up and down from the ranges and the honeyeaters go out into the surrounding woodlands to breed and return to suburbia in winter. The Silvereyes, however, are an entirely different matter. A map of eastern Australia with the various movements of Silvereyes shown on it would be mind-spinningly complex. Worse, at least some of it would look different from year to year.

In this Nicholls yard, for instance, not far from Percival Hill Reserve, some of the Silvereyes have chestnut flanks, conspicuous as they hang and flit. These birds have battled across the terrifying blustery expanse of Bass Strait, struggling exhausted ashore east of Melbourne, recovering then making their way north along the inland flanks of the Great Dividing Range. During the day they drifted along, feeding as they went, and travelled more seriously at night. While migrating thus they need only a fraction of the sleep they require for the rest of the year. Some of this group have made the return trip four times now, breeding in the Tasmanian summer and leaving as the snows threaten. What is more, the core of the group is the same – Silvereyes have a remarkable faithfulness to their travelling companions.

This little Tasmanian party will now stay in Canberra for winter before heading south yet again. Others though, who travelled with them, have continued straight through the capital, not resting until they get to south-east Queensland. Also in this yard are many Silvereyes with pale buff flanks, mainlanders all. A few of them bred on Percival Hill and nearby shrubby gardens and have simply stayed on. One little group of these though, which have chosen to remain 'at home' this year, did no such thing last year. Then they headed off in April, over-wintering up near Inverell, returning to breed. Yet others now present, as the whole mixed flock begins to drift across the road, have moved up from Victoria. Some of their compatriots, however, also kept moving to the north, having swelled the Canberra population for a while in autumn.

This apparent wanderlust even took a party of Silvereyes across the Tasman Sea in the 1830s, supplemented by a bigger influx in the 1850s, to colonise New Zealand. The Maoris bestowed upon it the name Tauhou, or Stranger. A stranger no more in the Land of the Long White Cloud, they are now one of the commonest birds there.

There are over 80 species of white-eyes, as they are known throughout the Pacific, southern Asia and southern Africa, all looking very similar. They are the bane of grape growers, but the number of insects that they take easily compensates for that.

Abruptly the high, hard shrill of the White-plumed Honeyeaters cuts the air and warns everyone of the appearance of the speculating local Collared Sparrowhawk. Suddenly it is as if there has never been a Silvereye in the area.

BRUSH-TAILED ROCK-WALLABY (*Petrogale penicillata*)

ORORRAL VALLEY, 1930. The young Rock-wallaby flinches and crouches low to the rock ledge as the male Wedge-tailed Eagle rushes low overhead. In relieved panic the wallaby gathers to leap to the safety of the tumbled granite tors as the eagle hurtles out over the valley. He is inexperienced, however, and the eagle pair have been working together for many years. The female arrives at the precise moment that the wallaby springs into the air, seizes his head in her talons and follows her mate to the nest on the far side of the valley. All along the ridge, Rock-wallabies huddle in shelters until the birds are out of sight.

Their numbers have fallen severely in the past century, but that is not due to the eagles, who have hunted wallabies for millennia uncountable, and they are still common in the more rugged and remote rocky places of the ACT. Their ancestors were also those of the little scurrying rainforest pademelons. When the great drying of the land began, the rock-wallaby forebears sought refuge in the sheltered gorges of the desert ranges. More recently, rock-wallabies re-entered the forested land of the Great Dividing Range and evolved even more rapidly; when Europeans arrived there were at least 14 species. Nearly every mountain range and rocky outcrop in Australia had its rock-wallabies. As numbers built up in the smaller populations, younger animals left the safety of the outcrops, travelled across the valleys and plains and blended their genes with those of other populations. Dingoes, eagles and human hunters took their toll, but life was good and rock-wallabies prospered.

Then things changed. Hunting, for fun and for furs, was intense – millions of rock-wallabies were shot. The country was cleared, making gene exchange between colonies much more hazardous; foxes greatly increased this hazard. Goats and rabbits competed for their food, and the goats forced them from their hitherto unassailable cliff-side shelters. The small outlying populations disappeared and their fastnesses could not be recolonised from the now isolated ranges. Nonetheless, in larger areas they persisted.

Among the huge granite boulders that edge the rims of the Ororral Valley the rock-wallabies are starting to emerge, freed for now from the eagles' shadows. Among them is the mother of the adolescent which is now nourishing the female eagle, soon to lay her own eggs. The

elegant wallaby seems to glide, almost flowing up the rock faces, pushed not by a long fourth toe as her lowland ancestors were – this would be a real hindrance on the rock surface – but by tough, leathery ridged soles. Her tail does not pump up and down behind her for balance, but is a heavy untapered rudder, carried arched high over her head to help with rapid direction changes. She does not allow her semi-independent joey to follow her about, as do the Eastern Grey Kangaroo youngsters in the grassland far below. That would be too hazardous and he is tucked away safely at the back of a low cave.

Far below numerous rabbits are feeding in the grass too; their coming scourge will unwittingly be the catalyst that seals the rock-wallabies' fate. When the *Myxoma* virus shatters their numbers in the 1950s, the desperate foxes will move up into the rocks and the end will be close. How can the mother, now grazing in the open forest behind the rocks, dream that her kind's future will one day depend on humans in the Tidbinbilla valley, fostering babies onto captive Tammar Wallabies so that captive rock-wallabies can produce more young? Or that a great fire 73 years hence will nearly – but not quite – end even that slim hope?

How can she dream that in less than 30 years all of her scattered colony will be just wisps of memory flowing over the great granite tors?

Note: The Brush-tailed Rock Wallaby is listed as a threatened species under Commonwealth, ACT, NSW, Victorian and Queensland legislation.

WEDGE-TAILED EAGLE (*Aquila audax*)

SHEPHERD'S LOOKOUT, MURRUMBIDGEE RIVER CORRIDOR. High above the Murrumbidgee an extraordinary and thrilling display is being presented, but on a winter Tuesday the metal platform with its stunning views north along the river into NSW is deserted.

The huge eagles are flying in a wide arc, he staying just behind and above her. As she dips a wing and swings to the left he does likewise, mimicking her every move. Suddenly he swings away and begins a near vertical rollercoaster series of shoulder-wrenching climbs and closed-wing stoops. He is showing her his stamina and sheer muscular power, his fitness to be the father of her chicks. She is clearly impressed, because now she introduces her own seemingly impossible aerobatics, swinging beneath where he is plunging down yet again. As she arrives directly under him she flips over so she is flying on her back, talons extended. His response is instant and as he pulls out of the dive he reaches out with his own claws and touches hers. They repeat the show with variations, until suddenly they are wheeling over and over towards the ground, talons locked. The inertia of the fall would seem fatal but they separate just above tree

level and plunge into the foliage, uttering strange wild little yelps. This is early in their annual courtship and all the proprieties must be observed, so they crouch and rub bills, mewing loudly. Then he mounts her briefly, holding his claws closed to avoid damage. Later on, renewed familiarity will permit them to dispense with the preliminaries.

These are mature birds, almost black, and they have held this territory for over a decade. They rest and preen for a while, then take off together to resume the more mundane work of nest repair and refurbishment. In fact they are upgrading three nests this year, of the eight in various states of repair around the territory. Soon they will focus on one, but meantime they keep their options open; the others will be used as lookout points and roosts. She suddenly stoops, not onto a rabbit or raven, but onto a sturdy dead branch which cracks beneath her accelerating weight and is borne off to the most developed nest. This is carefully sited high in an Apple Box fork on the south-eastern slope of a hill, sheltered from the prevailing winds and the hottest afternoon sun. When complete it will be lined with large sprays of eucalypt foliage. This is a statement of occupancy, but it also performs the essential function of repelling parasites.

When these birds were young they fed mostly on rabbits, food which their distant grandparents had adjusted to as the native medium-sized mammals – such as bettongs and bandicoots – disappeared. In their lifetimes though the rabbit numbers have dropped; even though rabbit calicivirus has not had the same impact here as in the dry lands, it and a number of drought years have had their effect. The eagles are survivors and adaptors though. In the absence of Australian vultures the Wedge-tail sups well on road kills and stock deaths. They pluck ravens, galahs, currawongs and magpies from a perch or as they take to the air, often stooping out of the sun to approach unseen. The attendant large birds which so often harass wedgies know just how dangerous their giant neighbours are. Bearded Dragons are taken from fence-posts and goannas from tree trunks. Young kangaroos and even adult wallabies are hunted by the pair working in tandem. This pair's chicks will feed only on fresh meat, not carrion.

For now they fuss over details of the nest. The ravens though, make sure to know exactly where they are.

SILVERFISH (Order Thysanura)

HOME LIBRARY, INNER NORTH CANBERRA. It is a dilemma. I don't like killing things. On the other hand my library is invaluable to me and I care about the natural history prints on the wall – none of any commercial significance, but all of value to me, either done by friends or selected to commemorate a place or event. And at the moment my beliefs and my needs are incompatible, the broken link being due to Silverfish. These ancient and brazen little survivors are eating bindings and nibbling the backs of the prints. At the moment I'm contemplating one which is itself being nibbled; in the ceiling corner one of the house huntsman spiders is demolishing a 20-millimetre-long grey insect, despite its protective grey shedding scales.

This is a useful reminder to me in case I was thinking of weakening my resolve not to use broad insecticides – apart from other considerations the spiders would be among the first victims, thus eliminating my major and ongoing pest control system.

In making my moral decisions about killing things, I discriminate unhesitatingly in favour of native species and against exotics – and fortunately for me these silverfish are exotic. There are native silverfish, found from the ground litter of Canberra Nature Park to the central deserts, but like the often colourful native cockroaches, these have no interest in coming indoors.

Silverfish are of an incomprehensibly ancient lineage, the most venerable of all insects. They are so ancient that they arose before the common ancestor of nearly all other modern insects and as a result have never had wings. Apart from the few species of equally ancient litter-dwelling bristletails, all other living insects, winged or flightless, have ancestors which flew. When the first fish-like amphibian clambered uncertainly ashore some 380 million years ago, chances are that its first meal was a silverfish. Two hundred million years later, the silverfish which scuttled nimbly between the toes of dinosaurs, eating plant products from the forest floor, didn't look very different. Nor do the ones in my library. Essentially the silverfish got it right for the lifestyle they'd adapted to and very little fine-tuning was necessary, notwithstanding cataclysmic worldwide changes in climate and a meteorite strike which took out some 85% of all animal species on earth. The tapered flat body, shiny slippery scales to clog the jaws of an assailant, little eyes, long antennae and three 'tails' haven't altered much in almost the entire time that animals have lived on land. Unlike more modern insects, baby silverfish look exactly like miniature adults, moulting a dozen times or more before attaining maturity.

The biggest change to the silverfish world came just a few moments ago, in silverfish terms, when humans started living in dwellings. Silverfish found that human habitations were dry, warm – and full of goodies like starch and cellulose. Flour, glue, paper, sugar and other processed carbohydrates suited them perfectly and they followed people around the world – even to my library. The six commonest indoor Australian silverfish can be found in any country on earth. They can live for years, and if times are tough in the food cupboard or library, can go a year without eating.

Cellulose, the complex sugar which forms the cell walls of plants and which enables a tree to push its photosynthesising leaves a hundred metres into the wind, is utterly indigestible to any organism bigger than a bacterium – except for some silverfish. Cows, koalas (and most silverfish) must employ a gut-full of cellulase-producing bacteria. We have recently learnt, however, that some silverfish, perhaps uniquely among animals, can make their own cellulase, the enzyme essential for digesting cellulose. They are really a special group of creatures.

Unfortunately my library is special too, so it looks like the borax and sugar for them. I don't really feel all that guilty – I have little doubt that they'll be around long after all traces of me and mine are gone from the earth.

LITTLE PIED CORMORANT (*Phalacrocorax melanoleucos*)

JERRABOMBERRA POOL, JERRABOMBERRA WETLANDS. I am sitting in the Fulica Hide looking out at the big deep pond in Jerrabomberra Creek. There are never as many birds here as in the shallower waters of Kelly's Swamp, but it's only an extra five minutes walk and worth a look for cormorants, darters and shelducks, and sometimes small birds in the surrounding willows. (Not to mention of course the ubiquitous coots for whom the hide is named.)

Today it's quiet, with only a solitary Little Pied Cormorant hanging its wings out to dry on a snag in front of the hide, but I always find bird-hides restful places to contemplate the world, so I'm happy to sit and ponder. A duck would never need to waste time drying its wings, for the simple reason they never get wet – their feather oils are entirely waterproof. As ever if I want to understand something about an organism I must start by thinking about what it does. A cormorant fishes. In particular it fishes by actively chasing the fish underwater. This alone is a key to explaining a lot about what I can see on the log in front of me now. Oil is great for keeping dry and thus warm, but it has a major defect for a diver – it floats. The cormorant can't afford all the extra effort it would need just to keep a buoyant body below the surface, so it puts up with being waterlogged – come to think of it that could even be a plus, in terms of keeping it below the water – and dries out later.

One way in which early birds shed some non-essential weight to make flying easier was to dispose of the heavy teeth and associated jaw muscles of their ancestors. Fish are notoriously slippery though, so the cormorants (along with some other fishers, such as pelicans and albatrosses) have invented an artificial tooth in the form of a hook on the bill tip, to grip the elusive prey. There is something funny about the cormorant's feet too, now that I've started this inspection. For a start they're much further back on the body than I might expect to see. This again relates to the swimming – it makes sense for a swimmer's propulsion to be right at the stern, like a propeller. It is not good for walking and cormorants are pretty hopeless at that, but evolution is all about compromises and they need to swim far more than they need to walk. The webbed feet make sense of course – lots of groups of swimming birds have developed these, independently of each other. There seems to be an awful lot of webbing here though, relative to a duck for instance. The reason here is that cormorants (like pelicans and darters and gannets) have improved on their paddles by having the hind toe move around to the side, so there is an extra segment of webbing to propel them.

If I wished to muse on matters not related at all to the bird itself, I could reflect that this black and white bird gives the lie to the somewhat tortuous origins of its English name. Originally applied to the sooty Great Cormorant, it comes via French from the Latin *corvus marinus*, the sea crow! I recall reading too how the vast guano harvest of the Peruvian cormorant colonies, for fertiliser in North America and Europe, provided the backbone of the economy of Peru for much of the 19th century. Twenty million tons of droppings were exported in just 30 years. The industry provided Peru's first railway and the large Chinese Peruvian population, whose ancestors were brought in to help with the mining when indigenous slaves and convict labour became unavailable.

But, back to the bird … I am especially fond of Little Pieds – apart from their very petiteness (they are in fact, by the weight of a down feather, the world's smallest cormorant) they seem to turn up everywhere. Partly perhaps due to their small size, they can make a living on any small farm dam or narrow creek. I've seen them on the coast, in mountain streams and far inland billabongs. Both Great Cormorants and Little Blacks are also common around here, while I can usually find some of the bigger, fine-billed Pied Cormorants around the National Carillon.

Now a darter joins the scene, looking a bit like a cormorant but not closely related – it shares a lifestyle though, which will always produce superficial similarities. Hunch-backed, this white-breasted female splashes heavily into the water where she rides very low, just her head and neck protruding – 'snake bird', she has been dubbed. She is not an active pursuer of fish, yabbies, tadpoles and small turtles like the cormorant but a stealthy skulker and stalker along the bottom of the river or pool, so she has heavier bones than the cormorant to keep her even lower in the water. Her bill is not hooked, but needle-tipped. Now she slips quietly under to go about her business.

Time I did too, but I nod before I go to acknowledge the cormorant's role in some productive and enjoyable contemplation.

PLATYPUS (*Ornithorhynchus anatinus*)

LOWER MOLONGLO RIVER CORRIDOR. At around 6°C the river is very cold indeed by the standard of most mammals, and there is a bitter evening breeze drifting down from the ranges, but the Platypus is oblivious to it. She has two dense layers of highly specialised fur – the outer one, of coarse guard hairs, keeps the inner layer dry. This one is thick and soft and provides near perfect insulation. Her vulnerable parts are the unfurred ones – feet, bill and tail – but she can cut the blood flow to them to reduce heat loss.

As she forages across the bed of the river pool her eyes are tightly closed, but she is still finding and even pursuing small animals. A major part of her diet comprises insect larvae, especially those of the cryptic caddis flies and mayflies. Worms are important and in winter she enjoys the shrimps which are now feeding on the bottom; in summer they are free-swimming and avoid her attention. She is using a sense for which mere humans do not even have a proper name, so alien is it to their own perceptions of the world. Her sensitive flexible bill has thousands of very sensitive receptors all over the surface, detecting the faintest of electrical impulses, such as those given off by the muscle contractions of a worm. That part of her brain which is given over to senses is dominated by the bill department. All her other senses are insignificant by comparison.

She eats about a fifth of her body weight per day – equivalent to a human female tucking away 13 kilograms or so of high protein food! As she swims, using only her powerful webbed front feet, she is sifting the mud from the food and storing the nutritious small animals in her cheek pouches. When these are full she comes to the surface, ignoring the biting wind, and lounges on her back with legs spread out munching her takings. She has no teeth but grinds the mass of living protein between her muscular tongue and a series of hard ridges and plates on her palate.

She will feed throughout the night and when light comes will retreat to her burrow, dug back into the bank two kilometres upstream and accessed by an obscure entrance just above the water level among the roots of an old River Oak. This camping burrow is only two metres long with a chamber at the end just big enough for her to turn around in. Come spring though she will dig out a 10-metre-long breeding tunnel with a slightly more spacious chamber at the end which she will line with wet leaves and where she will lay two sticky parchment-shelled eggs about 15 millimetres across. They will hatch in not much more than a week and the babies will stay there for another three or four months, secured by mud plugs to the burrow which their mother will replace as she comes and goes. This creates problems of course as oxygen levels drop and carbon dioxide rises. To compensate they have unusually high levels of haemoglobin in the blood to maximise use of the existing oxygen levels.

She is a true mammal and her babies will feed on concentrated iron-rich blood which is excreted from glands and which they lap from her fur. They will emerge from the burrow in autumn and spend a busy time learning to hunt and building up enough fat to help them through winter.

For now though her only responsibility is to keep up her own strength. With a flourish and a rolling swirl she dives again to create havoc among the small creatures of the Molonglo.

BLACK SWAN (*Cygnus atratus*)

LAKE TUGGERANONG. These swans are lucky. Unlike some of their abused companions in parts of Lake Burley Griffin, these are not subjected to mass feeding with loaves of bread, full of unnatural and unfamiliar salts, sugars and fats. The Lake Tuggeranong Black Swans are instead upending in metre-deep water, grazing on green water weeds which are their exclusive natural diet. Their long reach gives them access to a much larger grazing area than the Pacific Black Ducks swimming with them, which can only dabble-feed in much shallower water. The musical whistling bugle that is their contact call rolls across the water from other swans scattered across the lake, as it rolls across any Australian stretch of water from Tasmania to the central deserts, from the south-west to the Top End.

Out in the middle of the lake is an odd huge pile of greenery – a swan's nest. Black Swans start breeding perhaps earlier than any other Canberra bird and downy grey cygnets can be seen on the lakes in most months of the year. Swans have strong family bonds; youngsters will stay with their parents until they are well able to fly, though they are able to feed themselves from very early on.

The pair now starting to display their courtship intentions on the bank has been together since their first year of maturity and will remain so until one dies. Egged on by his mate, the male has slipped into the water and is advancing on the neighbouring male, spreading out his white wings and curving his neck forward and down to present his white-tipped red bill. The rival reacts, swimming up to him until their breasts and head are touching. In this position they swim up and down their mutual boundary for some minutes until, honour satisfied, the instigator breaks away and returns to his mating. His clamber ashore is awkward – his powerful swimming feet are too far back on his body for walking to be very effective. Once on land though he triumphantly approaches his approving mate, trumpeting with head pointed up and wings spread out until he flaps them vigorously and accepts her admiration.

This pair returned some weeks ago from Lake Bathurst where they had joined a great raft of swans moulting in the safety of the broad open expanses of the lake. Most birds can only afford to moult one feather per wing at a time, but swans are big enough to survive flightless for the time it takes to grow a complete new set of flight feathers, as long as they can stay out in open water. When they were ready to fly they exercised their wings, then ran across the water surface for 50 metres until they had enough momentum to lift their heavy bodies into the air and swing towards Canberra. Once up though, their flight is powerful and impressive.

Across the world, only the Australian Black Swan is not white (the Black-necked Swan of South America is in fact the only other one with any black on it). Europeans were not willing to extend their concepts of intrinsic swan purity to these antipodean aberrations, which were surely a living embodiment of metaphorical evil. When the Dutch explorer Willem de Vlamingh reported them from Western Australia in 1697 he was generally disbelieved. Black Swans probably did as much as any other creature to cement Australia's place in European minds as a perversity of nature.

The Lake Tuggeranong Black Swans though are not in a position to doubt or even consider their existence or place in European folklore. Nomadic children of El Niño, they just accept the existence of such artificial water bodies, not even judging them as compensation for wetlands drained.

And it's courtship time …

SPOTTED-TAILED QUOLL (*Dasyurus maculatus*)

GUDGENBY VALLEY, NAMADGI NATIONAL PARK. A small flock of Crimson Rosellas is feeding chattily on the ground among the rocks, foraging for wattle seeds. Unluckily for them, they have chosen to do so within hearing of probably the rarest predator capable of threatening them. In fact none of them have ever seen anything like the powerful hunter slipping closer to them on the other side of the rocks, though they would have no trouble in recognising it as a threat.

He is considerably bigger than them, dark rusty red with white spots over his five kilogram body and long bushy tail. Now a sudden rush, a flurry of red feathers and a shrieking explosion of parrots off the ground. The quoll carries his limp prey back to the shelter of the rocks to start feeding. He is a wanderer and an opportunist; last evening he was hunting rabbits along the edge of the valley below.

He is the largest carnivorous marsupial on mainland Australia and his kind have been so since the Thylacine and Tasmanian Devil eventually succumbed to the pressures of the introduced Dingo. Thylacines disappeared about 2000 years ago, while Europeans were only 400 years too late to share the mainland with the devils. The quolls' experience though would strongly suggest that the big pouched hunters would not have benefited from the newcomers' intervention, even had they survived the Dingoes. Spotted-tailed Quolls have declined greatly in the last couple of centuries, while their smaller relation, the Eastern Quoll, has followed the devil and thylacine into extinction on the mainland in just the past few decades. Quolls saw chook runs as some compensation for loss of traditional prey, and widespread use of strychnine baits led to an enormous slaughter of quolls in the nineteenth and early 20th century. In more recent times aerial baiting with fresh meat for wild dogs has also hit Spotted-tailed Quolls hard, even in national parks.

This big male is a survivor though, one of a scattering of his species through the rugged ranges of the southern ACT. Unbeknownst to him, some years ago his grandfather created a minor stir many kilometres away by following the Murrumbidgee down from the ranges, being distracted by the Ginninderra Creek and wandering into a backyard in suburban Macgregor.

His line is set to continue. Some kilometres to the south, his mate – who he will not see again until next year – has just given birth to four embryonic young which occupy the deep pouch that only develops when she needs it. This follows an exhausting all-night mating three weeks ago. By late winter they will have left the pouch to await her return in a grass-lined hollow log, riding on her back when she shifts hunting grounds. By mid-spring they will be tumbling in energetic play outside the den and undertaking their first hunts, stalking grasshoppers and skinks. Next year they will be seeking their own mates, wandering very far and wide in the quest.

Meantime their father, whom they will never see, has finished his meal and climbed nimbly up onto the rocks, thence into the lower branches of the eucalypt to bask in the late afternoon sun and gaze out over the valley. He yawns hugely, displaying his intimidating big canines, and dozes.

Note: The Spotted-tailed Quoll is listed as a threatened species under Commonwealth, ACT, NSW, Victorian, Queensland and South Australian legislation.

Superb Lyrebird male, see page 139

JULY

SULPHUR-CRESTED COCKATOO (*Cacatua galerita*)

HAIG PARK, SUBURBAN TURNER. As I drive along McCaughey Street with Haig Park on each side, I am forced to slow down by a gratingly deafening white cloud of birds flurrying across the road and settling again on the ground under the Pin Oaks. They spend a lot of winter here, harvesting what must be a huge crop of acorns. Deferring my errand I drive round the corner and stop to watch them, over 300 in a fairly tight flock. A few cockies screech at me from the trees, flaring their big yellow crests in warning – these are the sentinels of Australian folklore, though here the flock is more tolerant of intrusion than a rural one might be. The power that must be in the bills, to allow them to crush acorns to extract the seed, is phenomenal; it is aided by the hinge of the top mandible where it attaches to the skull, allowing extra leverage.

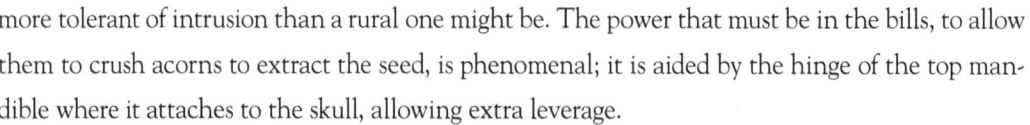

This flock is sharing the booty too. Among them is a group of a dozen Little Corellas, slightly smaller with a short white crest and blue skin around the eyes. These are refugees, now settled in Canberra. Some of them have escaped or been freed from backyard cages, others came from the west in a time of drought and stayed on. Their numbers increase by the year; in time they will become as familiar as Galahs to Canberrans. There is also a considerable scattering of King Parrots, shockingly bright red and green males and all-green females and immature birds, with a brilliant lime-green wing slash.

One unfortunate Sulphur-crest is infected with beak and feather disease. Most of the feathers of its head have disappeared and the upper mandible has grown well over the lower one, making foraging and preening difficult. As a result it is thin and unkempt and other birds tend to keep away from it, perhaps in instinctive acknowledgment of the fact that the virus is readily spread from the infected bird's droppings and shed feathers. I am sure this one won't last the winter; as well as affecting the cells of the bill and the feathers, the virus also damages its immune system. Some years ago I used to see many more affected cockies (as well as Galahs and King Parrots) but I suspect that there is a strong selective pressure for birds carrying an immunity to the disease.

I don't see the cockies here much in summer, when they are breeding in tree hollows in the paddock woodland remnants around Canberra, and further afield in the mountain forests. The youngsters have mostly given up their unremitting rasping begging by now, to the undoubted relief of their parents. These parents remain together throughout the year, unlike most birds (and virtually all other animals) which bond only for the breeding season.

As I'm standing here the flock is starting to stream away, not in any panic but methodically. By now, late in the morning, their crops are full and they're off to roost and digest the load. By the time I get home there will be a few loafing around, probably chewing on something that I'd prefer they didn't. Another symptom of this trait is in the street lights along this stretch of road; many of the covers are dangling in the breeze, where the cockies have chewed away the rubber seals! I'll cope, because I know they don't have a lot of choice. (I am not sure if Urban Services is that philosophical, but they too don't have a choice.) Cockies' beaks, on which they totally depend, must be kept sharp and trimmed by gnawing on whatever is handy; like fingernails they grow constantly and must be maintained. They are also intelligent animals and seem to simply get bored while waiting for their crop to empty!

In contrast I can't imagine ever being bored while there are cockies around to be entertaining.

SNOW GUM (*Eucalyptus pauciflora*)

MOUNT AGGIE, NAMADGI NATIONAL PARK. This ancient tree, vast and sprawling in the snow, is over 300 years old. It has clung to the rocks of Mount Aggie since before William Dampier became the first Englishman to set foot on Australia and coined the name 'gum tree', far, far to the north-west of here. Growing in a slight dip on the east side of the ridge it was one of the few trees here to avoid the fullest power and fury of the fires that exploded up the steep western slopes in January of 2003. Its leaves have now grown back and new stems from the base are well-established. When the foliage instantly vaporised in the appalling heat generated by the fire, their absence sent hormonal messages to the epicormic buds hidden and insulated under the bark, instructing them to start producing shoots so that the essential photosynthesis could continue.

It was a similar huge fire which created the open space that allowed this tree to become established more than three centuries ago. Gradually the thickets of saplings thinned out to form the open grassy woodland which was the norm for Snow Gums before increased European burning practices changed the structure.

The snow is piled on the branches and the foliage; unlike the drooping northern hemisphere fir trees, the Snow Gum's branches are erect and the thick, greyish leathery leaves also hold snow, rather than shedding it. In winter it simply endures, waiting until summer when it must do its growing and flowering in a scant three or four months until the cold again slows its systems down. It has evolved some remarkable strategies for making the most of the brief summer though. Its preferred temperature for photosynthesis changes over the course of the summer, following the mean air temperature, so that the current temperature is always the best one for growth to take place. In addition, the preferred temperature up here is considerably lower than that at which lower altitude Snow Gums grow best.

Despite the layer of snow across the landscape, the old tree is not alone. A party of Crimson Rosellas is squabbling in the branches, and a pair of White-browed Scrubwrens is foraging in the foliage of Leafy Bossiaea protruding from the snow. They are even pushing between the leaves to work beneath the snow – indeed they will roost tonight in the foliage under the insulating snow blanket.

Inside the tree there is activity too, beyond its own cycles. Remarkable tiny caterpillars, only a couple of millimetres long, are chewing along the surface of the cambial layer under the bark. It is here that the tree is laying down new tissue to increase its diameter, so it provides a nourishing environment for an animal hardy enough to use it. When the caterpillar has chewed a certain way it will turn and burrow back again parallel to its own track, perhaps taking advantage of the new growth stimulated by its previous depredations, like a burglar coming back to steal items replaced since his last theft. At intervals the little grub moults its skin and grows into a new enlarged one, necessitating a wider tunnel. Behind it the passageway is filled with its droppings. In summer it will burrow out and drop to the litter to pupate. The minute grey moth which emerges will lay its eggs on the tree's bark and the little caterpillars which hatch will burrow in to start a new mine. Only when the bark drops later in summer will the evidence appear in the form of long-abandoned mines on the tree surface; the burrows that are active now will not appear on the surface for a few years yet.

It is a slow dance but one that will be repeated for millennia yet to come. Across the distant jagged Bogong Peaks the sun is lowering. The scrubwrens start to go to roost and the rosellas hurtle, shrieking, down the slope. And to the south, over Mount Gingera, winter storm clouds are building.

BLACK-TAILED WALLABY (*Wallabia bicolor*)

CORIN DAM ROAD, NAMADGI NATIONAL PARK. Finally leaving the pines and ill-sited developments behind, we have entered Namadgi National Park by the Square Rock Walking Track car park and descended the hill. By now Mount Gingera is dominating the skyline ahead.

As soon as the dark hump-back shape hop-scuttles across the early morning road, it is obviously different from the numerous Eastern Grey Kangaroos we've been seeing. Aside from its near-black back, the Black-tailed Wallaby has a small head and ears which it holds low to the road, and its tail doesn't 'pump' as much as that of a roo. We pull up before we reach it and are readily able to admire it as it stops among the bracken by the roadside and gazes back at us. Its white cheek stripe stands out in the misty morning and the lovely rusty underside contrasts with the chocolate back and sides. While it contemplates us, it absent-mindedly reaches out and pulls in a bracken frond to nibble on. This would be a bit startling if I'd not seen it often before – in other mammals, including humans, bracken can lethally suppress white blood cell counts and destroy thiamine, leading to beri-beri like symptoms. It can also cause intestinal cancers; altogether not ideal tucker, one might think! On the other hand these characters have tough tummies – I've also seen Black-tailed Wallabies snacking on Hemlock, a common enough weed in the ACT. Poor Socrates could have used the trick. As we watch now it hops back onto the verge and begins to chew on a rounded white fungus. (This Horse Dung Fungus only resembles its decidedly unpalatable name when it ages!)

All of this supports the impression of an 'unwallaby-like wallaby'. Swampies – I grew up calling them Swamp Wallabies, and though this is a much less informative name than Black-tailed, old habits don't die easily – are indeed only relatively distantly related to the other common roos and wallabies in the area. Both the swarming Eastern Grey Kangaroos whose numbers have burgeoned with increased pasture and water and reduced Dingo predation, and the Red-necked Wallabies we've been seeing along the forested verges this morning, belong to the 'main line' of macropod evolution. 'Macropod' means 'big foot' and the whole group takes its name from this section, the genus *Macropus*. The Red-necks are grey with rusty neck and rump; their pale tail immediately distinguishes them from the Eastern Greys, whose tails are black-tipped, and the descriptively named Black-tails.

All this emphasises the essential truth that 'wallaby' and 'kangaroo' are interchangeable terms. We tend to use 'wallaby' for smaller ones and 'kangaroo' for bigger ones, but there is lots of overlap. ('Wallaroo' is not a hybrid term, but the name of a big, blue-grey, shaggy muscular hill kangaroo that occurs in quieter parts of the ACT. To assist confusion, west of the Great Divide the same species has a reddish-grey coat and is called a Euro.) And of course even these names are just luck – we learnt them from Indigenous Australians and there were probably scores of different names for kangaroo in the wealth of languages across the land. For instance, had Cook not learnt the name 'kangaroo' up at the mouth of the Endeavour River, we would probably be using 'patagarang', that being the name used around Sydney Harbour.

We are busily digressing – but not really. There is no 'point' to the bush, it just is, so it's all digression really.

As I start the engine again, the wallaby is off, powering down the road on its big strong fourth toes. With each bounce the hind leg tendons contract and, like springs, store the energy and release it to power the next hop. At over 15 kilometres per hour, this is more efficient than conventional running. As I ease out into the road I have a last wallaby-powered thought. This one, on land, is incapable of moving its hind legs independently of each other. But, when forced to swim, it suddenly works out how to do so. Hmm.

AUSTRALIAN PELICAN (*Pelecanus conspicillatus*)

YARRAMUNDI REACH, LAKE BURLEY GRIFFIN. A couple of the morning joggers and cyclists slow to admire the dozen or so pelicans coming in to land, one after the other, on the lake. Each one holds its great two and a half metre wing span to face the wind and splays its broadly webbed feet to catch the air and slow it down before skiing to a halt in a splashing wave. It is an impressive sight but what the watchers cannot know, as they already move on, are the details of the remarkable journey these birds have made to get here. Just a few sparse weeks ago they were fishing for Yellow-belly, Catfish and Bony Bream in the waterholes of the King Creek, a tributary of the Georgina near Bedourie in south-west Queensland. Lines of pelicans and cormorants, like living nets from side to side of the channel, day after day wreaked havoc on the wealth of life brought by the previous year's floods. Overhead great flocks of woodswallows and martins harvested the air for the richness to be found there. But now the cycle was coming to a quieter phase, the waters were dropping and the birds were beginning to disperse.

One morning, after feeding, this group had found a nearby dune where the morning sun was rising and they had ridden the thermals up, up until they were nearly invisible from the ground, powering themselves on the solar energy in the rising air. Then they had set out to glide for scores of kilometres towards the distant south-east coast, imperceptibly losing height as they went until they found another thermal to boost them onwards again. In all the history of life on earth, until a few of the largest birds attained the trick only one group of reptiles, the unrelated great ptero-saurs, had learnt this soaring, the very epitome of flight. And now, with a minimum of expended energy this group was splash-ing down into distant Lake Burley Griffin.

Their life journey had been even greater than this one though. Most of them had hatched on islands in the distant Coorong, the long tongue of water separated from the sea by a narrow spit of sand and fed, albeit sporadically these days, by the floodwaters of the Murray. Some had been to the east previously, before heading north-west – like many Australian waterbirds the inland was their preferred place when it could support them. Among them though are three much older birds who, over 15 years ago, had hatched in a vast cacophonous rookery of pelicans under the blazing blue sky over Lake Eyre, the last time the endless salt pans had been full of water and fish, brought down the Cooper by huge floods. Between them these three had seen most of Australia, from the Kimberley to Tasmania.

But they have travelled far and need refuelling, so in a well-practised move they form a line and start to swim towards the shallows of the banks, wings part-opened, stabbing the water with their bills. Immediately every nearby Little Black Cormorant starts rushing to join the hunt, to seize fleeing fish that are too small to interest the pelicans. As they approach the bank the outer pelicans swim in to form a tightening circle, now immersing their bills side on, coming up with a huge pouch of water. By contracting the pouch they sieve out the water and toss back down their throats the carp they've retained. Fish is a high protein diet and it only takes a while to get all they need.

Later, as the evening approaches and the still lake surface starts to pick up the orange sunset tones, the pelicans preen their travel-battered plumage on the pontoons, preparatory for a restful stay in the national capital. And next year? Not even the pelicans know.

COMMON WOMBAT (*Vombatus ursinus*)

FISHING GAP TRACK, TIDBINBILLA NATURE RESERVE. Like furry bulldozers the two wombats push through the snow on a sparkling clear morning, puffing steam into the air. A branch cracks and drops under the piled weight; the smaller animal leaps incongruously into the air, gallops a few steps, then stops, looks around and trots back to his impassive mother. She has seen eight winters and it takes more than a snow-laden branch fall to ruffle her phlegmatic disposition. This is the young-ster's second, but his first was spent as a fur-less tiny embryo-like baby in the snug security of her pouch. He is now almost exactly a year old. He left the pouch in February and has fol-lowed her closely since then, still suckling from the back-opening pouch which evolved to avoid filling with earth in a burrow. Even after he has completely weaned in spring he will continue to stay with her until late the following summer, when he will set up his own burrow and commence the solitary life of a male Common Wombat. Not until then will his mother again seek a mate to start the two-year cycle all over again.

Now though she has more immediate concerns. The nights are hard at the moment and it makes sense to focus her foraging in the slightly less harsh mornings. With broad feet and hard claws she digs down into the snow. Given that they can excavate hard soil and shift recalci-trant boulders in the process, the snow is a very easy proposition, though some mornings the effort of digging out from under a metre of it is wearing. Under it the tough Snow Grasses survive the winter and she commences to graze, nipping the grass blades with her strong inci-sors and passing them to her broad ridged molars to grind up. The tough grass fibre constantly wears her teeth, but alone among all marsupials a wombat's teeth grow continuously, like a rodent's, to compensate. Her son is now taking experimental nibbles, but he still prefers her rich warm milk.

By early afternoon the wind is rising and the wombats retreat to a nearby burrow to doze. Snow-walking is hard work and she follows well-tramped tracks where the surface has been hardened by her constant passage. The burrow she is heading for is a minor bolt-hole, only four metres deep; she is going out again later to feed and has no need of one of the elaborate multi-chambered homes she also maintains throughout her territory. She has three of these, dug into the sides of banks and under tree roots, the sides compacted to hardness with her solid flattened rump and head. The biggest is nearly 20 metres long, with four sleeping chambers, several tunnels and three entrances.

The first bolt-hole she approaches though is occupied, as notified by a pile of fresh cube-shaped droppings near the entrance. This is the part of the territory that she shares with her neighbour and in this area they often share burrows – though never at the same time! Now she just turns and moves deeper into her homelands to find the next shelter of the six minor ones that she keeps. During most of the year, when she is feeding only at night, she will visit at least a couple of them each night just to check up on them – over a few weeks she will have been to all of them at least once.

It is here in the hours within these shelters that the youngster is learning his own digging skills. And now he restlessly enlarges the tunnel while she dozes, with no concept that one day he will return and occupy it as a full shelter burrow himself, after a couple of years of roaming. A life of digging has begun.

STRAW-NECKED IBIS (*Threskiornis spinicollis*) and ROYAL SPOONBILL (*Platalea regia*)

TURF FARM, FYSHWICK. Heading south to visit the Jerrabomberra Wetlands I have pulled off the Monaro Highway extension where it passes the sweeping turf farms. I have been attracted by the opportunity to watch two members of the same wading bird family whose ancestors took somewhat different paths. Across the green expanse are upwards of a hundred handsome dark-bodied, white-bellied Straw-necked Ibis, moving slowly and purposefully on long red legs. Through the binoculars I can see the sheen of their wings and the yellow straw-like plumes hanging under their throats from the white collar. They are probing their long down-curved bills into the soft soil, but although they can't see where their bills are working this is no random probing. Both the interior and exterior of the tip of the bill are absolutely packed with nerve endings, thousands of them to a square millimetre. There are at least four different types of these receptors which between them are giving the bird a remarkable 'touch and taste' picture of what their bill is contacting. It can immediately determine the difference between a small living animal and an inanimate object or seed; when it does sense a food item the bill automatically snaps shut and the ibis tosses it back. Periodically one will break into pursuit of a larger fleeing victim – cricket or frog perhaps.

These ibis are very common on sports grounds and golf courses around Canberra, and I confess that I probably wouldn't have stopped just for them; however, in the shallow pool that forms near the road at the lowest point of the farm are two black-billed, pure white Royal Spoonbills, ibis relatives who are frenetically rushing around in the water, using the same system of bill tip organs to find their tiny aquatic prey. In their case though, their bill is not a long slender probe but a broad flat organ with a round tip. They are hunting by sweeping their bills from side to side in a zig-zag fashion, snapping them shut when they contact little aquatic insects or snails. In winter their superb drooping white head plumes are absent – they will develop them when breeding season comes around.

Thinking of that I sweep the ibis flock again with the binoculars and sure enough there is quite a sprinkling of immatures, with plain dark wings and dark tails, and no straw on their necks. Some of them have bills notably shorter than their parents' though they are now curved. When they were younger these bills were short and straight, to enable them to probe deep into their parents' throats for regurgitated food. As to where they hatched, my best guess would be in the swamps of the Riverina or central northern Victoria in the Kerang area in a colony which may have exceeded 50 000 pairs. With them would have been large numbers of White Ibis – and right on cue at least 20 of these wing in from the south and land in the wettest part of the paddock, not far from the spoonbills. These newcomers are all white with bare black heads and necks. They have this in common with the Straw-necks, to avoid clogging their head feathers with mud. I should have said that their plumage is distinctly off-white, suggesting that they are newly arrived from the Mugga Lane tip. In recent times ibis, and particularly White Ibis, have adapted in dramatic ways to the bounty supplied by our cities, from dumps to city parks, where they fight the long-established Silver Gulls for scavenging rights.

As I drive on it occurs to me that 'ibis' might just be the only English word in common use derived from the Egyptian. When the almost identical African Sacred Ibis followed the great Nile floods the ancient Egyptians confused cause and effect and venerated them (i.e. mummified great numbers) for their role in bringing the essential waters. Feeling a touch jaundiced by certain recent environmental decisions taken in Canberra, I'm not entirely convinced that our society understands the connections of nature in a much more sophisticated way.

LICHENS

MOUNT MUGGA MUGGA, CANBERRA NATURE PARK. It is a whole new meaning for 'rock garden'. The rocks don't provide the setting for the garden bed – they are the beds! I love getting down (though that doesn't get easier, sadly) to look at the little things. We miss so very much by just standing back and looking at the large and obvious. It is a sunny mid-winter morning up here and the granites themselves provide an ameliorating factor, soaking up the sun's energy and re-radiating it. Small animals find this very valuable, but the lichen gardens are quite immune to cold. If your close relations can live on rocks on the Antarctic Peninsula or near the summit of Mount Everest, Mount Mugga Mugga is not going to be very intimidating.

Close up, even my untutored eye can see several obviously differ-ent species within a few square centimetres. There are spreading pale grey sheets and bright orange ones and more compact and defined dark grey patches. There are olive green, dry leafy forms and others which consist of long tangled threads. These last encourage me to take some deep breaths – they will not grow where levels of air pollution, especially of sulphur, have risen even by a few percent. It doesn't take much to encourage me to sit back and ponder on what I can recall of what I'm watching. It is hard to imagine, but these modest and largely over-looked organisms are among the most remarkable and the most successful on all of earth. It has been claimed that there is 10 times as much of the world covered by lichens as there is by tropi-cal rain forest. Not of course that there aren't many lichens in these forests too, but there are also lichens to be found in the Atacama Desert where no rain has fallen for a hundred years. Here they get all the water they need from the fogs which roll in from the cold Pacific currents. The vast Arctic reindeer herds are sustained by them and everyone who has used litmus paper in a science lab is indebted to lichens.

But it is the very nature of lichens that is perhaps the most remarkable part of their story. Every lichen comprises a fungus and an alga growing in an extraordinary symbiosis. The fungus provides the structure of the organism, while the alga contributes the unique capacity of plants to fix the sun's energy directly by the wonderful chemistry of photosynthesis and to store it in the bonds of sugars. The fungus too takes up food via its network of mycelial threads and both alga and fungus lose some nutrient through its cell walls, which the other absorbs. The two components are not just casually associated; in fact the fungal partner in particular has long since lost the ability to even survive alone. Another indication of the integral nature of the relationship is that together they – i.e. the lichen – produce 'plant' structures and many chemicals that are not found in the worlds of either fungi or algae. And the partnership predates any life on land, as evidenced by 600 million year old lichen fossils which lived in a shallow sea in what is now southern China.

And now I've recalled the Peter Rabbit connection. Beatrix Potter was a truly remarkable woman, an excellent self-educated naturalist and botanical illustrator. She had the perspicacity and courage that the professional men of the time lacked, to see what was really there, even though conventional wisdom said it couldn't be. As a mere woman she wasn't even allowed to attend the meetings of the august Linnaean Society and she was abused and ridiculed, her convincing drawings utterly ignored. A shy person, she found the humiliation unbearable, and she put her microscope and studies aside to seek the safer world of writing children's stories. Within 30 years she was vindicated. How passionately I wish that the luminaries of the 1897 Linnaean Society could have been compelled to attend the meeting a century later which issued a formal apology to her for their treatment.

Unfortunately my backside is not as at home on a winter granite boulder as the lichens are and it's time to rise, albeit a little stiffly, and move on. Wherever I go though, I will not have left behind the lichens.

YELLOW-RUMPED THORNBILL (*Acanthiza chrysorrhoa*)

GOSSAN HILL, CANBERRA NATURE PARK. Ghostly in the frosty morning mist, the little gang has lost its leadership. The pardalotes are drifting off in small groups and the silvereyes are scattering into the nearby gardens. The young Golden Whistler which has strung along with them for the past few days is now foraging alone in the reserve, as is the pair of Grey Fantails. The core of the mixed flock, which has fed together in ever-changing combinations of species and individuals for much of winter, was the tight group of bright busy little Yellow-rumped Thornbills. Dozens of birds of several species could be found on occasions feeding together and swarming through the foliage but always either among them in the branches, or more often on the ground below, were the Yellow-rumps, swirling into the air like butterflies when disturbed. Now, with the frosts still hoaring the leaves well into the mornings, the thornbills have broken off into pairs to breed and the cohesion of the flock has dissolved.

Like a tiny mute ghost one appears through the cold fog, the black and white circlet around its forehead glimmering above the load of bark fibre in its bill. Silently it flits by and vanishes again to its chosen site, the bright yellow rump flashing briefly before the fog devours it. This nest is deep in a prickly grevillea in a garden bordering the reserve; its neighbours are building in mistletoe clumps, in eucalypt foliage and even in dense garden exotics. The Yellow-rumps are ambitious builders. No delicate little cup like the silvereyes or honeyeaters, but a huge scruffy hanging structure three times the length of the owner-builder. It is not unsubtle though – the side entrance is an inconspicuous narrow slit, sheltered from the elements by a protruding hood and inside is a cosy chamber lined with possum fur and rosella down feathers. Most peculiarly though, it is topped with a little cup-shaped false nest on top. Mere humans have not been able to come up with an explanation for this that can be supported by observation. Attempts have included suggestions that it is a decoy, either for cuckoos seeking to lay their eggs in the thornbill's nest or for nest robbers, a watching post for the male while the female broods, or a safe roost for the newly fledged young. The thornbill is too busy to elucidate, even if it could.

In the reserve the closely related Buff-rumped Thornbills have not yet started to breed, though will be doing so by next month. Their system is a complex one, starting as their close winter clan breaks into pairs or even groups of three or four which scatter through the clan territory to start nesting. As the attempts fail – and most of them do, victims of accident or currawong or cuckoo, often several times – the unsuccessful parents turn to assisting the successful clan members to feed their chicks, ensuring that at least something will come from the season.

Meantime though the Yellow-rumps continue their spectral flights through the freezing mist, lining the cosy chamber into which they will very soon lay three tiny brick-speckled eggs; by the time the earliest chill spring days appear, their chicks will already be fledged. And next year they too will be leaders of the little winter-foraging packs.

DADDY LONG-LEGS (*Pholcidae* sp.)

INNER NORTH. I know that White-tailed Spiders probably do not have flesh-eating compounds in their venom and that the weight of evidence is that there is no definite link between such sores and their bites. Caution is always sensible though and decades of urban mythology can be hard to shake off; while I won't kill them myself I'm quietly relieved to see this one being steadily devoured in the corner of the ceiling. I also appreciate irony and this is the hunter hunted – the White-tail itself specialises in tickling other spiders' webs and seizing the owner when it comes to investigate. Its own nemesis, this über-predator, is sprawling, spindly and fragile, an unlikely assassin, but I am happy to leave its tangled webs in these corners in return for its pest control services. Throughout much of the world Daddy Long-legs is found lurking in its untidy shelter, from whence it emerges to seize often more powerful prey by use of a spider's ultimate weapon, a portable net of silk, in which the careless White-tail is currently being enveloped. The Long-legs (though I can't really make this out) will now be biting a hole in the webbing through which it will bite the victim, further immobilising it, and then injecting tissue-dissolving chemicals to make digestion easier. Another piece of folk mythology concerns the supposed potency of this venom – it may be that it is harmful to humans, but since the spider's fangs are far too tiny to make an impression on human skin the point is academic.

If I were to somehow rid my house of other spiders, silverfish, flies, mosquitoes and clothes moths, the Daddy Long-legs will set out on hunting expeditions and start eating each other; they are not at risk of that fate in my house though. I don't really know of course if this is actually a Daddy or Mummy, as they are of much the same size and appearance – well, to me anyway! I could find out if I hung around and kept an eye on it long enough, as he only lives for a year and dies when his conjugal duties are done, while she can be around for some years. He never sees his children but they are well cared for. She bundles the eggs, less than 30 of them, into a silk net (of course) and carries them, then the babies when they hatch, in her jaws until they can feed themselves.

Curious now, I go for a walk through the house to see who else is around. In the corner of the kitchen window the Black House Spider is lurking in her funnel-shaped web. She is a true web-builder and no relation to the more primitive Funnelwebs. All three of the species I've seen so far are deadly enemies of Redback Spiders, which may be one reason I never see them in the house. (On the other hand the Black House Spider is a common victim of the White-tail's web-tweaking trickery.)

In the corridor, now actively looking for my eight-legged tenants, I am momentarily taken aback to see a large dead spider hanging from the ceiling. A better look confirms, however, that it is just the transparent shed skin of the resident big female Huntsman – she has again grown too big to fit inside her skin and has grown a new one inside the old, which during the night has split to let her out. I find her behind the lounge-room curtains, paying her rent by devouring a Silverfish, notwithstanding the loose shedding scales with which the book-nibbler tries to protect itself. She does not build a web to aid her hunting, but relies on her long-legged speed to run down her prey, most of which are much less welcome residents from my point of view. Her natural habitat is tree trunks and rocky ground, but given that she's lost that living space around here she is willing to accept the alternative I'm offering.

All seems well and I return to see how the Daddy Long-legs is progressing. He appears to have taken a rest from dining and I get too close, trying to see how much he's eaten. Immediately he goes into a paroxysm of alarm, vibrating the web around him so that he appears as a shimmering blur within it – I'm not sure what effect it has on other predators but it makes me back off. My very welcome pest control team all seem to be working well.

SPOTTED PARDALOTE (*Pardalotus punctatus*) and STRIATED PARDALOTE (*P. striatus*)

BENDORA DAM ROAD, NAMADGI NATIONAL PARK. I have pulled off the road where the gully of Collins Creek flows under the road to enter the Cotter River. Above the riot of ferns the Ribbon Gums and Narrow-leaved Peppermints are recovering vigorously from the 2003 fires. It is mid-morning and the birds are mostly quiet – so quiet in fact that that I can hear a steady pattering on the leafy tea-tree understorey, though there's not a cloud in the sky. Alerted I can now make out a constant movement in the foliage of the trees, which are alive with small birds fluttering between the leaves. They are pardalotes, tiny little feathered jewels with stubby bills and stubby tails, giving an oddly ladybird-like silhouette. There are two species locally and both are working the leaves here. The Spotted Pardalotes constantly call 'whit WHITty', a hugely powerful sound for such a tiny bird. The Striateds, in smaller numbers today, have a busier, less measured, repeated 'whitticher'.

Spotted Pardalote (above), Striated Pardalote (below)

They specialise in nipping the sugary covers – lerps – from psyllids, tiny sap-sacking bugs on the eucalypt leaf surface. The insect wants the tree's precious nitrogen, but this is so dilute in the sap that the bug must excrete large amounts of carbohydrates to get what it needs; some of this surplus is constructed into a beautifully intricate shelter. It is the showering of these covers to the ground that I can hear around me. (Other sap-suckers solve the problem by producing the prolific and delicious sweet honeydew.) Both pardalote species are also gleaning an array of other animals from the leaves as they swarm over the tree, seizing spiders, beetles, tree crickets and ants, clambering along the outer twigs and hovering at the leaves.

Both species have black heads, brown backs and yellow undersides. Spotteds also have red rumps, orange throats and white spangles on the crown and wings; the more sombre Striateds have thin white streaks on the back of the head, a yellow eyebrow and broad white wing streaks. Females of both are somewhat plainer. It is the spots which caught the attention of our fore-bears, fancifully bringing a leopard to their overwrought imagination – hence Pardalote. Other early names included Panther-bird and Diamond-bird.

Most of these birds will have spent summer higher in the ranges, up through the high wet gullies of Brown Barrel and Alpine Ash and into the Mountain Gums and Snow Gums of the ridges. Many more of their colleagues have moved lower down still into the suburbs and surrounding dry forests and woodlands – indeed there was a somewhat smaller mixed flock in my own garden yesterday. Yet others head north for the winter, joining flocks moving up from the inhospitable south.

I am always amazed to think of the tiny, exquisitely spangled Spotted Pardalotes digging out a nesting burrow in roadside or streamside banks, or in garden compost heaps and sand heaps. They begin by pecking a hole, then continue the tunnel with their feet, hurling out dirt up to a metre away. The tunnel in the end can be over 50 centimetres long and can take up to three weeks to complete. Elsewhere in Australia Striated Pardalotes also dig burrows, but for some reason in the ACT they always use tree hollows (or artificial alternatives). On the other hand I've known Spotteds to use roof cavities too – my neighbours were bestowed the honour of hosting such guests a while ago, though I had the best views of their comings and goings from my backyard eating area.

As I am about to leave to continue on to the reservoir a brilliant male Spotted Pardalote flutters down to a sapling at eye level about five metres away, peers sideways at me then dismisses me in favour of a small beetle on the leaf. These are his forests, not mine.

AUGUST

SUPERB LYREBIRD (*Menura novaehollandiae*)

LEES CREEK, NAMADGI NATIONAL PARK. She scratches vigorously in the litter, hurling leaves and twigs out to the side with her powerful feet and periodically seizing worms and fleeing beetles, native cockroaches, spiders and centipedes. She is working methodically up the slope among the ferns, sweeping material to each side in turn, turning over rocks and fallen branches in her efforts. Close behind her a Pilotbird, small and softly rusty, follows along to take advantage of prey that the lyrebird has missed. A pair

of Eastern Yellow Robins is also harvesting her leftovers, perching sideways on trunks just above her and pouncing regularly to the ground.

A little further up the gully the local male is displaying on a low mound of soil and ground litter, one of many he maintains throughout his territory. He is emitting an extraordinary cacophony of sound, comprising a tumbling potpourri of bird calls, each delivered with considerable virtuosity. Grey Shrike-thrush follows Pied Currawong and Kookaburra, the weird metallic rasping of Satin Bowerbirds juxtapose with a whoosh of Crimson Rosellas through the foliage, their multiple voices and rushing wings clearly audible, distant wailing Yellow-tailed Black-cockatoos alternate with nearby grating Gang-gangs. She is no longer interested, because two months ago she succumbed to his message – and the message she heard among all the bird calls was not what another species might have interpreted. To her his concert was an announcement that 'I have lived a long time to learn and perfect all this repertoire, and I have been able to practise very long hours to get it right; I am a survivor and strong and would make a great genetic contribution to your chick'. This message was reinforced by his remarkable dance, the mimicry emerging from under a shimmering silvery veil of his tail feathers cascaded forward over his back, and culminating in a leaping climax.

The same message was received by the other four females whose territories are also included in his much larger one, as well as by other birds along the valley. Once she has started breeding though, a lyrebird will not tolerate another female on her patch, so he must then go searching, risking the wrath of neighbouring males.

Now she makes for her nest and the single chick, her cheek pouches full of food. Flying heavily up to the big stick dome in the crown of a tree-fern, she pushes the food deep into her youngster's mouth. His father's role in his rearing began and ended with the mating on the display mound. Even the nest had already been prepared by her to receive the egg. This egg, left in the winter chill while she foraged for her own food, cooled to a degree that other birds' eggs could not have tolerated, and as a result it was a slow incubation by others' standards. Perhaps the difficulties of winter breeding are made worthwhile by avoiding the marauding goannas which are found through much of the lyrebird's range, and which are torpid in winter. Whatever the reason, it is clearly a successful strategy because the uniquely Australian lyrebirds are among the most ancient of all songbirds.

A mist is now rising in the gully and from it explodes the Pilotbird's piercing 'tippety-teeeep'; perhaps even he was momentarily fooled by the lyrebird male's rendition of his call. As if in response the female now leaves the nest and glides down the hill again to resume foraging.

ECHIDNA *(Tachyglossus aculeatus)*

MOUNT TAYLOR, CANBERRA NATURE PARK. A strange silent afternoon procession is moving earnestly across the mid-slopes of Mount Taylor, beneath the casuarinas. Five Echidnas, in single file, are ambling along, the leader in usual vaguely whiffling echidna fashion, the others tracking her with more purpose than they usually show. Every now and then she stops and pushes her leathery snout into the soil. At one point she senses the minute electrical impulses of a contracting body near to her probe; her snout engorges with blood, greatly increasing its sensitivity and she homes in on and extracts a white beetle larva. With the tip of her snout she mashes it against the ground, then swallows it. Now she is distracted by a small termite colony beneath a hollow log, only established last summer. She tears into it with her powerful shovel-like front claws, ripping into the partly decayed log in the process. She has no jaws and no teeth, but her flickering 15 centimetre tongue explores the recesses of the nest, dragging back juicy eggs and larvae, along with frantic workers and lots of soil, to be mashed against the hard plates on her palate and swallowed entire. Later the soil component will be left behind as characteristic cylindrical droppings. Meantime the rest of the train disperses, searching for its own food, but as soon as she is ready to move on they fall into line, the two largest of them – all are males – shoving and shouldering to get the prime position immediately behind her. In the time they are following her they can lose up to a quarter of their body weight by missing meals in their desperation to stay close behind her.

They have been following her scent trail now for nearly two weeks and it will be another two before she is fully ready.

When that happens she will lie flat and the two lead males will start to dig a trench on either side of her; eventually they will meet head to head until the strongest male has sole access. Things are still tricky for him and she doesn't make it easier until finally he is able to lift her tail and get his under it. After that she will lose her interesting aroma and the males will wander about their business, which at this time of year primarily relates to joining another train.

Meantime she will busy herself in digging a metre-deep nursery burrow between the roots of a casuarina. In a little under a month she will lay a small leathery egg directly into the pouch which is starting to form now on her abdominal wall. For 10 days she will carry the egg until it hatches to produce a minute hairless blind puggle which, for the only time in its life, will have a tooth, a single forward-pointing blade to help it tear the egg case open. From then on, fed on enormously high-protein and iron-rich milk, it will grow to about a thousand times its birth weight in two months. This female is over 20 years old (though still only halfway through her life), large and healthy, which is the most important start to life her youngster could ask for and its rapid growth will be a direct result of that. At that point, with the baby weighing nearly half a kilogram and, equally significantly, its bundles of soft hairs beginning to fuse into hard spines, she will deposit it in the nursery burrow. Here it will spend the rest of spring and half of summer sealed in and alone, its mother visiting every few days to fill it with the milk which, in time, will comprise 50% solids. Eventually she will remove the plug from the burrow and let it out to make its way in the world.

This youngster, for reasons only an Echidna could know, will wander south through the suburbs and reserves over the next couple of years, crossing roads and swimming across the Murrumbidgee, using its snout like a snorkel. Eventually it will settle in the bush behind Tharwa.

But now a cold wind is rising, blowing from the Brindabellas which are snowy from a late season fall. The Echidnas cannot maintain their body temperature as readily as most other mammals. Beneath the distant snow are Echidnas which have gone into hibernation for a couple of weeks, reducing their body temperature to that of their surrounds and slowing their functions to almost nothing. Things aren't that tough on Mount Taylor and these five seek shelter in logs and by digging in between tree roots to settle down for the night. The morning sun will rouse them and the train will reform.

AUSTRALIAN RAVEN (*Corvus coronoides*)

The battlefield, two days after the ambush, was a terrible place. The chill wind sighed among the pines and the soggy sun trickled through the clouds. Among the tumbled granite rocks of the hillside it coldly lit a sprawl of bodies – men and horses – and gear that hadn't been worth plundering. As the band of warriors warily approached the place where their compatriots had died, a flock of strong-billed black birds flapped heavily upwards, croaking from deep in their shaggy throats. The warriors cursed them as harbingers and associates of death, not considering that the ravens weren't the bringers of that death …

A score and more of centuries later, across the world, some of that superstitious fear of the clever opportunistic crows and ravens came with the European settlers to Australia, and was transferred to their close relations that inhabited the largely unfamiliar land.

URAMBI HILLS, CANBERRA NATURE PARK. In the clear wintry skies above the hills rising over the Murrumbidgee, far from any battlefield, two big black birds tumble through the air, renewing the bonds of their life-long partnership. Swooping easily down to perch close together on a bare branch they lean forward and with throat hackles flaring, let their powerful falsetto pulsing wail drift over the open ground to the nearby houses. Early breeders, despite the climate, they already have four brown-blotched eggs in the big rough stick nest lined with wool and grass. Despite the sun, the pair can ill-afford to leave them uncovered for much longer and she slips onto them, settling so that the bare brood patch on her belly brings engorged blood vessels into warming contact with them.

Meantime her mate flies to a nearby yard, where the householders would probably be somewhat startled to know that this morning he cached, in the flower bed, some surplus rabbit meat from a road kill that he'd scavenged. There is not a lot, from a bird's perspective, to identify the houses from each other but unerringly he lands in the relevant yard and swaggers straight to the precise spot where he'd buried the booty. He belongs to a very intelligent group of birds, quite capable of such feats of memory and more besides.

In Europe, Carrion Crows are known to pull up fixed fishing lines to remove catch or bait. In Japan the same species has learnt to place walnuts on the road when lights are red so that when they turn green the cars will crack them. In New Caledonia, in order to extract grubs from hollows, crows use a small 'tool kit' of gadgets from which they select the most appropriate tool for the particular job. These tools are fashioned by the bird, including a stick carefully snipped just below a side twig to make a hook, a serrated 'rake' snipped from a stiff leaf, and even probes from moulted feathers. When offered wire they are able to form that into tools too.

Here in Kambah the male takes the morsel back to feed his mate. Part of their success lies in their ability to feed on almost anything. The golf balls at the foot of the tree are the result of ill-judged attempts to bring eggs back to the nest – sadly these were a considerable disappointment to them. As well as carrion (not healthy lambs, despite nearly two centuries of persecution for the alleged crime) and insects, they are happy to eat fruit and seeds. Along the river drifts the sound of a flock of the much more gregarious Little Ravens, deeper voiced insect hunters who follow the Bogongs into the mountains or turn to the cicadas when they have a bumper year.

With the sun overhead the male Australian Raven now settles to preening, carefully straightening the vanes of every feather in turn. His clever white eyes are missing nothing though.

YELLOW BOX (*Eucalyptus melliodora*)

ELLERY CIRCUIT, AUSTRALIAN NATIONAL UNIVERSITY. The tree towers above the road, most of the lower branches lopped as a precaution against accidents. Its coarse yellow-tinted fibrous bark covers trunk and branches. It began its life in an abandoned meat ants' nest, germinating after the nest was flooded in a severe thunderstorm. Its tiny cotyledons, paired leaf-like food storage structures, appeared on 10 October 1725. This was also the date on which across the world a Scottish farm labourer named James Cook married Grace Pace in Cleveland, Yorkshire. Three years later, when the sapling was already a metre and a half tall with broad greyish juvenile leaves, they had a son, also called James, who would be working on the farm by the time he was five and leaving school at age 12 to work in a haber-dashery. When he was 17 and start-ing his apprenticeship on the coastal colliers, the first step of the sea career which would bring him to the land of the Yellow Box, the 20 year old sapling was 10 metres high and well established. In 1770 the sapling had become a handsome young tree; in April that year the Yorkshire farm boy guided the *Endeavour* up the forested coast just 140 kilometres away.

The tree was part of a beautiful and bountiful woodland, dominated by huge ancient Yellow Boxes and Red Gums, scattered so their canopies were barely touching and the sun poured down into the waving grasslands that formed the understorey. A full array of ages of trees was present, from those which had been young when Chaucer wrote the *Canterbury Tales*, to newly established saplings. Every few years the understorey burnt, a hot summer flash which was soon gone and in whose wake new growth burgeoned. In summer large flocks of Swift Parrots and Superb Parrots sought nectar and lerps, along with myriads of Regent Honeyeaters. Diamond Firetail finches rose in swarms to escape hunting Eastern Quolls, while bettongs bounded through the grasses.

Now all those birds are threatened with extinction; the quolls and bettongs have long gone. When the tree was a century old, broad and spreading, its world changed forever. Sheep came, and cattle, in numbers far greater than those of the kangaroos and wallabies which had previ-ously grazed the grasses. They were held in place by herders, and later by fences, so the grass never got a chance to recover. In attempts to increase the grazing the land was burnt yearly. For some decades the trees were spared, in the belief that they attracted rainfall, but by the end of the 19th century people had changed their minds and decided that instead the trees 'stole' water and sunlight and nutrients that the (now exotic) grasses needed. Most of the tree's companions were felled or ringbarked and left to die of starvation and thirst, as their long tubular cells were severed so they could no longer carry essential sugars down from the leaves or water and nutrients up from the roots. The final death blow to the woodlands came with ploughing; not a plant or small animal – lizard, moth or grasshopper – could survive that.

The tree, already well over 150 years old, was still spared – perhaps the nearby blacksmith's forge valued its shade for animals awaiting shoeing. Then came the city. Finally the sheep began to retreat before concrete and bitumen and increasing noise. And still the tree remained, though apart from a very few scattered others of its kind not a trace of its whole world remained with it.

Then just last year a single Regent Honeyeater came and stayed for a few brief days foraging in its foliage, as uncountable of its ancestors used to do every year. Just one. And was gone again.

MASKED LAPWING (*Vanellus miles*)

SCHOOL OVAL, TUGGERANONG. It is Monday morning and two small boys are moving very fast indeed. In fact they are covering the ground across the frosty oval a lot faster than either has done before. Behind them an angry bird is pulling out of a pursuit, shrieking its clattering annoyance to the sky. Not that the boys had actually done anything to it; they had just wandered across to the far side of the oval, retreating from the chattering mass of girls in the quadrangle. Suddenly they were faced with an even more intimidating cacophony and the intimidating spectacle of a large brown, black and white, yellow-billed red-legged bird, hurling abuse and itself into their faces. What has changed since they came here on Friday, unmolested, is the advent of three greenish-brown dark-spotted eggs, in a flat bowl of dried grass. And once the Masked Lapwings have claimed a breeding area as their own – be it oval, small island, nature strip, aerodrome, paddock or even a flat roof – they demand precedence and enforce it with very effective and vigorous bullying. For the next four weeks this section of school grounds will be out of bounds, as dictated by both the school principal and the birds themselves. At the end of that time the fluffy mottled brown and white chicks will hatch and will immediately be led away into the longer grass at the school boundary, to the immense relief of small boys who will no longer have to pretend to a nonchalance they definitely don't feel. And they would be even less nonchalant as they tease the birds from a safe distance if they knew that the angles of their wings bore sharp forward-pointing spurs of bone with which they can back up their threats.

The birds are plovers, a large and worldwide group of essentially shoreline waders, some of which, including the lapwings, have diversified to inland habitats. A few kilometres away at Jerrabomberra Wetlands a dozen little related Black-fronted Dotterels are busily probing the mudflats; their ancestors adapted to the inland waterways as the country dried out.

The boys might be entitled to feel, albeit anthropomorphically, that the plovers usurping their oval could show a little gratitude. The advent of ovals and other open space has given them foraging and breeding opportunities that they did not previously have and in the past century or so they have extended their range to Tasmania, New Guinea and New Zealand, where other small boys are doubtless less than thrilled. One spin-off of this expansion is that humans have (again) disrupted evolution. In northern Australia a separate race, with big fleshy facial wattles and no wing spurs, was evolving into a separate species until their long-separated southern cousins were enabled to move north along the cleared coast. Around Townsville they came together and were still able to interbreed; the northerners' and southerners' journeys towards separate species status were over.

Back in Tuggeranong the parents spend their days – in between intimidation displays – in foraging the oval for worms and insects, and even taking some seeds for their oil content to help fight the cold. Earlier in winter there were up to twenty of them at a time on the oval, but before activation of their hormones they were content to share the space and the small boys had not noticed their existence.

They are noticing now though, and showing a distinct lack of empathy for the unfortunate dog which had absconded from its yard and tried to take a short-cut through the school grounds. The laughter of many small boys accompanies its high-speed retreat; it won't be back for some time either.

MAGPIE-LARK (Grallina cyanoleuca)

CIVIC. As I step off the footpath and onto the raised area by the GPO boxes to collect my mail, I am outrageously abused. My eardrums feel as though they've been perforated. My assailant is a medium-sized black and white bird, raising her wings and being totally unambiguous about her feelings at having to step out of my way. (Actually I would have walked around her, but she didn't give me a chance.) I know she's a female from her white forehead and throat.

Now, with a moth in her bill, she flies up to a nearby Plane Tree. At home these particular east European trees on the nature strip are the bane of my frontyard's life, dropping vast quantities of leathery leaves to form a waterproof layer, with an apparent half-life of about a decade, across my garden. They are beloved of town planners, however, for their apparent immunity to drought and air pollution and the city. Magpie-larks, in the absence of tradi-tional alternatives, are happy to build their nest on their branches. The nest, a mar-vellous mud brick construction, is pro-gressing well. There wouldn't seem to be a very promising source of the essential building materials in this concrete waste-land, but I assume they're utilising a garden bed or perhaps even mud from an upper level

window-box. As I watch, her mate – black forehead and throat – arrives with a beakful of mud held together with dry grass and applies it to the cup of the nest.

'My' backyard Magpie-larks (or Peewees, as I think of them) are doing the same thing in the neighbours' biggest eucalypt and I know that all over Canberra the process is remarkably coordinated, triggered by last week's warm spell. As accidents befall some of these attempts and some have to start again the synchronisation will become ragged, but at the moment it's a strong sign that September is only a week away. I am not sure how these city-dwellers will manage to guard their youngsters – probably three of them – from the human traffic when they start to explore the ground, but I know that my home family will divide the task. He will park one or two in the backyard while he forages for them nearby, while she does the same thing out the front. The young birds, both male and female, curiously have a black forehead and white throat and sort it out when they first moult.

Now there is another barrage of sound from the tree, high-pitched shrieking trumpet blasts with the brain-piercing qualities of Miles Davis at his most challenging. This time both birds are contributing, but not in unison. One starts the fanfare and the other immediately responds to complete it; it is so tight that if I were not watching them (and with some prior knowledge) I would have no idea that more than one bird was calling. Their message is directed to any other Magpie-larks in hearing, that the territory is still occupied and defended. This is a call I have heard pretty well all over Australia, save only the wet closed coastal forests and the driest west-ern deserts, for this giant flycatcher is one of Australia's most successful birds, limited only by a supply of mud for nesting and some open ground on which to forage.

But now they're both off, in apoplectic pursuit of a raven which dared to fly over. And next month, with eggs and chicks to defend, the stress levels around here are going to get even higher …

BLACK CYPRESS PINE (*Callitris endlicheri*)

MOLONGLO GORGE. The wind is whistling along the gorge in the dull afternoon light, shepherding little flurries of sleet. No walkers are out today. Birds are sheltering deep in the foliage, fluffing up their feathery doonas to increase insulation. Lizards and insects are deep in torpor under rocks and logs and the Wallaroos are lying among the boulders out of the wind. But the trees growing among the exposed rocks have seen it all before. On the steep scree slope spilling down from the railway line cling the rough-barked Spearwood Wattles, whose greyish foliage appears oddly out of focus from a distance. They are essentially a tree of the western slopes, with only a couple of ACT populations on sun-facing northerly slopes. Among them are the tall, slender, dark green cones of the Black Cypress Pines, tips whipping in the gusts. On one a disconsolate Little Eagle hunches, its little crest blown forwards.

The pines' lineage though, that of the conifers, is at least twice as long as that of either wattle or eagle. Three hundred million years ago their ancestors grew in forests of giant ferns and lycopods, and other groups of plants now long gone from the face of the earth. Dragonflies with 60-centimetre wingspans flitted across the lush landscape and 30-centimetre-long cockroaches foraged beneath them. Small reptiles were a prelude to what was to come, but the largest animals in the landscape were dog-sized amphibians – the dinosaurs were still far in the future.

The conifers were the beneficiaries of a huge development in the evolution of plants – the seed. This was a sealed case within which the embryo was protected from dehydration and which also contained a food supply so that the embryo could wait until conditions were suitable for it to develop. Fifty million years later the greatest of all mass extinctions occurred and the conifers benefited from the removal of competition. Their seeds enabled them to adapt well to the new and less well watered conditions and for another 150 million years they ruled the drier plant world along with the seed-bearing cycads; the ferns still held sway in the wetter areas. 100 million years ago the conifers were at the height of their powers all over the earth. Then a new group came along with another revolutionary advancement – they rewarded and trained animals to carry their pollen efficiently and accurately to others of their kind. But these flowering newcomers could only function where insects or birds could live, and in vast cold areas near the poles and on mountains the conifers held their own, casting millions of pollen grains to the wind and to chance. Only a very few of these grains ever land on female cones, but those are enough.

These Molonglo Gorge cypresses are of ancient ancestry, but are not one of the truly venerable Gondwanan conifers. Those, like the Bunya and Hoop Pines and the podocarps and the old Tasmanian pines, are mostly restricted to their ancestral habitats, the rainforests. The cypress ancestors arrived here more recently and have spread to drier habitats. West of here vast area of White Cypress Pine woodland still dominate parts of the western slopes and plains, occurring both alone and with box eucalypts. Cypress Pine timber has long been valued for its rot-proof and termite-proof timber, though these days much of it goes to fence posts. Most of the great historic shearing sheds of the west were built of it, and are still going strong after well over a century.

The eagle gives up and allows itself to be swept with the wind down the valley. In the concentrating gloom the wattles fade against the hillside. The cypresses still loom though, as their line has done since creatures like giant tadpoles snuffled around their roots.

RED WATTLEBIRD (*Anthochaera carunculata*) and NOISY FRIARBIRD (*Philemon corniculatus*)

UNIVERSITY OF CANBERRA. One could be forgiven for thinking that a ghost from the recent past was stalking the campus. From the flowering shrubs in the garden border comes a rasping snarl which would not have disgraced the late lamented and magnificent leopard-sized and leopard-like carnivorous marsupial possum Thylacoleo. A mere 20 000 years ago maybe, but on a bright late August day in the early 21st century? Now the branches waver and the snarling mystery appears. If the passing students were a bit more alert, they would be seeing a medium-sized, white-streaked brown bird with yellow belly and a distinctly grouchy attitude with regard to its current feeding bush. If they were to look even more carefully they would, at this range, notice the pair of red wattles hanging below its eyes which gives it its name; Red Wattlebirds are not red and do not especially frequent wattle trees! It has been attracted by the hybrid early-flowering grevillea, with huge yellow spikes of flowers. Any honeyeater would love to dip its four-pronged brush tongue into their copious nectar, but this giant of the family has no intention of allowing that. Except when it's breeding it doesn't hold a fixed territory – wherever it's feeding is home and it defends it ferociously with prolonged and furious chases.

Some wattlebirds join the annual vast exodus of birds to the warmer north, tagging along with the flocks of smaller honeyeaters streaming along the Murrumbidgee in April. Many, however, stay in place over winter, a bonus of being large. A larger bird (or any other object) has relatively less surface area than a smaller one, so doesn't lose heat as readily and can cope better with a Canberra winter. The wattlebirds currently soaking up the rarefied intellectual atmosphere of the campus have stayed here right through the hard winter days and nights, giving them the advantage of being in place to set up territories when spring returns. For the first time in over four months though, they are about to be seriously challenged for their jealously guarded food sources.

From the eucalypts above now erupts again the raucous blast which has drawn the wattlebird from deep cover. The song echoing around the campus is, to the jaundiced ears of students, even less musical than that of the wattlebird, an imposingly shrieking, croaking gobble of noise. The world is made very forcibly aware that the aptly named Noisy Friarbirds are back. These are also honeyeaters, as big as the wattlebirds, but they are total migrants – very few stay behind when the flocks depart. The reason lies with their bald pate. Birds as well as students lose a lot of heat through their heads, and their black featherless crowns would be too much of a liability when the frosts bite. Vultures and ibis also have bare heads, to avoid getting unpleasantly gummed up when probing into carcases or mud. The Friarbirds' problem is a sweeter one than these, its nemesis being large, mostly tropical, nectar-laden flowers. Later in the year they become the scourge of Christmas Beetles, flying out from summer evening perches to seize their prickly snacks.

For now though a serious blue would seem to be brewing. The Friarbirds, with their manic red eyes, black dome and menacing knob on the bill, might appear to have the edge in intimidatory appearance, but the Wattlebirds are in possession. In practice though they will yell and skirmish for a while, then settle more or less comfortably into campus life. Their altercation wouldn't even register in the Friday night bar.

AUSTRALIAN WOOD DUCK (*Chenonetta jubata*)

AGISTMENT PADDOCKS, FAIRBAIRN AVENUE. I pull off the road – fortunately the regular idiot driver who is usually on that stretch is talking on his mobile and not tailgating me

– puzzled by the behaviour of a young horse in the paddock near the road. It is stretching its neck out low to the ground, investigating something in the grass. Now I too can see a vague lump there, but only through the binoculars does a duck become apparent, crouched low to the ground. Without the curious horse to blow her cover, I would never have noticed her. She seems injured, and starts to move away, dragging a wing. I've got a fair idea what's going on now, so I wait for a while until the duck stages a miraculous recovery, prompted by the realisation that the skittish horse is no threat. She returns to her starting point, creeping through the grass in a most unducky manner,  then continues. She is not alone. There are other lumps, tiny, scurrying along behind her. At least a dozen little brown and white mottled ducklings are in the parade, with their father slinking along in the rear. They are heading for the dam across the paddock – a long hike for tiny legs, but at least this family does not have to cross the road to reach its goal.

I am sorry that I missed the prelude to this trek, for the emergence of Wood Duck babies from their nest hollow is truly breath-stopping drama, but I can readily envisage it. A feature of winter around Canberra is the noisy performance of Wood Duck pairs selecting their breeding site – they must start early as there is a lot of competition. Both male and female perch, rather incongruously, near a likely-looking hollow, abusing with their somewhat whining honk others who might also be fancying it. Once the right hollow has been selected and claimed, the eggs are laid straight onto the wood, but covered with down for insulation. The female, pale-headed and heavily spotted with pale crescents below, incubates alone. The task of her handsome consort, with his deep coffee-coloured head and little crest, is to take charge of the nearest available dam or pool so that it's available for his family's use when they are ready.

When the babies hatch they are ready to walk and feed immediately – but there is no food 10 or more metres up the tree! They come to the edge of the precipice and gaze out at the ground so very far below, where their mother is calling encouragingly. Eventually one takes the leap, spiralling down, a tiny scrap of fluff which bounces slightly as it hits the ground. Others follow, urged by their increasingly anxious parents who know that this is a very dangerous time for them – the longer the babies are on the ground the less chance they have of reaching the safety of the dam. The mother is now flying up to the nest and down to the ground to emphasise her entreaties. When the last timid baby has hurled itself into space, the journey begins.

As I re-enter the traffic I muse that though this is the commonest and most familiar duck in Canberra, most of us don't see the excitement of this saga and really only see the birds when they are loafing the day away in their chosen camps, by dams or urban ponds. They are very loyal to these camps, which they only abandon when breeding. At night they leave them to graze on grassy areas, ovals or crops, coming back to the same dining room night after night until it is eaten out. But for a few months now I must forego the pleasure of hearing the flocks 'ngow'ing loudly as they pass over in the night. The Wood Ducks will be busy with their babies for a while to come.

VELVET WORM, or PERIPATUS (*Euperipatoides rowelli*)

BLACK MOUNTAIN. She is the undisputed ruler of her small world, a matriarch who demands subservience. Her universe is largely confined to the moist interior of a gently mouldering tree trunk in a shady clearing on the sheltered southern side of Black Mountain. If she were able to look out she would be gazing over the lake, where rowers pass through the narrow section between Weston Park and the cars on busy Parkes Way. She doesn't get out much though, certainly not in daylight, and her eyes are not designed for looking over such distances – she has no need of that. Sometimes at night, if it's damp out, she goes hunting in the leaf litter around her log-world but in all her life she will move only a few metres from here.

The old Red Stringbark came down in a storm decades ago and is slowly returning to the soil, aided by a vast community of fungi, slime moulds, bacteria, beetle larvae and termites. This community provides an enduring food source for the matriarch and her community, a dozen or so Peripatus, comprising adult females, a few males, and some youngsters; all of them are smaller than her, though she's only a few centimetres long.

Her lineage is the most ancient on the mountain; even the scorpions must grant her precedence. It is some 540 million years since her ancestors appeared in a shallow sea – and Peripatus from half a billion years ago, preserved in the famous Burgess Shale deposits of Canada, looked very like this one. Hers is one of the great dynasties of life; her kind was already ancient when the dinosaurs arose, dominated and vanished. Nonetheless most humans are unaware of her existence. Until recently regarded as a 'missing link' between two other mighty dynasties – the segmented worms (earthworms and leeches for example) and the vast legions of arthropods (insects, spiders, centipedes and crayfish, among many others) – we now know that Peripatus are either true arthropods themselves, or are very close to them. Belying external appearances, their brains are remarkably spider-like, though their bodies have only a thin veneer of the chitinous armour that has enabled their modern cousins to carry all before them. Much of the work of teasing out the matriarch's secrets is being done just across the mountain at the Australian National University, but to her that might as well be the moon.

To an untutored human eye she looks a little like a chimera of centipede and deep blue caterpillar, but in reality she is not like any other living thing. Her body is soft, which is why she must avoid situations where she could dry out, but is covered with glistening tubercles. These tubercles are giving her messages about the world, as are a pair of simple eyes and her rubbery-looking antennae. Her slightly tapered, stumpy hollow legs flow over the ground with surprising grace, powered by inner pressure as fluid is forced in and out of them. The hunting Peripatus must be a nightmare to other denizens of her log-world. She senses prey – most often termites, but in practice any beetle, cricket or moving creature – from a distance and needs go no closer to immobilise it. Remarkably she squirts a complex chemical cocktail from glands alongside her jaws, shaking them so that it snakes out like writhing cables. When it drops over the victim it hardens, so that the prey can only wait helplessly while the hunter approaches, pierces its carapace and injects saliva which turns its organs to soup … She can even tackle dangerous spiders by glueing their fangs.

After the kill, the matriarch has first turn at the table; the others must accept her leftovers. When she is satisfied, the other females take their turn, followed by the males and youngsters; the feast may last for hours. She forcefully exerts her authority with kicks and bites, backed up by superior size and strength. Sometimes she will allow a subordinate to ride on her back, but perhaps only because this helps her reduce water loss by evaporation. If a neighbouring family is encountered, the reception is even more violently aggressive.

Given all this it is no wonder that her reproductive behaviour seems bizarre to humans too. Within her paired uteri are strings of embryos. Those near the entrance will start emerging soon, one or two a day for about six weeks; there will then be a hiatus of another six months, while those further back wait their turn. They are encased in separate membranes which supply their needs, but will break out of them just before birth to emerge live and white. Later they will achieve their mother's rich velvety blue skin. Different species of Peripatus use different mating strategies, but her mate placed a package of sperm on her back. Her adjacent body wall broke down as an ulcer, allowing the sperm to enter her body cavity, where astonishingly they found their way through the vast complex to special chambers where they were hosted until required – which might take years. Nor do all the embryos within her have the same father.

Some of these fathers truly were peripatetic, in a way that the matriarch herself will never be. They wandered far in their search for her, but in recent years few have come. She can never know why, but the mountain has become isolated by development, and with the new burning regime on the mountain fewer logs remain on the ground to break down slowly and provide a Peripatus citadel. Here on the sheltered southern slopes, far from houses, she is relatively safe, but she is increasingly alone.

It would be a tragic irony if the extraordinary Black Mountain Peripatus was to disappear after 540 million years, just as we are beginning to understand them.

Note: It is recognised, through genetic research, that the Black Mountain population represents a separate undescribed species, but for now it is referred by this name, which describes a species found in wetter forest to the east, notably in the Tallaganda range. We can only hope that by the time the matriarch's kind is formally described, the name has become not that of another lost species.

Red Wattlebird, see page 149

SPRING

SPRING, FOR MOST LOCAL SPECIES, IS THE FOCAL POINT OF THE YEAR, A TIME OF NEW LIFE, A TIME WHICH DEFINES WHETHER THE YEAR — OR PERHAPS A WHOLE LIFE — HAS BEEN SURVIVED IN VAIN. IT IS A TIME OF URGENCY, HIGH RISKS AND, FOR MANY, HIGH REWARDS.

In milder climes, such as are found in the coastal heaths and forests, or in the open lands further west, winter is kinder and many plants flower and set seed then, so that those that rely on them may themselves reproduce. Spring in such a setting is less dramatic by contrast; in tropical areas spring is hardly acknowledged. In the valleys and on the hills and plains of the lowlands around the bush capital however, very little flowering or plant growth takes place in the frost months and, as spring melts the icy restraints, life burgeons. Here, life truly springs. If it has been a heavy winter in the mountains the streams and rivers are rushing with melting snow.

From the earliest misty spring days with frost still glittering on the grass, the migrants start to return from their sojourns in the warm frostless north. One morning we awake and are informed, either loudly or softly, melodiously or jarringly, that the friarbirds, cuckoos, orioles, gerygones and a score of others, are back to start the serious business of raising chicks to extend their line for another generation. They are not philosophers and in any measurable way this is the entire point of their existence.

Nests of mind-challenging complexity are woven and constructed, burrows are dug and they and tree hollows are lined.

By November every woodland and forest patch at the foot of the ranges is vibrating at sunrise with the urgent call of male birds of a hundred and more species, exhorting their mate to faithfulness and threatening dire consequences to their neighbours if they dare to trespass. As the season progresses this chorus rises into the mountain forests until even the high snow gums are echoing with it.

Every pool and streamside and boggy patch of sedges and reeds is alive with frog calls until our ears are humming, each striving to shout down his neighbours and inform the listening females that he alone is a fit father for her tadpoles. The message is repeated, in sound and movement and colour and scent, by every male wallaby, possum, lizard, snake, insect, spider –

indeed by most mature males of almost every animal group – across the countryside and suburbs, by day and by night.

Meantime the plants are doing much the same thing. From September onward more and more plants – grasses, lilies, orchids, creepers, shrubs and trees – come into flower, silently screaming with colour and pattern and scent to attract insects, birds and small mammals to come and receive a nectar reward. Unspoken is the trade-off – for an essential energy hit, the animal will carry pollen to another flower and fertilise it.

Millions of insects hatch or emerge from their winter torpor. Birds and lizards, spiders and frogs, feed on this insect feast, and their young, born or unborn, get fat and strong on it. One morning we find Bogong Moths hiding in cupboards and dark corners, resting from their arduous journey from hot northern plains to cool granite peaks.

Young Eastern Grey Kangaroos, born the previous summer, are starting to emerge from the pouch.

As the days get longer and the temperatures rise the sound levels begin to abate, at least from the birds, as the focus is on brooding the eggs and then young chicks, and on keeping a low profile to avoid predators. At the same time the real work begins in earnest, feeding several hungry mouths which represent the genetic return on all the vast and hazardous investment of time and energy that breeding represents.

And the hot days yet to come will go a long way to determining if the investment will pay.

Tiger Orchid, see page 205

SEPTEMBER

SPECKLED WARBLER (*Pyrrholaemus saggitatus*)

CAMPBELL PARK, MOUNT AINSLIE, CANBERRA NATURE PARK. The two beautifully patterned little birds – mottled brown above, brown mask on a dull yellow face, lines of dark arrows flowing up a pale yellow underside – move steadily across the ground, picking tiny animals from the litter. Campbell Park is one of the few places near the city where we can still watch Speckled Warblers. Suddenly she seizes a caterpillar, which she breaks apart by repeatedly dropping it and snapping at it before it hits the ground. Soon afterwards he proudly presents her with a small moth, whose wings he's already rubbed off on a twig. These little supplements that he provides enable her to get back to the nest and eggs as soon as possible. She only started incubating this morning, having laid the third of the three richly glossy, deep brick-red eggs. It's now Thursday; the first was laid on Sunday morning, the second on Tuesday.

The nest itself is exquisitely hidden and it needs to be, because it lies directly on the ground. It is a lovely grass and bark dome, cunningly placed in a slight dip among fallen branches under the edge of a large grass clump. The warbler wants to get back to incubating, having been away for nearly 20 minutes, but the nest is so vulnerable that she won't even approach it when potential danger is near. Two walkers on the nearby path are causing her considerable anxiety. These bird watchers though are currently more absorbed in conversation than in their purpose, so they soon follow the path into the distance. Only then does the warbler slip onto the eggs via the short tunnel at the side of the dome. Though the pair has been together for three years now, and will stay faithful to each other and the territory until a Collared Sparrowhawk intervenes during the winter after next, she does all the incubation.

Speckled Warblers have not done well from European settlement. They need patches of woodland of at least 100 hectares to survive and even then predation is severe. This nest will be found by a prowling fox before the eggs even hatch. The parents will escape though and start again. This time one chick will leave the nest to make its way in the world. In a way this is a small miracle – it has to survive undetected on the ground in the nest for two and a half weeks in the egg and then for the same time again as a flightless, helpless bundle. The determined parents will have yet another go late in the season, but this time a Shining Bronze-Cuckoo will find the nest. The cuckoo chick will hatch before the warblers and will evict the little red-chocolate eggs onto the ground. So, all the work of this season will produce just one warbler chick, but in fact that's pretty good. In their whole lives they only need to produce two chicks that grow up in order to break even. Any more than two is a bonus, and the only definition of 'success' that's meaningful to a bird.

RED-STEM WATTLE (*Acacia rubida*)

BOBOYAN ROAD, NAMADGI NATIONAL PARK. I always stop here when I can. Like most of us mere limited humans I am challenged by the concepts involved in geological time. My brain can know that the first proto-birds (really just another group of feathered dinosaurs) flapped clumsily in flowerless branches 150 million years ago or that 'Australia' broke its last ties to Gondwana some 65 million years ago – but I can't really comprehend it. But here by the roadside, 28 kilometres from the Namadgi Visitor Centre near Tharwa, I can see a leap of 50 million years. Just behind me in the gully is a massive granite outcrop that I like to explore when I have time; those same granites appear in the road cutting. Their crystals formed when uncountable millions of tonnes of molten rock and mineral, squeezed upwards from deep sub-terranean ovens 400 million years ago, cooled slowly underground. Immediately adjacent to them here in the road cutting are the older rocks of the area, formed from sediments which washed 50 million years earlier from uplands to the south into a sea in which swam the first strange jawless fishes, whose children include us.

This is also a good stretch of road in early spring to enjoy the wattles flowering and to ponder time and origins again. These are true Gondwanans; *Acacia* (or its close relations) are found in Africa, Madagascar, India and South America, and fossils of ex-Acacias are known from New Zealand. Since their seeds have not evolved to drift on currents of either air or sea, nor to be carried by birds, their ancestors must have been present in Gondwana before the components drifted apart, starting with Africa over 100 million years ago. Despite the fact that Australia has nearly 1000 of the 1500 known species, evidence gained from studying the sub-groups suggests that the ancestral home was the African-South American tropics.

Just down the slope from me the Black Wattle is about to flower. With its dark green feathery-looking foliage of compound leaves it superficially resembles *Acacia* from Africa or South America. Only superficially though, and here is something else that puzzles me. Why do Australian wattles not have the almost universally wicked thorns found elsewhere? Sure, a few species have evolved prickles and spines from phyllodes or stipules, but nothing compared with the weapons which shredded my shirt sleeve and arm when I first inadvertently tangled with them in Namibia. It is suggested that Australia doesn't have the big browsing mammals found elsewhere, but we certainly did until just a few tens of thousands of years back – yesterday in fact. Furthermore, to the same end *Acacia* species in Africa, India and South America have a variety of strategies to attract ferocious ants to defend them, including stem glands delivering nectar and even hollows in the thorns for the ants to live in. Why not here? After all we have a more diverse ant fauna than those places.

The Wedge-leaf Wattle whose bright yellow flowers have been brightening the roadside and the Red-stem Wattle I'm now admiring differ in another major way from their Gondwanan cousins too. They don't have the compound leaves, each comprising numerous tiny leaflets, that the Black Wattle and overseas wattles have. The Wedge-leaf has tough little triangular 'leaves' and the foliage of the Red-stem in my hand looks and feels remarkably like eucalypt leaves. It seems that their ancestors responded to the drying of the continent by dispensing with the soft desiccation-prone leaflets and instead developed these phyllodes from flattened leaf stalks endowed with the essential chlorophyll. Since their African cousins were facing similar challenges, I wonder why they didn't come up with a similar response? As this Red-stem Wattle is demonstrating though, these Australian wattles tend to have five bob each way, a strategy not alien to we newcomers too! The seedlings tend to have the ancestral compound leaves – presumably these are more efficient at photosynthesising and this is the imperative when getting established. After a year or so the long-term need for water conservation apparently gains precedence and the leaf stems flatten and the leaflets disappear. I am particularly fond of the Red-stem Wattle because it demonstrates this so well. The one I'm holding has a spray of little soft leaflets at the tip of many of the phyllodes.

The very ability to thrive here on the harsh road verge is an *Acacia* characteristic too. Like the related peas their roots contain lumpy nodules full of nitrogen-fixing bacteria which enable the wattles to take their essential nitrogen directly from the air, freeing them from the need to find soils containing soluble nitrogen salts.

I love wattles, but it's time to move on – there will be plenty more wherever I go anyway.

LATHAMS SNIPE (*Gallinago hardwickii*)

JERRABOMBERRA WETLANDS, CANBERRA NATURE PARK. Suddenly, they are here. As soon as I look out of the first hide at Kelly's Swamp I see half a dozen handsome black, cream and tawny-streaked birds with long, heavy black bills prob-
ing busily in the mud near the safety of the grassy island in front of me. They weren't here yesterday, but that strong sea-sonality is one of the joys of Canberra. Winter temperatures are grim, so plants don't flower then but save it for a con-centrated spring display; animals leave for winter and arrive back en masse as the days lengthen and warm. Among them are these snipe.

Their feeding borders on the frantic, and while this sewing machine action of bill into mud is typical of the shore waders, these particular birds have some very seri-ous energy needs to fill.

Not many weeks ago they were still in Hokkaido, finishing off their breeding season with about four fluffy chicks leaving the nest to forage on the dry grassy hillside or fir forest clearing. I marvel at the extraordinary story, as I do every time I see or think about the snipe. For a start they live a totally different lifestyle, in terms of their habitat, from one hemisphere to the other. From these dry breeding grounds they revert to the wetland wader life when they reach Australia.

But it's the odyssey itself that really challenges my imagination. As soon as chick-rearing duties are done, the birds start eating until they are gorged so much that their skin is stretched tight by the fat layer and they have trouble taking to the wing. My imagination is essential from here because we really don't know the details of the journey, but timing alone suggests that they fly directly across the ocean from Japan to here in just a few days. This is a bird weighing around 150 grams – quite amazing. Perhaps they make brief staging stops en route, but there are very few options and very little evidence of it. Guam might be an obvious choice, but despite the constant human presence there, these snipe are only very rarely reported. No, apparently they don't stop for the most part until they get to New Guinea, where they fly over the towering ranges and make landfall in north Queensland. From here they move quickly down the east coast, to Kelly's and the Namadgi bogs, and beyond to Victoria, Tasmania and South Australia.

And of course in early autumn they're off again, back across the equator to the now-thawing northern Japanese uplands.

As I watch and wonder a Swamp Harrier swings over the swamp and the snipe take to the air with jarringly harsh exclamations, dodging erratically across the sky before plummeting into cover. This defence, ironically, brought terrible devastation to them, exciting as it did the attention of so-called 'sportsmen' who responded to the challenge of shooting them. These original 'snipers' were responsible for the deaths of some 10 000 snipe a year in Australia alone until they were belatedly protected only in the 1980s. I shake my head, totally baffled by the mind which finds entertainment in killing.

Despite them being the subject of an international treaty between Australia and Japan their numbers do not seem to have significantly increased since the legal slaughter ended. Perhaps developments in their breeding grounds, continued wetland loss in Australia and even unknown factors affecting the migration routes are having an impact. Be that as it may, for now at least I have the utterly remarkable spectacle to enjoy of these transglobal peripatetics re-emerging from cover to feed on the mud with the national capital icons as a backdrop. It is all a bit surreal actually.

GREATER GLIDER (*Petauroides volans*)

BULLS HEAD CREEK, WARKS ROAD. It is a truly remarkable sight, or would be if there were any humans to see it. The odd car passes along the road below, but the huge owl is hidden among dense Blackwood foliage, safely out of sight of mobbing Pied Currawongs and Australian Ravens, as well as the mid-week drivers. From her right claw dangles a large possum, taken last night from a branch as it moved along it to the succulent eucalypt leaves at the tip. The Powerful Owl is enormous, 60 centimetres high – bigger than a Little Eagle – and the entire ACT can only support 10 pairs. This is probably as many as there ever were; because they rely on such big prey they need vast territories.

The victim is a young Greater Glider, though at 700 grams it is still more than half the owl's weight, a big prize and a big challenge for the owl. Further, Powerful Owls can even prey on adult gliders.

Greater Gliders are common animals in the rich wet forests of the ranges – since the demise of ACT Koalas they are the only mammal here to subsist totally on the limitless food supply offered by eucalypt leaves. The trouble is that, while abundant, these leaves must be

among the worst food in the world. They are high in fibre and low in nutrient and are full of very nasty chemicals indeed. It takes the quiet gentle gliders a week to break down the horrid food in their huge bacterium-fueled caecum, while their enlarged livers work on the toxins.

Night. The light has now faded and a white furry face with big ears emerges from a hollow in the trunk of a big old Ribbon Gum down by the creek; a moment later a dark face follows. They are unaware of the owl, but she has last night's meal to work on still, so is no danger to them. The glider pair share the hollow and have done so since mating time back in autumn. They have just begun to leave their growing baby in the den while they go out to forage; this is the signal for father to move into single quarters and tonight is almost their last joint foray. Both adults are white beneath but he is creamy grey above, she sooty; the species varies greatly and these colours are not related to their sex. One after another they climb easily up the smooth trunk and out along a branch – then suddenly hurl themselves into space.

True flight has, perhaps not surprisingly given all its inherent unlikelihoods, only evolved four times in the whole history of the earth. Insects and mammals only discovered the extraordinary trick once each; in insects many groups have arisen from a single flying ancestor, but bats remain the only flying mammals. Reptiles managed it twice; the wonderful pterosaurs, which were not dinosaurs, took to the air 220 million years ago, but are sadly no longer with us. The descendants of flying dinosaurs, however, are all around us. The Powerful Owl is one. On the other hand, many groups of animals have learnt to glide, increasing their air resistance to slow their rate of fall and even steer their direction of fall. Gliding is still glorified falling, without the powering that is the hallmark of true flight, but can be very efficacious. In fact the majority of vertebrate groups have members, living or dead, which have taken up gliding. These include fish (on extended fin rays), snakes and dragon lizards (on extended ribs), frogs (on big toe membranes) and mammals, including the Old World squirrels and Australian possums (on skin flaps between the front and hind legs). In the Australian possums in fact, it seems as though it has been invented on at least three separate occasions. The little Feathertail Glider seems to be out on its own, while the Greater Glider is related to the ringtail possums. The Sugar Glider group contains four gliders, of which Yellow-bellied and Squirrel Gliders, as well as Sugars, are also found in the ACT.

Unlike the ankle-to-wrist gliding membranes of other gliders, the Greater Gliders' membranes attach to the elbow and they swoop with paws clasped in front of them. Some 70 metres into the smooth shallow descent, the female now leading, the gliders suddenly change direction, banking to the left around a dense stand of Hazel Pomaderris and towards the base of a rough-barked Narrow-leaved Peppermint. As they seem about to crash into the trunk they stand upright in the air and hit the trunk with all four feet, gripping with their claws and scrambling up the trunk to make another leap.

Soon they will settle to a night of eucalypt nibbling, big ears always tilted for the sound of deadly wings.

BROWN GOSHAWK (*Accipiter fasciatus*)

THE PINNACLE, CANBERRA NATURE PARK. The chase started on the lower slopes of the Pinnacle, but crossed Springvale Drive and ended abruptly – especially for the unfortunate pigeon – in a Weetangera backyard. Later the owners would wonder about the grey feathers on the lawn, but would never guess the drama that led to them being there.

Half a dozen Crested Pigeons had been feeding quietly on the ground in the reserve when the sudden shrieking of rosellas hurled them into instant flight; a bird must always know its neighbours' alarm calls. The pigeons scattered, their short rounded wings evolved for this very eventuality, enabling explosive take-off and rapid flight at least over short distances. Their wings are powered by immensely strong breast muscles, representing more than a third of their entire body weight. Unfortunately for them, the big female goshawk streaking after them has similar adaptations. Her wings too are short and rounded and they, together with her long tail for steering, make her a formidable pursuer, particularly when manoeuvring through her wooded habitats. She is not designed for a long chase, but she was already beginning a low fast approach to the feeding pigeons when the rosellas startled them. Typically, she had become aware of them from her sentinel point just within the outer foliage of a big eucalypt and had dropped almost to ground level before accelerating towards them, hidden by bushes. The pigeons had taken to the air just as she rose over the bushes, so she was able to adjust her line upwards slightly without losing speed, while the selected Crestie was starting to climb above the traffic of Springvale Drive.

In desperation the pigeon started to dive for shelter in the nearest garden but the goshawk had precisely the right angle of attack now and as the bodies merged just above the ground an explosion of grey feathers hid them briefly. Then she was standing over her dead prey on long yellow legs, beak agape, glaring round defiantly with golden eyes made to look more ferocious by the heavy brows. Half a metre long, with barred undersides, she dominated the yard, now

shocked into silence. Before feeding, she plucked the pigeon, leaving the pile of feathers for the residents to puzzle over later.

This was a substantial meal though, even for her, and before finishing she was discovered by the local currawongs and forced by them to retreat to the shelter of her tree in the reserve, taking the remains with her.

This pair 'owns' The Pinnacle. As well as harassing the pigeons she commonly uses her stealthy low approach method to take rabbits feeding in daylight, and glides around the foliage of trees looking to ambush unwary birds. Her much smaller mate concentrates more on striking terror into the local honeyeater and starling populations. Soon now they will be repairing their flat stick nest from last year, high in a tree in a quiet section of the reserve, and lining it with leaves in preparation for three eggs.

After that, life will become even more fraught for the local birds and rabbits – and any intruding walkers had better wear a good hat and keep their eyes well and truly open!

GREY SHRIKE-THRUSH (*Colluricincla harmonica*)

THARWA. In the backyard is a small pile of brick pavers, left over from the laying of the shaded patio. No-one was sure what was going to happen to them, but in true Australian style they were kept, 'just in case'. The shrike-thrush knows exactly what they are for though. They provide excellent shelter for an array of many desirable snacks. The snacks, however, – beetles, ants, spiders, moths, snails and even lizards and small frogs – know very well how to utilise the shelter and are not apt to expose themselves to the heavy hooked bills of the pair of shrike-thrushes which are currently even more than usually dangerous, with three rapidly growing chicks to be fed.

Today the male bird is doing something that most humans would find remarkable, though if it were in its nature to do so, the bird would wonder why. He has in his bill a flexible twig some 10 centimetres long and is probing with it into a crevice between the pavers. This has been going on for a couple of minutes, but now – success! A slightly damaged Grass Skink wriggles out of its sanctuary and is immediately snatched by the powerful hook-tipped bill (which in fact is not dissimilar to that of the unrelated old-world shrikes, as noted by early British settlers). The tool is discarded.

Poor self-deluded humans. Not so long ago we were so sure that we had a monopoly on tool use that we used it as a definition of humanity. Then in 1960 Jane Goodall found that

Chimpanzees not only used, but fashioned tools according to requirement. Other mammals were also subsequently admitted to our club – then it began to be realised that many birds (especially but by no means solely crows) were also practitioners. Ah, it's hard if you're determined to see yourself as the pinnacle of evolution and the sole Holder of Innovation. The world just isn't going to help with that particular delusion.

He returns to the nest with the crushed lizard. To reach it he must fly in through the opening at the end of the enclosed verandah and land on the large hanging pot of geraniums, among the stems of which the cup nest of tea-tree bark, leaves and twigs is placed. For extra support the birds have jammed a piece of bark down one side of the pot, between soil and terracotta, against which the nest rests. Perhaps feeling pleased at his offering, he now hops onto the wooden table and breaks into a truly breathtaking song, rich and powerful, the fluting notes accelerating in a crescendo before ending with a strong statement. Each repetition of the call differs slightly from the preceding one, introducing tremelos and new notes. This song is one of the reasons the human users of the verandah are happy to lend the pot to the bird family for the duration – and if the plant suffers somewhat in the process, well after all it's only a geranium. (These people have in fact never heard a European Song Thrush, which was the source of the other half of the hybrid name applied by the settlers, but if they had they would be somewhat disappointed in its musical skills by comparison with 'their' bird.)

Meanwhile the female has waited patiently – and probably somewhat admiringly, since she is an important target of his singing prowess – on the rim of the pot, where she perched to make room for him to feed the most strongly begging baby. Now he takes the hint and settles down to do his share of brooding while she goes out to find food, both for herself and the chicks. She flies across the road to pull bark from tree trunks, hunting insects, while the Murrumbidgee flows busily with melted snow and Mount Tennent lours darkly above.

BROWN TREECREEPER (*Climacteris picumnus*) and WHITE-THROATED TREECREEPER (*Cormobates leucophaeus*)

Yankee Hat car park, Namadgi National Park. Time's mists are opaque and to catch a glimpse of ancient birds we need tools to pierce the murk. Such tools have been fashioned variously from studies of body form, fossil evidence, skeleton, behaviour, distribution and more recently from peering at different aspects of the basis of the very codes of life itself, including DNA from both within and outside of the cells. Using these scopes in unison, we can peer far,

far back through tens of millions of years to catch a glimpse of an ancient songbird, perched in a Gondwanan rainforest above where a proto-lyrebird is scratching on the ground. Our tools cannot yet trace the details of its immense time journey, but we can see where time has brought it – to a nearby woodland.

From the car park at the end of the Old Boboyan Road the walking track wanders across the open valley, crosses Bogong Creek and Swamp and eventually leads to the wonderful Yankee Hat art site. Around the car park though is some truly lovely woodland through which rings the clear 'bink' of the Brown Treecreepers, a sound sadly silent in much of the region, gone with the lost woodlands. One of the birds is assiduously working a line of ants, snapping them up with the thoroughness of a vacuum cleaner. Ants are a bit like eucalypt leaves, appall-ing food but if you can get past the hard shells, bitter taste and formic acid they provide an almost infinite supply of

Brown Treecreeper

nutrient. This is a young male, taking some time off from helping his dad feed his mother, who is incubating two eggs in a small tree hollow five metres above the ground. His father is hopping along a fallen log, searching for insects and spiders – beak now full, he flies up to the nest. She does all the incubating and brooding, but he feeds her for all this time. And now he does some-thing truly curious. On the ground is a piece of battered, shed snake skin and he flies down, picks it up in his bill and returns to perch on the lip of the hollow. Carefully, he wipes the skin all around the entrance to the nest, continuing for 20 minutes. Why? No mere human can answer that nor can we ask the only ones who know …

Other calls fill the woodland too, especially the harsh chapping of the Dusky Woodswallows who also nest here, crankily swooping any intruders. But another, clearer call filters through the woodswallows' spattering of sound, a rapidly repeated piping which slows and even briefly stops sometimes, but always starts up again, extending almost interminably. This is the call of the White-throated Treecreeper, smaller than the Brown, dark above and white below, with no white eyebrow. It is much more widespread than the Brown too, favouring the commoner open forests which, unlike the woodlands, are not under particular threat. In places like the Yankee Hat car park, where the woodlands grade into forest on the slopes, the two treecreepers come together. They do not compete, however, as the White-throateds work the trunks and branches, above the heads of their Brown cousins. In fact the pair of Browns and their four stay-home sons share the top portion of their territory with three pairs of the tree dwellers, who have much smaller territories, though these territories also extend further up the hill than the Browns go.

They differ in other ways too. The White-throateds evict both sons and daughters from the territory when they are six weeks out of the nest, doing without the subsequent help that they could offer. On the other hand the Brown Treecreeper sons will never leave home. They will take up their own territories nearby, or within the parental territory, or inherit their father's when he dies. Meanwhile they assist not only their parents, but their brothers in adjacent territories. In winter members of the associated territories wander into each others' territories, while the White-throated pairs do not even spend time together within their own territory.

Now the White-throated male's song has changed and got louder, a shorter series of strong trembling notes. He has flown to the base of a thick branch and is standing with erect tail and spread wings, flicking them open and shut with audible clicks. He is expressing his renewed interest in his mate, especially after their winter sabbatical from each other.

Time has led these two treecreeper species down quite different, equally effective, lifestyle paths – but then they have had more time than nearly every other Australian songbird to perfect them too.

Note: The Brown Treecreeper is listed as a threatened species under ACT and NSW legislation.

WATER RAT (*Hydromys chrysogaster*)

It had been a nightmare journey. The little group of refugees was wet and starving; fortunately the monsoonal rains were warm which meant that there was no danger of dehydration and minimal risk of hypothermia. On board the battered raft were three species of forest rats and a tree snake. The snake and rats had reached a stand-off, but other passengers – geckoes, stick insects, smaller snakes – had succumbed to their hungry companions. The voyage had started nearly three weeks earlier in

eastern Indonesia, when a violent tropical storm had flooded the forest floor, washing many animals into the river before they could climb to safety. Many perished, but some clambered onto debris being washed downstream. Some of these came back to the bank kilometres downstream, but others were not as fortunate. This group had been on the largest of the many rafts – a full forest tree augmented with other debris tangled in its branches. Fruit and leaves (and fellow passengers) had sustained them until a few days ago, but things were now critical and only the chop of shallower waters and a dark line on the horizon gave any hope. When the raft lodged among the mangroves the survivors scrambled unsteadily ashore. They had a whole continent to explore and populate, where no rodent had ever set foot. Over the subsequent few million years their descendants would spread throughout the drying continent, diversifying until they represented a quarter of all the Australian mammal species, in every conceivable habitat.

Much later, perhaps only a million years ago, another group of invaders arrived, closely related to the rats which have now become part of human life all over the world. Another seven species derived from these, including the delightful Bush Rats, but they have not been here long enough to penetrate the deserts.

LAKE BURLEY GRIFFIN. The handsome big rat – some 60 centimetres long – paddling along the edge of the lake wall is a child of that long ago and far away landfall. So successfully had his ancestors made themselves at home that he has achieved in a mere five million years or so what no marsupial had managed in 65 million years of isolation from the rest of the world. Of some 200 land-dwelling Australian mammals, only the Water Rat and the Platypus have taken to the water as an essential part of life.

He swims with his partly webbed back feet, and his streamlined flattened head with eyes and nostrils high up in it, tiny ears to reduce drag in the water and thick waterproof fur are all adaptations to his lifestyle. His distinctively sinuous style in the water, and white-tipped tail, make him unmistakable. At the moment he is heading for the little island to the west of the Carillon, leaving the wall and heading across the open water. In his front paws is a large freshwater mussel; he can readily crush young ones but this one is too tough. He knows a trick or two though, and the mussel is doomed. Coming ashore, he shakes himself dry and places the mussel on a rock in the sun – and waits. He knows that patience will earn him a meal. In time the mussel will open in search of relief and then he will pounce. The area around the mussel is littered with yabbie and small mussel shells and fish bones. This is his favourite feeding table and he habitually brings food back here to eat at leisure.

His mate is nearby, though he will take no further interest in her until her current three babies are big enough for her to breed again. She is now suckling them in a burrow which opens among willow roots on the far side of Aspen Island. This is not just any old burrow, but a complex and comfortable one indeed. It runs parallel to the bank with a bedroom lined with bark and grass, a pantry to store snacks and beyond these the breeding chamber where the babies are being fed.

As soon as they are finished she will go out to find something for her own hunger twinges. Out on the rock the mussel is giving up. The mangrove landfall of the rats' ancestors is indeed very distant.

PURPLE SWAMPHEN (*Porphyrio porphyrio*)

Over a period of 40 years in the 19th century, the French naturalist and polymath Georges-Louis Leclerc, Comte de Buffon published a remarkable 36-volume compendium of all that was then known of natural history. (Another eight volumes were added after his death.) His Histoire Naturelle, Générale et Particulière featured the best artists he could find and was translated into most major European languages. One painting in it is a striking representation of a Purple Swamphen, obviously at home in a Roman temple, snacking on a pear lifted from a flat basket – perhaps an offering plate, albeit probably not one intended for the bird. It is holding the pear aloft in its ridiculously long toes.

LAKE GINNINDERRA. The one in front of us now almost seems to be mimicking its distant relation, except that instead of standing on a marble bench it is on the end of the picnic table and the pear is replaced by half a croissant, carelessly left briefly unguarded. Perhaps concentrating too much on us – though 'nervous' is certainly not the appropriate word – it drops the plunder and flaps down to the ground after it. Here, instead of simply picking it up in its massive red bill, it fiddles about until it manages to pick it up again between its toes and resumes nibbling. This is literally an in-your-face bird, though ironically it is a member of the family of crakes and rails, which are notorious for their clandestine skulking behaviour.

Two other conspicuous smaller family members are visible from where we sit too. Currently picking along the lake edge, the Dusky Moorhen divides its time between land and water, duller in colour and with a fine yellow-tipped red bill without the massive red forehead guard of the Swamphen. Out on the lake is a raft of sooty Coots, with white bills and flanged toes to assist their mostly aquatic lifestyle.

The Purple Swamphen – or perhaps closely related species, the taxonomists are still at work on the question – is found from New Zealand through Australia, Indonesia, south-east and southern Asia to the Mediterranean and southern Africa. Apparently satisfied that it has scrounged all that's currently going, this one stalks back to the reed beds which are its stronghold, flicking its white undertail pointedly. Indeed, when pears and croissants are not available, the reed stems themselves are an important food item, snipped into sections with the strong bill and lifted delicately to the beak between toes. Their dietary preferences are broad though, and Swamphens are definitely not ideal neighbours. Many birds nest in the reeds for the shelter they offer, and these parents must tremble with apprehension when they hear a Swamphen moving through the thickets, spreading its considerable weight on its long toes. The big blue-purple rails are infamous egg thieves and they are quite strong enough to bend down reeds with hanging nests, such as the reclusive Reed Warblers build. They will also prey on incautious ducklings.

Reeds are bent down to make a nest too, with a platform of reed sections in the opening created. And as for what goes on during nesting time behind that merciful screen of stems – well! I grew up in free-thinking Adelaide in the infamous 60s and early 70s, but we had no idea … For some reason there are more males than females, but they're very broadminded about sharing her favours. Up to seven males and two females quite promiscuously court and mate each other, so that homosexuality and incest are standard. All eggs are laid into one nest and all care for the offspring.

Rasping shrieks now emanate from the reeds where our pilferer vanished. We don't need to know the details of what's going on in there though.

BLACK-FACED CUCKOO-SHRIKE (*Coracina novaehollandiae*)

VISITOR INFORMATION CENTRE, NAMADGI NATIONAL PARK. The little woodland remnant around and behind the Namadgi Visitor Centre, just south of Tharwa, often provides a cornucopia of feathered riches for birdos and I can rarely resist popping in if I'm passing, just in case … Spring is especially likely to be rewarding with woodland species returning and setting up breeding territories. Today though my first treat, heard before seen, comes as soon as I open the car door. My ears are suddenly filled with a bizarre mechanical whirring, rising and falling and accelerating, sounding for all the world like a knife blade on an old-fashioned stone grinding wheel. The bird emitting it – a bit like a peak-headed Willie Wagtail with a white chin – is hovering near the fence line, watching for insects. Because of this most bizarre call the bird I know as a Restless Flycatcher is also widely referred to as Scissors Grinder. I love the fact that, despite efforts to standardise Australia bird names, such folk names remain alive and well, telling us more about the perceptions and humour of our forebears – and often about the birds too – than many 'official' names do.

Further along the fence now another black and white bird bursts into a prolonged 'chewy-chewy-chewy-chewy-weet-weet-weet-weet-weet-weet'. I am always glad to see the White-winged Trillers back; apart from their intrinsic attractiveness it is a sure sign that spring is well-established. Actually this one is a bit early, as most of his companions won't arrive until next month. I also like the fact that we get to enjoy him in his very smart courting garb, while in winter tropical bird-watchers – far too spoilt in my opinion – see him in his off-season gear, brown with mottled wings, much as his mate wears all year round.

Among the trees Red-rumped Parrots and Eastern Rosellas flash up from the ground and Dusky Woodswallows 'chap' irritably. My attention is drawn though to an oddly cat-like soft musical yowling call as a dozen medium-sized pearly grey birds with conspicuous black face masks settle fussily onto the branches of a Yellow Box, shuffling their wings into an acceptable position before settling. Black-faced Cuckoo-shrikes seem psychologically unable to land without performing this ritual, every single time. These birds are just arriving back to breed and spend the summer here – I don't normally see them in flocks except in spring and autumn when they are migrating. Although I've had a couple around my inner north home through the winter, most of the local population leaves, especially those without the welfare benefits of suburban living. This little flock could even have spent winter in the balmy climes of New Guinea, though we're not well-informed about their travels. They are close relatives of the Triller, who is still trilling enthusiastically behind me.

I think that it's quite likely that at least some of these birds will hang around here – some breed here most years, building an apparently ridiculously tiny nest bound in spider webs and placed on a horizontal branch or a flat fork. I sometimes wonder how the two or even three eggs, much less growing chicks, can be fitted into it. (Actually they can't – after a week or so the chicks literally spill out of the nest, completely obscuring it.) As I watch, one of the birds takes to the air and seems to be emulating the Restless Flycatcher, hovering somewhat heavily at the eucalypt foliage before snatching something from it. I can't tell from this range what the prey is but one of their folk names is Caterpillar Eater; my father (who called them Summer Birds) reckoned that they eat woolly caterpillars, which would make them among the few birds which can do so. The strong bill, which has already engulfed the unfortunate caterpillar, gave rise to the second part of the clumsy and unhelpful hybrid name. The 'cuckoo' part is explained as the group suddenly takes off again and flies across the road towards Mount Tennent, dipping on folded wings between comfortable bouts of flapping. Well, perhaps these individuals aren't going to breed here this year after all; I should have known better than to predict that a bird might do next …

Australian Wood Duck male, see page 151

OCTOBER

AUSTRALIAN MAGPIE (*Gymnorhina tibicen*)

KAMBAH. This is a virtuoso flying performance and entirely unnecessary. He could of course simply have flown in from the park, passed over the decking and landed on the branch, but not a bit of it. Instead he starts a long glide from at least 50 metres away, swooping up over the fence. Just when it seems that a crash is imminent he folds his wings back, slips between the deck railings, flaps twice along the length of the deck, repeats the manoeuvre at the other end and finally swings up to land with a flourish on a favourite perch. Perhaps it's to impress his mate, or maybe he's constantly honing his skills. Or maybe just because he can.

Certainly his hormone levels are up, not only for breeding season but because he's just back from a whirling shrieking aerial border dispute with the neighbours who approached too close to the territory boundary. They wouldn't comprehend that humans can't discern the boundary – to them, no matter that it shifts over time, it is as obvious as a wall in the sky and as they approach it they veer off to the side or straight up but almost nothing will make them cross it. Nonetheless, that only applies to a properly defended territory so any approach must be challenged. In this the old male was assisted by his son and daughter from last season's nesting. They are permitted to stay around, helping with territory defence and later with caring for their young siblings, until they leave in hope of setting up a territory or are driven out when they get old enough to pose a threat to their parents.

Rather than emulate their flashy father, the two younger birds took the direct route to the big backyard eucalypt that is one of the essential components of the territory. High in it their mother is brooding three eggs which will hatch in the next couple of days. Laying was delayed this year by a frosty burst in September, but it's still possible that there will be a second clutch later in summer if conditions are good. To celebrate their victory – or rather to emphasise it to their neighbours, who of course don't see it that way at all – all three returning heroes break into the intense vibrato warbling that is as jingoistically and aggressively tub-thumping in its message as any human anthem. This is a song that can be heard in many areas now where it has only been made possible by human alterations to the environment – magpies need trees all right, but only a few scattered ones.

The other essential component of their territory, open areas of short grass, is something humans are rather good at providing. It is for this that these magpies defend the section of the neighbouring park so ferociously. All four birds – the old female judges that her eggs will stay warm enough on their own for a while – now fly down to the park to feed. They spread out so as not to interfere with each other, peering intently for any tiny movement in the grass that might indicate a grub or worm below, but also standing with head cocked, listening. And there it is – the unmistakable sound of a scarab beetle larva munching underground. A heavy white sharp bill homes in on the noise, plunges into the ground and extracts the grub.

Two children on bikes ride along the adjacent footpath but the birds take absolutely no notice. They have never experienced any harassment from small humans, especially in past breeding seasons when they have been defending chicks, so don't see them as a threat needing to be repelled. If a Goshawk or Wedge-tailed Eagle were to pass over, however, they would certainly join the mixed party escorting them from the premises; both raptors are a very real threat to adult and young magpie alike.

Deeper in the suburb some chicks of this territory from previous years roam with a group of several dozen birds, scrounging food where they can. Many of them are youngsters, a few are refugees from territories which succumbed to neighbours when a member of it died and it could no longer be defended. They cannot breed and are just waiting for a vacancy to arise in a nearby territory. Some will pair up and go travelling, hoping to make a space for themselves somewhere.

It won't be here though, not while this very desirable real estate is happily occupied and passionately defended.

SWAMP FROGS

KELLY'S SWAMP, JERRABOMBERRA WETLANDS. One of my favourite spots for sitting and thinking – as I've doubtless mentioned before – is any of the bird hides at Kelly's Swamp. Occasionally other bird watchers may drop by, some of them people I know to some extent, though that doesn't really matter. We will sit quietly and companionably, having checked what each other has been seeing, but often after a polite interval one of us will murmur a 'good luck' and wander off to another hide and solitude again. (Some of course just can't bear to sit still for long anyway, in case that elusive crake or transient wader has appeared in front of the next hide.) It is a refuge I've sought in the past when my life wasn't going the way I'd hoped and planned, but that was a while ago now and I still come here often.

Today there is just me and the inevitable Swamphens mincing about on the bank, and Pink-eared Ducks and Shovellers swimming back and forth sieving micro-salad from the water with their big flanged bills. A few Pelicans and a Royal Spoonbill are loafing on the big arched log, but there is no sign of last week's Freckled Ducks, rare and temporary refugees from the drought which has drastically lowered the levels of their favoured Murray-Darling swamps.

There are also, from the sound of it, about fifty thousand frogs out there in full chorus, encouraged by the recent rains. The terrible chytrid skin fungus, that mysterious worldwide frog plague which has dragged many species to the edge of the precipice of extinction, and even hurled some over it, does not appear to have affected them yet. Just below me a small coterie of Spotted Grass Frogs is sounding like a mob of soccer fans whirl-

Peron's Tree Frog

ing their ratchets in short bursts. The sports theme is continued further out where it would appear that someone is hitting a tennis ball back and forth in a particularly lethargic sort of way. This is actually a close relative of the ratchet-whirlers, a Striped Grass Frog. A swelling nasal rattle advertises a Peron's Tree Frog, though I'd usually expect to hear him at night. (I don't have to see him to know he's a he – only male frogs call like this, in order to attract a mate and to warn off rivals.) The real crowd though is provided by two closely related and similar tiny species which are still widely abundant. 'Neee neee neee' insists the Plains Froglet, while the even more numerous Common Eastern Froglets sound like thousands of snapping sticks and they have been snapping them right through winter. Frog calls are as distinctive as those of birds and easier to remember because there are less species of them in a given place.

In sheer numbers though they provide an enormous resource for hunters and hundreds of frogs enter the food chain every day here, courtesy of herons, egrets, ibis, cormorants, water rats and snakes. In spring though the pools are dense with spawn, floating masses of eggs fertilised by the favoured male who clasps her from behind as she lays them. From these frothy bundles will emerge millions of tadpoles to replace those who don't make it to the end of the year.

I have tried looking through a lens at tadpoles at the stage when they've developed legs but still have their tail, because this gives me some idea of how their ancestors, the wonderful and intimidating Labyrinthodonts, lived. The first known back-boned animal to live ashore left its tracks for posterity 360 million years ago in an East Gippsland swamp. Its kind still needed water but they had evolved some essential changes from their fishy ancestors. To find more food or to avoid even bigger teeth, muscled limbs hauled them onto the shore where tough skin stopped them from drying out and a primitive proto-lung let them take oxygen straight from the dreaded air. Their offspring though still 'breathed' water, with gills. At this time all the continents were temporarily joined, so they spread throughout the world. This was also the time of the great Permian Ice Age, which wiped out most of the other new land life forms, but the Labyrinthodonts were able to follow streamways to safety. With a temporal symmetry 'Australia', their cradle, also became their greatest and last stronghold – they seem to have survived here until just 110 million years ago, 80 million years later than elsewhere. The largest Laby known from anywhere was a monster nearly three metres long from eastern Australia. I am irrationally proud of such facts, but there is no good reason why my form of jingoism should be any more rational than anyone else's.

All four of the southern frogs present (all non-tropical native Australian frogs are either southern frogs, a homegrown contribution to world frogdom, or tree frogs) I have heard in my suburban backyard, but the sheer numbers here are thrilling.

A final thought occurs to me; wouldn't it be wonderful to see a three metre Labyrinthodont ambling through the reeds, scaring the skin off of all those smug predators who make his descendants' life hell? Obviously time to go home.

RAINBOW BEE-EATER (*Merops ornatus*)

THARWA SANDWASH, MURRUMBIDGEE RIVER CORRIDOR. It is a bad place to be an insect, and even the hunters have become the hunted. Big blue-grey dragonflies flash after midges and winged ants, almost vanishing in a blur of movement then, totally counter to intuition, hanging motionless in the air. One is hanging thus for what are destined to be the last moments of its life.

Well below the insect the Rainbow Bee-eaters are arcing above the broad sandy bed of the Murrumbidgee, banking and rushing down again in glorious flashes of copper and blue, yellow and green. Suddenly one swoops vertically upward and while still beneath the dragonfly, closes its wings in an astonishingly virtuoso display of aerial judgement. Perhaps the rush of wings would have warned the insect, but it might seem as though the bird has stopped flying too soon. Needless to say, it has actually timed it absolutely perfectly. It stalls at the top of its swoop just below the dragonfly, reaches up and plucks it delicately from the air and immediately drops, opening its wings again with a flourish some metres below.

All up and down the river its fellows are plundering the air, their mellow 'prrrrip' echoing along the valley. There are also sporadic bursts of harsh rattling 'takatakatak' from the Dollarbirds, distant relatives and superb aerialists in their own right, tumbling after their prey on hugely long wings emblazoned with a white splash on each. Their orange bills are short and broad to maximise catching ability.

One bee-eater has seized a wasp in its long forceps-like bill, and lands on a dead branch. Cautiously it taps the insect's abdomen on the wood; the body is hard-tipped, suggesting a dangerous sting. The bird responds by wiping it vigorously on the branch to remove the threat – had it been soft it would have tossed it straight down. This bird is a male, with a pair of long slender round-tipped feathers extending from his tail; his mate has much shorter ones. These shafts rarely survive the nesting season, but for now they are very smart indeed.

Bee-eaters seem to have an impossible amount of energy and their nest excavation is a blur of action. One pair is now constructing a nest tunnel just below the wasp eater. Clinging to the vertical river bank they started by breaking the surface with their bill, but when they got into the opening they started to tunnel in real earnest. Spurts of soil now emerge from the opening as if from a sandblaster. Balancing on a tripod of beak and wing 'elbows' they pedal furiously with their feet, hurling the beak-loosened earth out behind them. Even so it may progress at only eight centimetres a day, until it is 1.5 metres deep. She does most of this work, though later he pulls his weight with regard to egg incubation and chick feeding. Some of their neighbours have a young male 'helper' to assist with nest defence and chick care, but the diggers have managed successfully on their own for three years now. This year three of their five eggs will hatch; two of the hatchlings will leave the nest to fly north with the flock soon afterwards.

Meantime though their parents are not long back from the annual great odyssey up the east coast. Their northern relations stay in place all year round, and many of these southern birds pass through those territories and keep going, across the Torres Strait to New Guinea and even beyond to Indonesia. The Dollarbirds undertake very similar movements.

The sun is sinking now, but the frenetic activity of the bee-eaters does not abate; they simply switch their focus from bees, wasps, beetles and dragonflies to the later fliers such as moths. And the river seems lit by the flashing colour of their wings.

MISTLETOES (Family Loranthaceae) and MISTLETOEBIRD (*Dicaeum hirundinaceum*)

GOOROOYARROO NATURE RESERVE, CANBERRA NATURE PARK. I am always fascinated by the yellowish leafy cascades of mistletoe that festoon trees of many species almost wherever I go in Australia. They are parasites, but who are we to make moral judgements about another organism's lifestyle? If it comes to that, every animal on Earth is a parasite of plants, relying entirely on the uniquely plantish trick of fixing sunlight as available energy.

Goorooyarroo is one of our newer and most exciting reserves and I love visiting its woodlands. Now, with the late afternoon sun turning canopies golden, the surging activity around the flowering mistletoe clumps is evident. Butterflies, moths, beetles, wasps, flies and bees visit the flowers, along with a young Eastern Spinebill. A small flock of restless Brown-headed Honeyeaters moves through, gleaning insects from the leaves, and an exquisite male Mistletoebird flashes red and calls with an urgent 'zzee' as he flies between clumps. This busyness around mistletoes truly reflects their importance to the landscape. David Watson, an ecologist working at Charles Sturt University, has done a lot of work on the role of mistletoes and this has led him to believe that mistletoes

Amyema pendulum

are a 'keystone resource'. By this he means that mistletoes contribute essential food and shelter to a wide range of other species, far more than the relatively small number of mistletoe species and individual plants might suggest.

The dense clumps provide important nesting shelter for many birds and the moist fleshy leaves are an important food for other animals, including several butterfly species which rely exclusively on them. Mistletoe fruit is also an important food source in many Australian habitats; many animals eat them and some – such as the Mistletoebird and the endangered Painted Honeyeater – rely on them. The mistletoe attaches to its host by a thick base called a haustorium which is easily seen from the ground, the seed having been deposited on the branch by a bird, most likely a Mistletoebird. Through this it diverts a small amount of its host's water and mineral flow, though it still does its own photosynthesis. Often the tree branch beyond the mistletoe dies. Many mistletoes don't survive – for one thing the growing tree fatally shades many of them out – and when they or the dead tree branch fall, these too become important habitats. For instance David Watson showed that ground-feeding threatened Brown Treecreepers disappear from woodland without mistletoes.

The very smart royal blue, white and red Mistletoebird is now back, singing lustily above me. Mistletoebirds are almost exclusively responsible for spreading the mistletoe; indeed, apart from feeding growing chicks on insects and spiders, they eat only mistletoe berries. The seed passes through with some sticky flesh still attached and to remove this annoyance from its feathers the bird wipes its backside on a convenient branch. One of the aspects of mistletoes which has always intrigued me is the way the leaves of a species seem to mimic those of its host tree, be it the sickle leaves of eucalypts, the round leaves of Kurrajong or the needles of she-oaks. Some say that it's to hide the leaves from browsing possums, but I'm not convinced; I think a possum's nose would be more useful to it at night than its eyes. No, I think it's down to the Mistletoebird again. It has just found a very yummy snack among leaves that look like eucalypt leaves, so where to look for another one? Yep, among leaves that look the same – and most of these are actually going to *be* eucalypt leaves. The plant is effectively 'sending' its courier to find another host tree for its seeds.

Time to go home, glad to know that the marvellous mistletoes are still enriching the landscape, partnered by a very busy little bird.

WHITE-WINGED CHOUGH (*Corcorax melanorhamphos*)

MOUNT TAYLOR, CANBERRA NATURE PARK. A grim drama is being played out in the grasslands below the casuarinas on the lower slopes, a border transgression which has a much darker purpose. If this were human soci-
ety, then the actions of the bigger group of choughs would be seen as ruthless and sinister, though well within the norm of human behaviour. Animals live and die by their own rules though, not those of any other species, and a human system of ethics is no more pertinent to a chough than is that of a wombat. What matters to a chough is that as many of its four

chicks as possible survive and this is definitely a question of numbers. Unless the parents have at least two helpers all the four are doomed. Their feeding strategy, of finding underground grubs, requires skill and meticulous application; the parents can't keep up the supply to the nest-bound chicks on their own and the youngsters inevitably die, one after the other. Young birds take four years to properly learn all the skills necessary to be an efficient chough and two help-ers may give one chick a chance of at least making it out of the nest; it takes at least eight help-ers to give all four chicks any chance at all.

This group, the Casuarina flock, has recently lost a couple of members to a speeding car on nearby Sulwood Drive and there is an uneasiness in the group as it works to keep up the food supply to its three surviving youngsters. The chicks accompany the group as it feeds across the ground, but are not skilled enough to survive without the older birds supplementing their food. They will need this help for another seven months.

The adults somehow 'know' that the number problem must be resolved for the long-term survival of the group and they have now deliberately descended from their Casuarinas heartland to provoke a fight with the neighbours, a slightly smaller group with just two fledglings. They have come right up to the boundary and shrieked a defiance which the neighbours cannot ignore. There is much threatening with spread wings displaying the big white flashes and red eyes engorged with blood and bulging apoplectically, and even some buffeting and pecking. The outnumbered neighbours are fully engaged and unable to notice that two of the offending flock are focused on one of their own confused fledglings, attracting it with feeding displays and even food. Too young to be sure yet who is who, it willingly follows the food – then the aggressors sud-denly break off the affray, close around it and retreat, the snatch having been made.

This is a deliberate and planned kidnapping, which can only work when the victim is less than a month out of the nest and still very naïve. The youngster quickly bonds with its new protectors, and next year it will be helping to raise a new lot of chicks. It may be too that one day it will even become a dominant in the group and bring some badly needed new genes into it; the current parents are father and daughter.

If these birds were human, they would be judged as ruthless raiders on more than one level. For instance the northern neighbours are based around a small dam. Last month a couple of the Casuarina flock took advantage of the Dam flock being harassed by magpies, a perennial hazard of choughdom. All members of the Dam group had rushed to form a protective 'plum pudding' of swollen red eyes and open beaks, temporarily leaving the nest untended. Into the temporary hiatus swooped the Casuarina birds; after an unsuccessful attempt to dislodge the magnifi-cently sturdy mud nest they simply tossed the eggs to the ground and retreated. The bereft parents later laid more, but they have been set back and will offer little competition to the Casuarina flock for the rest of the season.

But these birds, now feeding quietly again, and rushing to offer fat squirming delicacies to now four youngsters, not three, are not bad people. Just effective choughs.

MURNONG; YAM DAISY (*Microseris lanceolata*)

MULLIGANS FLAT, CANBERRA NATURE PARK. I am pleased to find a small patch of Yam Daisies – perhaps a dozen plants in a couple of square metres. These days this is almost a profusion, but my pleasure in them is filtered through the knowledge of what was, and will not be again. Some-times I wonder in fact if a little ignorance might not make life a bit more comfortable, but I usually decide that I don't really want to be falsely content.

We might, at first glance, mistake the Murnong for an exotic Dandelion but its dark green toothed leaves at the base of the flower stalk are long, slender and smooth, not flat to the ground and covered in bristly hairs. Dan-delions may have several flower heads per stem, but Murnong only ever has one. The single bud hangs modestly down until it opens, when the stem straightens and the flower faces the sky.

Now if I close my eyes I can see, through the eyes of those who saw and recorded it, golden fields of Yam Daisies nodding in the breeze to where the grassy plains blur into the horizon. I see groups of dark-skinned women and children squatting down and using pointed sticks to dig up the small white tubers beneath the plants. They eat some as they go, but most are piled onto shield-shaped wooden trays to be taken home and cooked into a delicious soft treacly mass. So abundant are the daisies that a couple of hours work will produce all that their families can eat – and there is scarcely a hole in the bright yellow carpet. Later others with paler skins would also learn to eat the yams; someone I know was regularly sent out to gather them for the family in the hills north-west of the Blue Moun-tains as recently as the 1930s.

Long-billed Corellas evolved their exaggerated upper bill specifically to hook the yams from the soil. When the new settlers arrived and yams became scarce the corellas starved and numbers crashed. They only recovered when they found they could eat the crops that replaced the Murnong – but they were shot for that. I also sometimes wonder if our sense of irony has atrophied, but maybe it's a defence mechanism to protect our conscience.

Again, because I have read the accounts, I can see a wagon hauled by wretchedly straining bullocks lurching gradually across a grassy black soil plain. The ground is soft after the winter rains, and the heavy iron-shod wooden wheels sink in. As the abused animals haul it onwards, the wheels churn up uncountable numbers of Murnong tubers, which will rot on the surface. In my mind the wagon fades as a long line of sheep works across the plain. They are eating the plants, but they have also learnt to push into the rich soil to eat the tubers. Soon there will be few tubers to find – then the ploughs will finish them.

I could get maudlin if I'm not careful and it's far too lovely a spring day for that. Around me the newly returned Rufous Songlarks are frenetically rushing between display perches to impress each other with their oddly metallic ringing calls. And the golden Murnongs still grow among the Kangaroo Grass. Far too few, but while Mulligans Flat remains as an island in the spreading urban tide, there is hope for them. And for us.

SATIN BOWERBIRD (*Chlamydera violaceus*)

MOUNTAIN CREEK, TIDBINBILLA NATURE RESERVE. The raiding goes on constantly while the bowers are being used. The old, deeply glossy blue male has just surprised a

younger bird attempting to steal his collection of blue feathers, which in turn were formerly the personal adornment of a Crimson Rosella. The youngster, still in green and brown female-like plumage, flees while dropping all but one of his prizes. Not that the aggrieved party would be in a position to claim any sort of moral outrage, were that to occur to him. He has just brought back a very nice piece of booty from a neighbour's bower half a kilometre to the north. He also took enough time to demolish several sticks of the bower before he went. This is not simple vandalism, but a very practical strategy. Firstly, with the pilfered decoration, his bower is now more attractive to the females whose favours he so desperately craves at the moment, and his neighbour's is less so. Further, the neighbour is currently having to do repair work, rather than do either of the things he'd prefer to be doing – that is, either displaying to the females or conducting a counter-raid to retrieve his lost treasure.

This treasure is valued by the bowerbirds – and it has enhanced several dozen bowers over the years – because it is so different from other decorations. It is a piece of deep smoky blue glass, removed by a very distant grandsire over 60 years previously from the dump at the back of the eucalypt distillers' camp. These men were Czechoslovakians, refugees from the Nazis, and the bottle had come with one of them before failing to survive a move. Stolen and re-stolen many times a season, it had gradually worked its way up the edge of the valley until now it was in an area where natural decorations were much more common than human-made ones. It survived the great fire thanks to the location of the bower it was in at the time, against the east side of a big granite boulder. Now it takes pride of place, at least temporarily, among some purple Apple Berries, the blue feathers, plus an apparently anomalous yellow one from a Sulphur-crested Cockatoo crest, a couple of snail shells, bracken fronds, several Nodding Blue Lily flowers and a section of shed snake skin.

The bower itself is a remarkable construction and it took him years of apprenticeship to attain the skill; it was only two years ago, aged six, that he attained his blue mature plumage. Until then, scores of his building attempts were destroyed by other birds, both his contemporaries and his seniors. This one is close to the remains of last year's bower, using some of the sticks from it. He started by laying straight sticks into a deep platform nearly a metre in diameter. Then he selected a series of thin curved sticks, each of similar length, jamming them into the platform to make an avenue of two parallel rows curving in towards each other. Finally he carefully painted the inner walls, using chewed leaves as a brush and a paint made, on different days, of chewed lichens, charcoal or leaves. He applies a new coat every morning. The avenue is carefully oriented so that it runs north–south, to maximise the lighting effect on the decorated display platforms at each end. This avenue is where the female will stand to judge his performance.

And now he is aware of an interested adult female which has quietly materialised on a nearby branch. Impressed by what she sees, she flies down into the bower and he immediately goes into a trance-like frenzy of display, his violet eyes bulging, his necked arched and wings alternately flicking rapidly and held stiffly above his back. He seizes the treasured glass in his bill, lowers his bill and raises his tail, standing on tiptoes, all the while buzzing and clicking more like a machine than a bird. After some time of this he suddenly goes quiet, stepping partly out of sight behind the walls of the bower, showing her just his head and the glass. He suddenly emits strikingly impressive mimicry of Yellow-tailed Black-cockies, Grey Shrike-thrush and Pied Currawongs, still with the glass in his bill tip and while doing 'push-ups' of his body. Finally she signals her acceptance, crouching with lowered head; quickly he moves round to the back of the bower and goes inside, and within seconds it is all over. She flies up to a perch and in the morning will lay in the nest she has already built.

His interest in her is over – already he is preparing for another conquest.

MURRAY COD (*Maccullochella peelii*)

LOWER MOLONGLO, 1833. The splashing startles him. This is not the minor water disturbance of emu, kangaroo or wombat fording the stream, but a prolonged churning of the nearby shallow water by a large number of unfamiliar big mammals. He has lived in this deep pool for nearly 90 years but nothing like this has ever disturbed his equanimity. Cautiously he sinks to the bottom, sliding under the big Red Gum log that is his home. The noise comes no closer and after a while subsides. It is not of his world and seems to pose no threat, so even before it fades altogether he relaxes. He is wrong.

Nothing in his existence or that of his innumerable ancestors could allow him to understand the significance of Dr Gibson bringing his cattle to follow this ancient human access route to the high country. Gibson's people have noticed his kind all right though, and would even rename it the Fish River in acknowledgment of its richness.

He is not long back from an annual journey up the river, past stands of ancient River Oaks and through frosty treeless plains to where the stream runs through a deep rocky gorge. Here the cod battle upstream through foaming rapids and granite slots where the weight of the river pounds on their backs. They push on through more forested stretches where the sun dapples the water, along another grassy valley which narrows until finally he stops at a place where the bottlebrushes hang low over the water. He and others of his kind make the journey each year when the waters are running high and travelling is safe and easy. In that sheltered spot, to which he has journeyed now for decades, eggs are spawned and stuck to rocks and logs to avoid being washed downstream. Each year he guards 'his' eggs from rival males and smaller predators until they hatch, whereon the tiny larvae, provisioned with a large egg sac to give them a start in life, must fend for themselves. While he is on guard, however, they are safe. He is over a metre and a half long and weighs most of 100 kilograms, and nothing in the river will challenge him. For the same reason he can be sure of resuming life in his home pool, beneath the same log to where he has returned for years beyond remembering.

Here he reverts to an easy life of lurking still and patiently under his log, waiting for yabby or crayfish, frog or fish or even duck to wander within reach of a short rush and those huge engulfing jaws.

It is many decades since he himself had enemies apart from occasional groups of wandering hunting humans, but his deep hole and sheltering log have protected him from them. For the first year or so his offspring must avoid the nightmare death masks of dragonfly larvae and the deadly grasping claws of Water Scorpions and Giant Waterbugs, as well as other fish. When they are larger and move downstream they run the gauntlet of hungry Water Rats, cormorants and Darters pursuing them underwater and herons and egrets waiting in the shallows. Not the least of their enemies are those of their own kind.

None of them can know, however, that their world has now changed forever. Not another cod in this river will ever grow to the size of their patriarch. In just a few decades fewer and fewer will make the journey upstream each year; even fewer will be allowed to survive it. And further ahead, but just a few years more than the patriarch has already lived, a deadly metal poison will sweep down the river from the collapse of unsecured mine tailings and not a single cod will survive it.

For now though it is a rich and tranquil life and no premonition disturbs that; the splashing of cattle is already forgotten.

Note: The Murray Cod is listed as a threatened species under Victorian legislation.

GRASS TREE (*Xanthorrhoea australis*)

TIDBINBILLA NATURE RESERVE. The stand of tall flower spikes gleams palely in the shadowy moonlight. Cloud shades slide across the scene, but the flickers on the creamy stalks are not all so insubstantial. A family of Sugar Gliders is working the stems, lapping nectar from the thousands of little three-petalled flowers. Swarms of moths are attracted by the beacons of colour and scent, and with them come the bats, intercepting the moths as they come in. In turn a young Boobook is fluttering around, making rushes at the bats, but with little effect; that is a skill that needs refining.

The feasting goes on all night, but doesn't stop when the moon dips and the sun lights up the Birragai granites. The gliders have gone to their shared tree hollow, the moths and bats have sought their day shelters; the owl had given up earlier and sought an easier meal. Now though the shift has segued almost seamlessly, as the Red Wattlebirds arrive with the sunrise. Yellow-faced Honeyeaters come too and there is a constant flurry as the bigger honeyeaters try to chase them away. They are less concerned about the small flock of Brown-headed Honeyeaters, knowing that these busy little relatives are more interested in the insects than the nectar. And there is plenty to attract them – a constant stream of native flies, bees, wasps, sawflies and butterflies wing in, and the Meat Ants march up the stalk to steal nectar from the base of the flowers without taking pollen.

This cornucopia of energy had its genesis last summer, when a small but intense fire raced across the hillside, burning the skirts of leaves from the Grass Trees and leaving the blackened stumps formed of rings of the leaf bases. Within days new thin wiry leaves appeared and during winter the plants put up slender woody stems to two or three metres high, which sprouted thousands of flower buds. They don't need a fire to flower, but post-fire flowering is always dramatic.

Two hundred years ago: the stand is much more extensive and the birds and insects have competition. Groups of women move around the stand, beating the bases of the leaf clumps and collecting the powdery resin on sheets of bark. Later they will melt the powder into big lumps, suitable for carrying on heads to be traded across the country for use as an invaluable glue to attach tool heads to handles. A pile of dried flower stalks will be carried away and fashioned into spears, though some will be set aside for use as fire sticks. Other women walk through the grove, pushing at the stems with their feet; most plants resist the push but one sags away, hollowed out at the base. Some quick excavation here produces several succulent wood-boring moth larvae. A child is carefully drawing a leaf up a flower stalk and licking the nectar from it. In summer the women will return and collect seeds to make flour; if they have need, they may also cut leaves to weave for shelter or baskets.

The light faded on the long-established lifestyle of these people, but their supplanters also found uses for the Grass Trees. Medicines, perfumes and varnishes were distilled from the resin and brake blocks for steel wagon rims fashioned from the trunks. It was even rumoured that in the earliest years of the 20th century Germany imported large amounts of the resin for the explosives industry.

These wonderful plants are archetypically Australian, but are far from being the ancient relics that they are often portrayed. In fact the 28 species belong to a relatively recent group of lily relations and are evolving rapidly. That could be regarded as good news for the wattlebirds, but right now they are much more concerned to repel an invasion by a group of hungrily pugnacious Noisy Friarbirds, just back from their northern winter resort and keen to share in the riches.

SHINGLEBACK LIZARD (*Trachydosaurus rugosus*)

GOOROOYARROO NATURE RESERVE, CANBERRA NATURE PARK. She was fully adult, had given birth many times before, and was wandering across the grassy woodland unaccompanied and looking for a mate at the start of breeding season. Suddenly, there he was; a handsome big glossy black male. But as she approached him, moving more quickly now, she paused. He wasn't the right one; he too backed off once he failed to recognise her and resumed his own search. On the face of it this is remarkable – these are not abundant lizards on the cold eastern slopes and there seems no reason why each would not have been a suitable mate for the other. However, each is firmly in a separate long-term relationship and only their own mate will do.

She found him the next day in the grove of old Brittle Gums, recognising him beyond doubt though they had not seen each other since the beginning of last summer. For most of those months they had been dormant, body functions just ticking over as they evaded the hazards of winter, one deep in a hollow log, the other in an old rabbit burrow, some 500 metres apart. This is the seventeenth spring that they've sought each other's company and unless disease or an eagle or fox intervenes there is no reason why they will not do so for another decade.

After some weeks together they will eventually mate, then go their own ways until next year. In her body will be growing just two babies, which by the time of their birth in autumn will be huge – half her length and each a quarter of her weight. They will be well placed to care for themselves, as they must, from the start.

This is the pair that we're watching now on the lower slopes of Burnt Stump Hill near Horse Park Drive. Well OK, it's a pair that might be them. I have an especially soft spot for Shinglebacks – or Sleepy Lizards, as I still think of them – and some of my earliest memories are of tracking them through the paddocks near the farm house that my parents rented north of Adelaide. I even kept some as pets in a big lizardarium that my father built, back when there was no protective legislation requiring a licence for this. These two are staying close together, seemingly content with each other's company. It seems odd, this close bond, given that they only spend these six to eight weeks of the year together. They are a rich glossy black; one is particularly shiny, having apparently shed his or her old skin very recently. Like all reptiles they go on growing as long as they live. Their skin doesn't, however, so they must grow a new roomier one under the old one which splits and is dragged and rubbed off. Sleepies are essentially lizards of the dry inland and in much of their range are blotchy brown and yellow, but these are at their climatic limits so must maximise the solar energy available to them by being sun-absorbing jet black.

The shiny one is focused on a flowering Hibbertia, tugging at the yellow flowers and eating them with jaws that are also powerful enough to crunch up beetle carapaces and snail shells. The other is aware of us and as I step too close it suddenly whips its body round into a curve and opens its mouth, poking out its inky tongue at us and hissing ferociously. It's all bluff of course – I've moved dozens of them from roads in my life and taken the opportunity to admire them up close – but there is no need to disturb this happy couple.

So we part, two couples with very different needs and world views. For us Goorooyarroo is not the whole world; we agree with the Shingleback pair that it's a good place to be though.

Kangaroo Grass, see page 61

NOVEMBER

WHITE-BROWED SCRUBWREN (*Sericornis frontalis*)

AUSTRALIAN NATIONAL BOTANIC GARDENS. Like busy mice, the scrubwren family work along the edge of the rainforest gully, gleaning the litter and hopping up onto the low stone wall to search crevices for tiny insects. A white eyebrow and moustache enclose the dark face (black in the males, brown on the female) and the white shoulder flecks gleam in the shadowy understorey, helping them stay in contact. There are four of them – the domi-nant male, his partner, and the patriarch's younger brother and two-year old son. These two are sub-ordinate to him and assist in feeding the chicks. This is a key time for the family; in the sheltered crown of a tree fern in the gully are three chicks,  just a few days out of the nest in which they hatched only three weeks previously. The empty nest itself remains on the ground entirely hidden in ferns lower in the gully.

All four adults are kept busy feeding the chicks, grabbing anything small and live, flying down to the crèche and stuffing it into the nearest gaping bill. Next week though this will change. The chicks will become mobile and will scatter, greatly reducing the risk that a calam-ity to one will be a calamity to all. When this happens, mother, father and uncle will each follow one of the chicks, taking full responsibility for it for the next six weeks. Their half-brother will be spared that responsibility, for now at least, though life for him has changed too now, much fuller of possibilities.

Last year his father was still mated to his mother and while their son helped out with feed-ing, it was only fairly sporadic. He was never going to mate with his mother, and the incentive to contribute was not as strong as it might have been. In autumn, however, things altered dramatically.

It was an accident that never should have happened, but perhaps it was no less likely than being struck by lightning, and wrens die that way. She was foraging on the lawn just across from the rainforest when a currawong swooping low over the opening startled her. Without looking she hurtled across the roadway and just clipped the slow-moving gardeners' vehicle

descending the hill. She wasn't badly hurt at all, but tumbled into the rainforest understorey –
immediately at the feet of a startled big male Water Dragon. He had never eaten a bird before,
but only because they were too hard to catch. This one was not, however, and he seized the
opportunity instantly.

The three males were unaware of the tragedy, but became aware of her absence. So were
surrounding scrubwrens, and when two days later a young female cautiously encroached,
having wandered since leaving her birth territory beyond the Eucalypt Lawn, she was allowed
to stay.

The young male now had a very good reason to be assiduous in his feeding of the territory's new female. Only his father and uncle now stood between him and the chance of fathering his own chick. Despite his attentions, however, the older birds seemed always to be there. His uncle in fact is the father of one of the three chicks now begging in the gully. Something deep in his dim little psyche, however, reassures him that his time will come. Scrubwrens can live for a long time, especially in such a utopian environment, and his chances are good of one day inheriting the territory and the privileges that go with it.

For now though there is a particularly plump brown caterpillar to deal with. The chicks won't be seeing that.

GOLDEN SUN MOTH (*Synemon plana*)

CRACE GRASSLAND RESERVE, GUNGAHLIN. It is early on a sunny afternoon towards the end of the month and the grasslands are spangled with the gold of daisies and long-stemmed Goodenias, purple Chocolate Lilies and the white tufts of Wallaby Grass flower heads. High on a grass stem a plain dark brown moth is sitting quietly, basking in the sun. Her wings seem small and indeed, while she can fly if she must, these wings won't carry her very far. She has conspicuously clubbed antennae, reminiscent of that small group of flashy moths which we know as butterflies; in this case the similarity is incidental though.

Her time is very limited. These last hours of her life are her only hours as an adult and since she now has only one purpose left – to find a mate and reproduce – she has no need of a mouth to eat and drink. Until now it has been a leisurely existence. Two summers ago her mother laid her creamy elongated ribbed eggs, not on the Wallaby Grass leaves but into cracks in the soil alongside the grass stems. The little caterpillars tunneled deeper down, feeding steadily on the rhizomes, safe from open-air predators and the harsh climatic extremes of their habitat. Then, about six weeks ago and still underground, they formed pupae, that amazing magic sack within which the components of a caterpillar's body reorganise themselves into the entirely different form of an adult.

Females of this species, like our moth, do something else remarkable too. Within the pupa, eggs were already developing to be ready for fertilisation almost as soon as she emerges. And now it's time. A coppery brown male is approaching. As he approaches she suddenly lifts her small top wings and reveals the reason for the name by which we know her – the Golden Sun Moth. The lower pair of wings is bright golden orange and it's the clinching signal to him that she is the one for him.

He alights alongside her and mating takes place immediately. Then she descends to the ground and with her long ovipositor – a tube extending from the tip of her abdomen – she delicately places the eggs into the ground. By tomorrow her body proteins will be returning to the soil, helped by the ever-alert ants. Here they will be taken up by the Wallaby Grass, which in turn nourishes her young.

Throughout much of the formerly vast range of her kind, the grasslands have gone and with them the many unique plants and animals which relied on them. Here in the Gungahlin grassland reserves though, including Mulanggari, a precious fragment remains where the Golden Sun Moth may still flash orange in the early summer sun.

Note: The Golden Sun Moth is listed as a threatened species under Commonwealth, ACT, NSW and Victorian legislation.

FAN-TAILED CUCKOO (*Cacomantis flabelliformis*)

MOUNT TENNENT, NAMADGI NATIONAL PARK. The measured descending trill never varies, and seems to be part of the very air of the open forest on the lower slopes of the mountain. In this creek valley where the Cypress pine walking track from the Namadgi Visitor Information Centre starts to rise, the shrub layer is a mass of scented long-stamened flowers. The yellow Forest Phebalium is in full bloom, while the pale pink-white Heath Myrtle is tapering off. On the hillsides many of the Black Cypress and Drooping She-oaks are stark skeletons, victims of the rampaging 2003 fires, but the seedling growth is healthy. It is hard today to imagine the intensity of that awful January morning, but the shattered granite boulders are reminder enough.

The male Fan-tailed Cuckoo is sitting high on a dead branch against the morning sky, grey back, rusty breast and long barred tail combining with his insistent message to proclaim his identity. Small nesting birds are well aware of it and are keeping a jaundiced eye and ear on him – which is exactly his intent. While they are focused on him they may be less likely to notice his mate who is being a lot more circumspect, staying low and quiet in foliage while she awaits her moment. She is currently watching a White-browed Scrubwren which she suspects has eggs deep in a dense phebalium. Eventually the smaller bird flies out of the shrub, glancing nervously up at the calling male cuckoo. The moment the scrubwren is out of sight the cuckoo female moves in, confirming that there is indeed a domed nest low in the shadows, seemingly part of its surrounds – grass, dried roots, bark and bracken leaves. Inserting her head into the side entrance she makes out dimly the two pale eggs within and removes one in her bill. Later she will eat it – no point in wasting protein – but the main point is that the scrubwren must find the right number of eggs when she returns.

Meantime the cuckoo turns and hastily deposits her own egg into the nest, its tough shell allowing it to bounce slightly without cracking as it lands. This is essential to enable her rapid getaway; if the scrubwren catches her there all will have been in vain. If the cuckoo had found no eggs yet in the nest she would have just gone away – the scrubwren would never have fallen for finding one where none had been before. The dim light in the nest is in the cuckoo's favour, as it makes it harder for the parent birds to distinguish any differences in the intruding egg, and she mostly chooses as host species which build such a nest. Nonetheless her lightly speckled egg matches that of the scrubwren pretty well.

A *fortnight passed*. The cuckoo egg hatched. If the scrubwren parents were surprised by the emergence, a few days earlier than they may have expected, or by the size of the chick that emerged, nothing in their behaviour suggested it. They just started feeding it. The next day the other egg disappeared. Perhaps they didn't notice it on the shadowy ground below and they certainly made no connection between its mysterious exit and the egg-shaped hollow in the middle of the demanding baby's back. Probably they were too busy bringing insects, grubs and spiders to fill the eternally gaping maw. By the third day, still naked and blind, it was already half their weight. In a week it weighed as much as either of them; by the time it left the nest after 16 days it weighed as much as both of them combined. Its begging was apparently irresistible, even when they had to stand on top it, dwarfed by it, to reach its pleading beak. On more than one occasion a passing Brown Thornbill was distracted by it and fed it at the expense of its own young.

A month after hatching the young cuckoo flew off. The parents were exhausted, but no more than their own two or three chicks would have rendered them. In three weeks they will start again and this time there is every chance that the result will be a couple of healthy young scrubwrens.

Cuckoos are a familiar and manageable scrubwren problem; on a nearby property on the other hand tea-tree regrowth is being slashed …

DAISIES (Family Asteraceae)

SHANAHANS MOUNTAIN, NAMADGI NATIONAL PARK. It was an extraordinary journey. Late last summer the Showy Podolepis daisy seed set off, with a myriad of others, from the meadows of the jagged Bogong Peaks, out of sight beyond the Brindabellas, far to the west in Kosciuszko National Park. The tiny hard seed (actually the entire fruit) was carried high on the prevailing westerlies, borne on a filamentous white parachute comprising the thread-like sepals. Most of the millions that embarked on the odyssey never had a chance. Some dropped short, into forests where the light was too dim for a light-loving seedling to survive. Others fell into streams either in NSW or deep in the Cotter or Gudgenby Valleys across the Brindabellas and were carried away, or were caught in heathy foliage and eaten by birds or insects. Still others sailed right over the ACT ranges into the unfriendly plains and forests to the east. Some even continued on and on and were lost in the endless Pacific. But this one did not. The wind dropped at exactly the right time and it settled in a Podolepis utopia, the open meadows on the eastern side of the Shanahans Mountain plateau, overlooking the Naas River valley and the rugged Clear Range.

Orange Everlasting

Here it germinated, the tiny twin cotyledons like miniature leaves providing nutrient until the true leaves emerged. The seedling was established by the time the first savage autumn frosts slowed everything down and it survived winter just ticking over. By mid-spring it was growing again and putting up several flowering stems and now, on summer's doorstep, the buds, just one on each stem, are beginning to open their yellow faces to the wide mountain skies. Scattered through the meadow are Billy Buttons, archetypal daisy flowers each comprising a golden globe. To the busy little hoverflies they appear from a distance as big glowing attractive balls but as they approach the ball resolves into a mass of separate florets, tiny tubular flowers, each with a minute nectar reward to entice the fly to take some pollen when it leaves. Perhaps only a few of the hundreds of florets will be fertilised to form a seed, but all are genetically identical and the role of the majority is to attract the insect to those few. The open Podolepis goes further in its efforts to be visible to the crucial pollinating insects. Around the flat disc of fertile florets is a ring of big, petal-like, tooth-tipped, sterile yellow ray florets, whose sole role is to further increase the flower head's visual appeal.

These insects see the world in yellows, blues, violets and other colours of even shorter wavelengths which humans cannot see and so just lump as 'ultraviolet'. The several species of Brachycome daisies take advantage of this with contrasting colours, again using yellow fertile florets but with mauve ray florets to arrest a passing insect's attention. In summer the striking Orange Everlastings join the silent advertising clamour by bringing totally different plant parts into play. Their shining papery surrounds are comprised of bracts, modified leaves which perform the same function as the ray florets.

As the focus swings up from peaceful Shanahans Mountain and pans out across the countryside, more and more daisies appear, from tiny herbs on the very summit of Mount Kosciuszko itself to trees in rainforest gullies. The curve of the earth appears on the horizon and still there are daisies; daisies in salt spray on seashores, daisies on scorching red central sand dunes, over 1000 of them native to Australia. The whole earth lies below now and there is no daisy-free corner of the globe, 23 000 species of them wherever there is ice-free soil. They travel by wind, and they hitch rides on animals, latching onto feathers and fur by burrs and hooks. Humans eat them (from lettuces to artichokes, turmeric to tarragon to sunflowers), grow them for their colour (*Gazanias* and *Gerberas*, *Zinnias* and *Chrysanthemums*) and hack thistles, dandelions, boneseed and a host of other weeds from their gardens and reserves.

A world of daisies, millions upon inconceivable millions of them. And on Shanahans Mountain the advertising hoardings are still out.

PRAYING MANTIS (*Orthodera ministralis*)

INNER NORTH. I am never certain if I really can hear the mantis crunching on the fly's inadequate carapace, or if that is just a fancy of my mind's ear. If one were prone to anthropomorphism, there could well be something horrifically macabre about the relentless munching on the still twitching body clasped in the nightmare spiked legs. The great staring eyes in the mobile triangular head are the stuff of some of the science fiction novels I used to read. I have heard people express horror at the mantid's 'cruelty' – but given that some of those people would quite cheerfully crush (and waste!) the fly, or spray poisons into the air in its direction, I'm not too swayed by them.

I have never seen the actual strike – given that it takes less than a tenth of a second, I don't suppose I ever will – but I remember reading that one of the great boxers (Joe Louis perhaps?) could pluck a fly from the air between finger and thumb. Any mantid can do that any and every day of the week. The rows of spines on matching foreleg sections provide a savage and inescapable trap once the leg snaps shut on the prey.

This is one of some 160 Australian species, though I'm likely to get a better selection as I head north. In the tropics there are some monsters who don't waste time on insect snacks, but eat small geckoes, frogs and bird nestlings. Some local mantids can be easily 10 centimetres long but this one is only four centimetres, somewhat flattened and strongly green, slightly brighter than the *Dodonea* foliage he's clinging to with his other four legs. A conspicuous blue-purple spot on the inside of each front leg might be used to warn off others from his excellent vantage point.

He's set himself up to intercept at will the traffic flow to and from the flowering *Phebalium* alongside. (I can say 'he' with some confidence because he has long wings – most mantis females have little or nothing in the way of flight apparatus.) And now I can see something else, confirming what I've read but never seen before. He is snacking on the fly in his left arm but in his right is another, awaiting its fate. Still, if my mum hadn't taught me better, I suppose I could grab a second chicken wing while still gnawing on the first.

Just the other day I'd come across one of the very recognisable mantid egg cases on the side fence, like a solid mass of foam. This is not a bad analogy actually as that's exactly how it is formed, hardening on contact with the air to protect the dozens of eggs within. These eggs were lucky, the hardening occurring before a parasitic wasp found them and added its own deadly eggs. They hatched at the end of winter, having been laid in autumn. The baby mantids, like flightless versions of their parents, left via cavities along the centre of the case. If there are random exit holes it is bad news for the mantids; it means that baby wasps have hatched, having eaten the rightful inmates.

Does that egg case belong to this muncher, I wonder? Maybe, though his continued existence weighs slightly against it. Female mantids are notorious for keeping their strength up by munching on their paramour's head during the act, though it's probably not as universal as the myths suggest. Apparently a male mantid's relevant nerve centre is not in his head, but at the rear of the body, so mere decapitation doesn't stop him from performing his duty. (Actually I've known a few blokes to whom that might have applied, but this isn't the place to pursue that thought.)

When this fellow resumes his hunting pose the 'praying' epithet becomes obvious; it struck the great Linnaeus who applied the Greek word 'mantis' for a prophet or seer. I recall reading that a mantis-god conducted the souls of the dead in ancient Egypt, and that the San people of the Kalahari see them as godly manifestations. I wouldn't quite that far, but as a great fan of mantids I can have some empathy with the idea.

GRASSLAND EARLESS DRAGON (*Tympanocryptis pinguicolla*)

MIKE'S HILL, JERRABOMBERRA GRASSLAND RESERVES, CANBERRA NATURE PARK.

March. It was a battle beneath the notice of much of the world. For the two protagonists, however, it was very literally life and death. The little lizard approached the spider hole cautiously, then tapped the soil in front of the burrow and moved sideways. Nothing for a moment, then with a rush the Wolf Spider emerged, but instead of a clumsy beetle in front of him, he encountered a quick and robust young dragon lizard hitting him from the side, jaws closing and twisting on one of his legs. Ruthlessly and skilfully, with tactics hard-wired into her brain, the lizard continued to attack the spider's legs, one at a time. As the fight progressed the balance swung further into the dragon's favour as the spider became increasingly disabled. Finally the unfortunate arthropod was totally helpless and the lizard began to devour his fat abdomen.

The meal was not, however, the main point of the assault. What she really wanted was the spider's deep burrow, within which she could survive the coming savage winter. At the time of the successful seizure of the shelter she was only two months old, but already full-sized – in her world this meant just 130 millimetres long.

This world consists of some 70 hectares of rolling Wallaby Grass and Spear Grass on the slopes of the hill between the Monaro Highway and the railway line marking the NSW border near the base of Mount Jerrabomberra. There are more grasslands and more of her kind across the railway line and also to the west across the highway, but she knows nothing of these. Beyond this though, there are very few places where the little grassland-specialising dragons survive. In fact, these other places are limited to Defence Department land north of the airport (the animals on and adjacent to the airport are constantly under threat from runway expansions) and to small sites near Cooma. There is a strong suggestion, however, that the Cooma animals are of a different species from the Canberra ones. They used to be found in Victoria too but haven't been seen there for a while.

She is rusty-fawn, with a wide pale stripe down her back and a beautifully patchworked body which disappears into the mottle of light and shade in the grass. Now, as summer looms, her five eggs are heavy in her belly. From the safety of the burrow she darts out to seize small passing insects and other invertebrates – ironically, much as the previous owner had done. She also regularly climbs up a grass clump to use as a vantage point from which to sight and seize prey.

Very soon she will scrape a hollow in the soil in the shelter of a grass clump and lay the eggs into it, carefully covering them again with soil and litter. This will be their sole protection until they hatch towards the end of summer. It will also probably be her sole contribution to the next generation of Earless Dragons – she may live through winter to breed again, but probability is against her.

Until very recently probability was against her even being here now, standing erect and alert in a clump of silvery Wallaby Grass. The shadow of the plough, the superphosphate bag, the massed hoofs of sheep and cattle, aggressively invading weeds and the incessant grinding advance of suburbia loured close and grim. The belated but crucial dedication of grassland reserves like this one offered her a last-instant reprieve. And neither she nor the inmates of the cars sweeping along the nearby Monaro Highway have any idea of each others' existence.

Note: *The Grassland Earless Dragon is listed as a threatened species under Commonwealth, ACT, NSW, Victorian and Queensland legislation.*

BOOBOOK OWL (*Ninox novaehollandiae*)

RED ROCKS GORGE, MURRUMBIDGEE RIVER CORRIDOR. 'Woo wuu … woo wuu'
rolls down the rocky gorge and back come the replies, one from each direction along the river
and another from the open country towards the suburbs. None of
them is very far away but each is where its neighbours expect
it to be and no remedial action is necessary. If, however, one
were to encroach on another's territory the response would
be swift and violent. All the callers are males. Their
mates rarely respond now that breeding is underway and
for a month the female of the gorge pair had been sitting
on two round white eggs in an erect hollow spout in a
eucalypt on the very edge of the cliff. Three days ago the
second egg hatched and she is now brooding two tiny
white owlets. She does all of the brooding, but he keeps
them supplied with food.

An hour ago he had delivered a Yellow-faced Honeyeater,
snatched from its roost among leaves where his remarkable light-
gathering eyes had made out its outline. Carrying the body to a branch above the nest he had
called with a soft growling 'cor cor cor cor' and his mate had come out, landed next to him and
returned to the hollow where she began to dismember the bird to feed morsels to the chicks.
Before that he had brought several cicadas to her, which he had hunted one at a time by landing
near foliage and listening carefully for their rustling among the leaves.

*This sense of hearing is astonishing. An owl can find a mouse in a totally darkened room
by sound alone. The big feathery facial disc acts as a sound collector; the ears are set asym-
metrically to enable better pinpointing of a noise.*

A little way across the river a Tawny Frogmouth is rolling out his incessant pulsating 'ohm-
ohm-ohm'. The owl, constantly scanning his surrounds, will continue to ignore him if he stays
away from the nest tree.

*The owl's eyesight too is remarkable, aided by a pair of very large eyes set close together
on the front of his face to give binocular vision. This is most unusual among birds, most of
which have eyes set on the sides of their heads so that they don't get the sort of overlapping*

images that humans take for granted. In fact it is quite likely that humans, in their ineffable arrogance, bestowed the mantle of wisdom on owls for this human-like face. The size of the eyes leaves no room for muscles to move them, so the whole head swivels instead; without moving his body he can turn his head completely around to gaze behind, or over sideways to look vertically up or down.

As he gazes around now he is suddenly aware of movement on a branch immediately below the nest hollow. The sight of the intruder is enough to hurl him silently into the air. Not a hint of whispering air betrays him, as it flows over softened feathers on both leading and trailing broad wing edges, and over super-soft body feathers. The Brush-tailed Possum's motives are entirely innocent – she is not even aware of the nest – but the owls take no chances. The possum is shocked and hurt when the needle claws strike her in the rump with absolutely no warning; she is much bigger than her assailant, but surprise is worth all. With an outraged and frightened snarl-shriek she drops six metres to the ground and runs into the undergrowth.

Satisfied, the owl resumes his perch and his inspection of his domain. And now his attention is attracted by movement on the ground. Focusing among the rocks he makes out a big yellow centipede doing her own hunting. His chicks and mate are fed for the moment, but he is not. Again he launches silently into the air, down now and down, to crush the hunter's carapace and life in his powerful claws.

SPRING ORCHIDS

BLACK MOUNTAIN, CANBERRA NATURE PARK. I am an incurable – and unrepentant – orchiholic and early November on Black Mountain is an ideal time and place to indulge my passion. These days I stay away from my former favourite sites on the west side; I don't like to be reminded of what the freeway has buried. The first orchids I usually see are the ubiquitous little Pink Fingers, with erect back sepal and four 'petals' pointing forward (they're a combination of petals and sepals, but let's not worry about that for now). They vary from deepest rose pink to virtually white, but each has the distinctive red stripes across the smaller forward-pointing petal that acts as an insect landing platform in all orchids – the labellum. The Blue Fingers, the essential and longed-for message to me that Spring Is Here, have finished flowering now, but there are plenty of another close relation, the scented white Musky Caladenias. Given their abundance I am always surprised how relatively little we know about the pollination of these finger orchids, but it seems that the tiny bees and flies I can (just) see are mistaking the lumpy calli on the labellums for anthers and investigating accordingly. They are probably encouraged by scents, but apparently there is no nectar reward for them.

This morning, the next species I come across is a relation of the fingers, a magnificent big wispy green and red Green-comb Spider Orchid emerging from a clump of Snow Grass. If orchids in general are the prime confidence tricksters in the plant world, the spiders are pre-eminent among them. The warty clubs at the tips of the long slender 'petals' are pumping a remarkable chemical into the air, mimicking the female scent of a species of small wasps. She emits this scent at a time when she wants males to be especially interested in her and it works very well indeed! So well in fact that the male wasp takes no chances and races upwind to find her before his rivals do; the big knobbly maroon-tipped labellum, fringed with the long green comb, nods in the breeze and he seizes on it enthusiastically. As he does so it rocks back, knocking him against the pollen packages. No rewards of any type for the wasp here.

Waxlip Orchid

The bright yellow Donkey Orchids are among my first memories of wildflowers, on picnics with my parents in the Adelaide Hills. I don't know if that underlines my enthusiasm for them, but they always strike me as notably cheerful flowers, with their 'petals' forming a donkey's face complete with ears, face and long whiskers. (Well, I can't help it if hairy donkeys don't actually have long whiskers!) These too are con-flowers, but in their case they are mimicking yellow pea-flowers to attract native bees; by the time that these dupes find that the orchid is not offering them the expected nectar treat, it's too late. The wide brown-blotched dusky golden Black Mountain Leopard Donkey Orchids are just about finished now, but the big, tall-flowered, bright yellow Tiger Donkeys are popping up everywhere. According to the most recent thinking, these Leopards are essentially limited to Black Mountain and its immediate surrounds.

Now, in a more sheltered gully, is a swathe of late-lingering big, blue-flowered Waxlip Orchids, named for the waxy white labellum base. Here again, we are still woefully ignorant of precisely what attracts the tiny native bees. Earlier in spring and in autumn the same moist shaded hollow is also reliable for several greenhood species, those wonderful green enclosed flowers with labellums like spring traps designed to lock an insect inside until it has collected pollen. And nearby a real treat – a Purple Beard Orchid, with long purple hairs on the labellum to again fool pollinators. Down the track a bit further in an open area the first sun orchids of the season are opening to the sun's warmth, dark blue spots on a bright blue flower. And scattered all about them, the tiny green flowers of Common Onion Orchids sprouting from the stems, waiting for ants to pollinate them – a truly remarkable occurrence.

Any spring visit to Black Mountain can easily produce well over a dozen orchid species, but given that there are nearly 60 species known from here – over half the ACT total – this is not so surprising. Unlike the orchids themselves of course, which never fail to surprise and delight me.

Note: Recent work divides the genus Caladenia *into several new ones, but only the most recent ACT field guide does not still use* Caladenia.

EASTERN LONG-NECKED TURTLE (*Chelodina longicollis*)

NAAS ROAD. I would like, as they say, a dollar for every time I've stopped and picked up a turtle off the road and moved it to safety – always in the direction it was heading, of course. Naas Road (the dirt section where it's diverged from the Boboyan Road bitumen and is following the Naas River south to Caloola Farm) is a touch quieter than the Hume Highway where I've performed the task with rather more haste than is required here. This character is probably pretty safe, but I'm sure that turtles are as prone to Murphy's Law as I am. Not that this one is more grateful than any other – the sudden stink of putrefaction is familiar. The animal is perfectly healthy, but presumably the smell, caused by a milky secretion from glands in the groin, persuades many predators that this is not fresh tucker. Sadly foxes are either not fooled or don't care.

'Turtle or tortoise?' my companion asks. It is a familiar question and one I only sorted out for myself a few years ago. The real answer is that it doesn't matter – as is so often it's only a human conceit. As if to concur, the creature folds its head sideways into the shell before I can answer, peering out with bright black eyes. Now *this* is the key distinction, identifying it immediately. I explain (trying not to sound too insufferably pompous) that this is the defining character of the Gondwanan family to which it belongs, dominating in Australia, New Guinea and South America. If it pulled its head straight back in it would be immediately marked as belonging to the other, mainly old-world, major freshwater turtle family. No chance of that here though – the only Australian member is the wonderful Pig-nosed Turtle of the Top End, only recently recognised by science though of course long known to Indigenous Australians.

I have both avoided the original question and acknowledged my own preferred answer to it by referring to 'freshwater turtles'. It has been traditional in Australia to use 'turtle' only for the magnificent big sea-going members of the group and refer to the clawed freshwater ones as tortoises. That puts us out of step with the rest of the world – that's no big deal in my eyes, but it does ignore a major group of tortoises just because we don't have to account for it here. The land-dwelling shell-bearers with club feet, including huge island dwellers and desert wanderers, are called tortoises in the rest of the world, leaving the term 'freshwater turtle' for their aquatic relations.

None of this is as interesting as the animal itself of course. The smelly chap in my hand will have spent winter in a torpor in a deep farm dam, which wasn't in danger of drying out, absorbing oxygen through its skin. That's not nearly as good a food source though as newly flooded areas and now that the air is warming up, it's time to move. It rained over the past few days, so the turtle knows there's food out there, but it had to wait for today's sun to navigate. Hard to imagine, but this is a pretty scary hunter if you're a snail, shrimp, tadpole or small fish.

The keratin shell presumably developed from the scales of their very distant reptile ancestors, as did both fur and feathers. It is fused to the spine and ribs and was clearly a very successful innovation, a long time ago when it was new. One of my exasperations is the use of 'dinosaur' as a metaphor for unsuccessful – they were around and in the premier league for some 160 million years! Nonetheless, the turtles and tortoises have already beaten their record by 55 million years and are still counting.

Accordingly it is with reverence that I place this venerable character over the fence – then attempt to wipe the smell off my hands. After that I'll resume looking for the Rainbow Bee-eaters that nest in the river banks along here.

LILIES

BLACK MOUNTAIN, CANBERRA NATURE PARK. After arriving in Canberra from South Australia very many years ago, it took me a while to stop wondering in September when spring was going to happen. I didn't twig for a year or two that, at nearly 600 metres above sea level, Canberra's spring does not fully spring, in terms of flowering, until mid-October and into November. Nonetheless it still seems a long time since I delighted in the first Early Nancies of the year back in September, as I pause now to admire the first Black-anther Flax-lily of the season. I am taking a spring stroll on one of my favourite Black Mountain walks, right around the mount just below the summit. Both Flax-lily and the Nancies are lilies, one of the most delightful groups of flowers both here and throughout the world (though curiously, South America is a bit light on). The exact nature of the group is a matter of speculation though. One of the things that keeps us amateur botanists on our toes is the constantly evolving understanding of the relationships of Australian plants. The traditional view is that throughout the world the lilies represent a sufficiently homogenous group to be included in one family, Liliaceae. In Australia at least though the general opinion is that there are actually over 50 related families, of which perhaps 20 are native to Australia and none of them being in Liliaceae. There is no question that they are related though, and the precise quality of that relatedness is but a human conceit.

Bulbine Lily

I take the opportunity now to sit and admire the view over the plain, trying, as ever, to imagine the scene as it would have been 200 years ago. Soon though I find myself musing over the lilies I've already enjoyed this spring. All have six colourful 'petals' – actually three petals and three sepals. The big Nodding Blue Lilies emerged on the hills not long after the Early Nancies, which are little white stars in the grass, with purple markings and separate male and female flowers. The blue flowers and yellow stamens of the Nodding Blue Lilies are similar to those of the Flax-lilies, but instead of a clump of grassy leaves the Nodding Blues have leaves clasping the stem all the way up. The Fringe Lilies, flowering more recently than those two with a long fringe of hairs around the mauve petals, are among my special favourites. The cheery yellow Bulbine Lilies, related to the African aloes, are now brightening the lower grassy slopes. Still to come, also in the grasslands, are the Yellow Rush-lilies and the curious little Yellow Stars, whose hairs are coiled when dry and uncoil in the wet, for no reason that mere humans can comprehend. And my nose is very fond of the multi-flowered drooping mauve Vanilla Lilies and the deeper rich lilac Chocolate Lilies.

But I also love lilies for their stories. As a cook I'd be bereft if deprived of onions and garlic (yes, both lilies) but I'm just one in a very long line. They have been cultivated for at least 5000 years around the Mediterranean and the Greek historian Herodotus wrote of an inscription on the Pyramid of Cheops detailing the vast sum spent on onions, radish and garlic for the labourers. I read somewhere that the first recorded sit-down strike was held at the Necropolis in Thebes because the onion wage hadn't been paid by the government for two months. (I'd have been on the picket line with them, too!) When Florence was a 13th century centre of world trade, their gold coins had a picture of a lily – it was called 'fiorin d'oro', meaning 'little gold flower', which came into English as 'florin'. A lily, the fleur de lys, decorated the sceptre of the first kings of France.

The tulip was brought to Austria from Turkey as a gift of the emperor in 1554 and spread throughout Europe. In Holland single bulbs sold for thousands of guilders and in Belgium speculators bargained at the Bruges house of the van der Beurse family, from whence comes the term 'bourse' for a stock exchange. 'Paper tulips' were promisory notes, of which ten million changed hands. When the dastardly government decreed that these notes actually had to be honoured, the craze waned and people were bankrupted. Another lily to begin a craze among bulb gardeners was the hyacinth, brought from the west Asian plains via the gardens of Arabia and Turkey to Europe in the mid-16th century. By the end of the 18th century there were 3000 varieties in Holland, though only 160 are now known.

High drama indeed, but as ever none of it was anything really to do with the plants or animals involved. We have an amazing knack for involving them without their consent or their wellbeing in mind. But I'll have to get back to the world of people soon enough. For now I'll stick to considering the lilies. A much happier pursuit, I often find.

APPENDIX – SPECIES LIST

African Sacred Ibis – *Threskiornis aethiopicus*

Albany Pitcher-plant – *Cephalotus follicularis*

Alpine Ash – *Eucalyptus delegatensis*

Alpine Pepper – *Tasmannia xerophila*

Alpine Shaggy-pea – *Podolobium (Oxylobium) alpestre*

Alpine Thermocolour Grasshopper – *Kosciuscola tristis*

Amazonian Giant Centipede – *Scolopendra gigantea*

Apple Berry – *Billardiera scandens*

Apple Box – *Eucalyptus bridgesiana*

Baobab – *Adansonia gregorii*

Bearded Dragon – *Pogona barbata*

Billy Buttons – *Craspedia* spp.

Black Box – *Eucalyptus largiflorens*

Black Cypress Pine – *Callitris endlicheri*

Black Fruit Bat – *Pteropus alecto*

Black House Spider – *Badumna insignis*

Black Mountain Leopard (Donkey) Orchid – *Diuris semilunulata/nigromontana*

Black Swan – *Cygnus atratus*

Black Wattle – *Acacia mearnsii*

Black Wattle, Sydney – *Callicoma serratifolia*

Black-anther Flax-lily – *Dianella revoluta*

Black-eyed Susan – *Tetratheca thymifolia*

Black-fronted Dotterel – *Elseyornis melanops*

Black-necked Swan – *Cygnus melancoryphus*

Blackwood – *Acacia melanoxylon*

Blakely's Red Gum – *Eucalyptus blakelyi*

Blue Fingers – *Caladenia (Cyanea) caerulea**

Bog Cricket – *Bobilla victoriae*

Bony Bream – *Nematolosa erebi*

Bracken – *Pteridium esculentum*

Brittle Gum – *Eucalyptus mannifera*

Brolga – *Grus rubicundus*

Brown Barrel – *Eucalyptus fastigata*

Brown Falcon – *Falco berigora*

Brown Goshawk – *Accipiter fasciatus*

Brown Pine – *Podocarpus elatus*

Brown Quail – *Coturnix ypsilophora*

Brown Thornbill – *Acanthiza pusilla*

Brown Treecreeper – *Climacteris picumnus*

Brown-headed Honeyeater – *Melithreptus brevirostris*

Brush-tailed Possum – *Trichosurus vulpecula*

Buff-rumped Thornbill – *Acanthiza reguloides*

Bulbine Lily – *Bulbine bulbosa*

Bull Ants – *Myrmecia* spp.

Bunya Pine – *Araucaria bidwillii*

Bush Rat – *Rattus fuscipes*

Bustard, Australian – *Ardeotis australis*

Buttercups – *Ranunculus* spp.

Carrion Crow – *Corvus corone*

Cauliflower Bush – *Cassinia longifolia*

Chocolate Lily – *Arthropodium fimbriatum*

Christmas Spider – *Gasteracantha minax*

Collared Sparrowhawk – *Accipiter cirrocephalus*

Common Eastern Froglet – *Crinia signifera*

Common Onion Orchid – *Microtis unifolia*

Common Shaggy-pea – *Oxylobium ellipticum*

Coral Fern – *Gleichenia dicarpa*

Crescent Honeyeater – *Phylidonyris pyrrhoptera*

Crested Pigeon – *Ocyphaps lophotes*

Crimson Rosella – *Platycercus elegans*

Dainty Greenhood – *Pterostylis reflexa*[#] (*Diplodium reflexum*)

Dandelion – *Taraxacum officinale*

Darter, Australasian – *Anhinga novaehollandiae*

Diamond Firetail – *Stagonopleura guttata*

Dingo – *Canis lupus dingo*

Dollarbird – *Eurystomus orientalis*

Drooping She-oak – *Allocasuarina verticillata*

Dusky Moorhen – *Gallinula tenebrosa*

Dusky Woodswallow – *Artamus cyanopterus*

Dwarf Ballart – *Exocarpus strictus*

Early Nancy – *Wurmbea dioicea*

Eastern Brown Snake – *Pseudonaja textilis*

Eastern Grey Kangaroo – *Macropus giganteus*

Eastern Quoll – *Dasyurus viverrinus*

Eastern Rosella – *Platycercus eximius*

Eastern Spinebill – *Acanthorhyncus tenuirostris*

Eastern Water Dragon – *Physignathus lesueurii*

Eastern Yellow Robin – *Eopsaltria australis*

Echidna – *Tachyglossus aculeatus*

Emperor Penguin – *Aptenodytes forsteri*

Emu – *Dromaius novaehollandiae*

Eurasian Coot – *Fulica atra*

European Song Thrush – *Turdus philomelos*

European Wasp – *Vespula germanica*

Eyebright – *Euphrasia collina*

Fairy's Apron – *Utrichularia dichotoma*

Fisch's Greenhood – *Pterostylis# (Diplodium) fischii*

Fishbone Fern – *Blechnum nudum*

Forest Phebalium – *Phebalium squamulosum*

Freckled Duck – *Stictonetta naevosa*

Freshwater Catfish (Cooper Basin) – *Neosilurus* spp.

Fringe Lilies – *Thysanotus* spp.

Fungus Gnats – family Mycetophilidae

Galah – *Eolophus roseicapillus*

Gang-gang Cockatoo – *Callocephalon fimbriatum*

Giant Tasmanian Crayfish – *Astacopsis gouldi*

Giant Waterbugs – Family Belastomatidae, Order Hemiptera

Golden Perch – *Macquaria ambigua*

Golden Whistler – *Pachycephala pectoralis*

Gorse-leaf Bitter-pea – *Daviesia ulicifolia*

Grass Skink – *Lampropholis delicata*

Great Cormorant – *Phalacrocorax carbo*

Great Crested Grebe – *Podiceps cristatus*

Great Egret – *Ardea alba*

Greater Glider – *Petauroides volans*

Green-comb Spider Orchid – *Caladenia* sp. aff. *tentaculata/Arachnorchis atrovespa**

Grey Currawong – *Strepera versicolor*

Grey Fantail – *Rhipidura fuliginosa*

Grey Shrike-thrush – *Colluricincla harmonica*

Hazel Pomaderris – *Pomaderris aspera*

Heath Myrtle – *Calytrix tetragona*

Hemlock – *Conium maculatum*

Highland Copperhead – *Austrelaps ramsayi*

Hoary-headed Grebe – *Poliocephalus poliocephalus*

Hobby, Australian – *Falco longipennis*

Hooded Robin – *Melanodryas cucullata*

Hoop Pine – *Araucaria cunninghamii*

Horse Dung Fungus – *Pisolithus tinctorius*

Hoverflies – Family Syrphidae

Huntsman – Family Sparassidae

Huntsman Spiders – Families Heteropodidae, Selenopidae

Huon Pine – *Lagarostrobos franklinii*

Illawarra Flame Tree – *Brachychiton acerifolius*

Jacky Winter – *Microeca fascinans*

Jumping Spiders – Family Salticidae

Kangaroo Grass – *Themeda australis*

King-Parrot, Australian – *Alisterus scapularis*

Koala – *Phascolarctos cinereus*

Kurrajong – *Brachychiton populneus*

Lace Monitor – *Varanus varius*

Laughing Kookaburra – *Dacelo novaeguineae*

Leafy Bossiaea – *Bossiaea foliosa*

Lignum – *Muehlenbeckia florulenta*

Little Black Cormorant – *Phalacrocorax sulcirostris*

Little Corella – *Cacatua sanguinea*

Little Eagle – *Hieraaetus morphnoides*

Little Egret – *Egretta garzetta*

Little Grebe – *Tachybaptus ruficollis*

Little Raven – *Corvus mellori*

Little Red Fruit Bat – *Pteropus scapulatus*

Long-billed Corella – *Cacatua tenuirostris*

Mainland Tiger Snake – *Notechis scutatus*

Maroonhood – *Pterostylis pedunculata*

Meat Ant – *Iridomyrmex purpureus*

Mole Crickets – *Gryllotalpa* spp.

Monkey Puzzle Pine – *Araucaria araucana*

Mother Shield-fern – *Polystichum proliferum*

Mountain Galaxias – *Galaxias olidus*

Mountain Grasshopper – *Acripeza reticulata*

Mountain Gum – *Eucalyptus dalrympleana*

Mountain Rose – *Pimelea ligustrina*

Mountain Spotted Grasshopper – *Monistria concinna*

Mud Dauber Wasps – Family Sphecidae

Mugga Ironbark – *Eucalyptus sideroxylon*

Musky Caladenia – *Caladenia gracilis/Stegostyla moschata**

Nankeen Kestrel – *Falco cenchroides*

Narrow-leaf Bitter-pea – *Daviesia mimosoides*

Narrow-leaved Peppermint – *Eucalyptus radiata*

New Caledonian Crow – *Corvus moneduloides*

New Holland Honeyeater – *Phylidonyris novaehollandiae*

Nodding Blue Lily – *Stypandra glauca*

Nodding Greenhood – *Pterostylis nutans*

Noisy Friarbird – *Philemon corniculatus*

Norfolk Island Pine – *Araucaria heterophylla*

NSW Christmas Bush – *Ceratopetalum gummiferum*

Orange Everlasting – *Xerochrysum (Helichrysum, Bracteantha) subundulatum*

Orb Web Spiders – Family Araneidae

Oriental Plane Tree – *Platanus orientalis*

Owlet-nightjar, Australian – *Aegotheles cristatus*

Pacific Black Duck – *Anas superciliosa*

Painted Button-quail – *Turnix varia*

Painted Honeyeater – *Grantiella picta*

Paper Wasps – *Polistes* spp.

Peaceful Dove – *Geopelia striata*

Pelican, Australian – *Pelecanus conspicillatus*

Peregrine Falcon – *Falco peregrinus*

Peron's Tree Frog – *Litoria peronii*

Pied Cormorant – *Phalacrocorax varius*

Pied Currawong – *Strepera graculina*

Pig-nosed Turtle – *Carettochelys insculpta*

Pilotbird – *Pycnoptilus floccosus*

Pin Oak – *Quercus palustris*

Pink Fingers – *Caladenia carnea/Petalostylis carneus** and *C. fuscata/P. fuscata*

Pink-eared Duck – *Malacorhynchus membranaceus*

Pitcher-plants – *Nepenthes* spp.

Plains Froglet – *Crinia parinsignifera*

Platypus – *Ornithorhynchus anatinus*

Powerful Owl – *Ninox strenua*

Prickly Starwort – *Stellaria pungens*

Purple Beard Orchid – *Calochilus robertsonii/montanus*

Purple Swamphen – *Porphyrio porphyrio*

Quandong – *Santalum acuminatum*

Queensland Bottle Tree – *Brachychiton rupestris*

Rainbow Bee-eater – *Merops ornatus*

Raven, Australian – *Corvus coronoides*

Red Fox – *Vulpes vulpes*

Red Stringybark – *Eucalyptus macrorhyncha*

Red Wattlebird – *Anthocaera carunculata*

Red-necked Wallaby – *Macropus rufogriseus*

Red-rumped Parrot – *Psephotus haematonotus*

Redback Spider – *Latrodectus hasselti*

Reed-warbler, Australian – *Acrocephalus australis*

Reef Egret – *Egretta sacra*

Regent Honeyeater – *Xanthomyza phrygia*

Restless Flycatcher – *Myiagra inquieta*

Ribbon Gum – *Eucalyptus viminalis*

River Oak – *Casuarina cunninghamiana*

River Red Gum – *Eucalyptus camaldulensis*

Rock Lily – *Bulbine glauca*

Rose Robin – *Petroica rosea*

Royal Bluebell – *Wahlenbergia gloriosa*

Royal Grevillea – *Grevillea oxyantha* (formerly *victoriae*)

Royal Spoonbill – *Platalea regia*

Rufous Fantail – *Rhipidura rufifrons*

Rufous Songlark – *Cincloramphus mathewsi*

Sandalwood, Australian – *Santalum spicatum*

Sarus Crane – *Grus antigone*

Satin Azure Butterfly – *Ogyris amaryllis*

Satin Bowerbird – *Ptilonorynchus violaceus*

Scarlet Greenhood – *Pterostylis*# (*Taurantha*) *concinna*

Scarlet Robin – *Petroica multicolor*

Scottish Bluebells; Harebells – *Campanula* spp.

Scribbly Gum – *Eucalyptus rossii*

Scribbly Gum Moth – *Ogmograptis scribula*

She-oak Mistletoe – *Amyema cambagei*

Shining Bronze-Cuckoo – *Chrysococcyx lucidus*

Shoveller, Australasian – *Anas rhynchotis*

Showy Podolepis – *Podolepis jaceoides*

Silver Gull – *Larus novaehollandiae*

Silver Wattle – *Acacia dealbata*

Silvereye – *Zosterops lateralis*

Silverfish – Order Thysanura

Snow Grass – *Poa* spp.

Snow Gum – *Eucalyptus pauciflora*

Southern Boobook – *Ninox novaeseelandiae*

Southern Corroborree Frog – *Pseudophryne corroboree*

Spear Grass – *Austrostipa* spp.

Spearwood Wattle – *Acacia doratoxylon*

Spider Wasps – family Pompilidae

Spitfires – *Perga* spp.

Spotted Grass Frog – *Limnodynastes tasmaniensis*

Spotted Pardalote – *Pardalotus punctatus*

Spotted-tailed Quoll – *Dasyurus maculatus*

Striated Pardalote – *Pardalotus striatus*

Striped Marsh Frog – *Limnodynastes peronii*

Suberb Fairy-wren – *Malurus cyaneus*

Sugar Glider – *Petaurus breviceps*

Sulphur-crested Cockatoo – *Cacatua galerita*

Summer Greenhood – *Pterostylis decurva*[#] *(Diplodium decurvum)*

Sun Orchids – *Thelymitra* spp.

Superb Lyrebird – *Menura novaehollandiae*

Superb Parrot – *Polytelis swainsoni*

Swamp Harrier – *Circus approximans*

Swift Parrot – *Lathamus discolor*

Tall Bluebell – *Wahlenbergia stricta*

Tammar Wallaby – *Macropus eugenii*

Tasmanian Devil – *Sarcophilus harrissi*

Tawny Frogmouth – *Podargus strigoides*

Thylacine – *Thylacinus cynocephalus*

Tiger (Donkey) Orchid – *Diuris sulphurea*

Triggerplants – *Stylidium* spp.

Tuatara – *Sphenodon* spp.

Vanilla Lily – *Arthropodium milleflorum*

Wallaby Grass – *Austrodanthonia* spp.

Wallaroo – *Macropus robustus*

Water Rat – *Hydromys chrysogaster*

Water Scorpions – family Nepidae

Waxlip Orchid – *Glossodia major*

Wedge-leaf Wattle – *Acacia pravissima*

Wedge-tailed Eagle – *Aquila audax*

Western Gerygone – *Gerygone fusca*

Western Spinebill – *Acanthorhynchus superciliosus*

Whistling Kite – *Haliastur sphenurus*

White Cypress Pine – *Callitris columellaris*

White Ibis, Australian – *Threskiornis molucca*

White-browed Scrubwren – *Sericornis frontalis*

White-naped Honeyeater – *Melithreptus lunatus*

White-plumed Honeyeater – *Lichenostomus penicillatus*

White-tailed Spider – *Lampona murina*

Willie Wagtail – *Rhipidura leucophrys*

Wolf Spider – Family Lycosidae

Wood Duck, Australian – *Chenonetta jubata*

Yabby – *Cherax destructor*

Yellow Box – *Eucalyptus bridgesiana*

Yellow Rush-lily – *Tricoryne elatior*

Yellow Star – *Hypoxis hygrometrica*

Yellow-belly – *Macquaria ambigua*

Yellow-faced Honeyeater – *Lichenostomus chrysops*

Yellow-rumped Thornbill – *Acanthiza chrysorrhoa*

Yellow-tailed Black-Cockatoo – *Calyptorhynchus funereus*

* Note that recent work, still controversial, divides the genus *Caladenia* into several new ones, but only the most recent ACT field guide does not still use *Caladenia*.

\# Note that recent work, still controversial, divides *Pterostylis* into several new genera, but most current authorities still use *Pterostylis*. Additionally the new proposal retains *Pterostylis* for several species.